The Archer's and Bowhunter's Bible

The Archer's and Bowhunter's Bible

H. Lea Lawrence

DOUBLEDAY

NEW YORK LONDON TORONTO SYDNEY AUCKLAND

PUBLISHED BY DOUBLEDAY

a division of Bantam Doubleday Dell Publishing Group, Inc.
1540 Broadway, New York, New York 10036

DOUBLEDAY and the portrayal of an anchor with a dolphin
are registered trademarks of Doubleday, a division of Bantam
Doubleday Dell Publishing Group, Inc.

Library of Congress Cataloging-in-Publication Data

Lawrence, H. Lea, 1930–
    The archer's and bowhunter's bible / H. Lea Lawrence. —1st ed.
        p.   cm.
    ISBN 0-385-42221-0
    1. Bowhunting.   2. Archery.   I. Title.
SK36.L28   1993
799.2' 15' 097 -- dc20   93-16901
                                                CIP

September 1993

10   9   8   7   6   5   4   3   2   1

First Edition

This book is dedicated to the late Ben Rodgers Lee, a valued friend and woodsman without parallel, and to Bob Foulkrod, one of the world's great bowhunters with whom I have shared many exciting adventures in the U.S., Canada and Africa.

Acknowledgments

I wish to acknowledge the invaluable assistance of my wife, Ardi, in every aspect of this manuscript's production; of Aubrey Watson, who took many of the photos in the book and whose personal friendship and abilities as a professional photographer were of special importance in developing the book's image; of Dennis Butler for his personal involvement in critiquing the material and suggesting alterations and additions; of the expert bowhunters who generously contributed tips on various facets of the sport; and of the many individuals in industry who supplied information, illustrations and professional advice and assistance throughout the project.

Contents

Introduction

No one knows where or when the first bow and arrow appeared, because it came into being long before recorded time. It's also possible that there was no single place of origin but that it evolved in several locations. The fact that it dates far back in time isn't disputed, and some evidence suggests that its inception may have been 100,000 or more years ago.

Some things clearly depict its early existence, though. There are paintings of archers in stone shelters in Spain that were done during the Mesolithic period approximately 10,000 years ago, and it is known that Egyptians were using bows and arrows as early as 3500 B.C. Assyrians produced the basic recurve design in 1800 B.C. that later became the model for the modern version.

But the earliest known cave drawings, discovered in 1940 at Lascaux in southern France, clearly show a bison with seven arrows protruding from its side. These drawings are from the Paleolithic period, some 25,000 years ago.

The contribution of archery to the progress of human history was of enormous significance. The earliest men were likely primarily vegetarians, eating foods that were readily available by scrounging things such as berries, fruits, nuts and whatever small living creatures they could gather by hand or with tools no more advanced than rocks or sticks.

With a weapon capable of bringing down larger game for food or to thwart an attack, and then to have the benefits of new raw materials for various domestic uses, primitive man was able to make larger strides toward survival and a more civilized existence.

Before the time of the first ancient Olympic games around 776 B.C., archery had become a game as well as a means of self-protection and food gathering. By 500 A.D. the Romans had improved archery by developing better shooting methods and stances that led to furthering it as a competitive skill as well as a vital weapon of war. At the same time, archery skills were being highly developed in Asia, and the invaders use of these weapons contributed to the fall of the Roman Empire.

The great stories and ballads about heroic figures like William Tell began to appear in England in 1300 A.D., and by the 17th century, archery competition was a tournament event at fairs and community festivals.

The invention of gunpowder influenced most of the civilized countries, but the use of the bow and arrow continued to play a prominent role in many of the less-developed parts of the world. The tiny, poison-tipped arrows of the African Bushmen and Pygmy tribes were vital to their existence, and for many centuries the American Indians had no other means of gathering game or defending themselves.

In America, the awareness of archery increased following the Civil War. Confederate veterans weren't permitted to own firearms, so two brothers, J. Maurice and William H. Thompson, resorted to archery as a means of gathering food. They became accomplished at this skill, and in 1879 they founded the National Archery Association at Crawfordsville, Indiana.

It was in 1900 that archery was made an official event at the Olympics, where it was also included in 1904, 1908 and 1920. This was its start as a recreational and competitive sport, and while at that time a few archers did some hunting with the bow and arrow, it was mostly on a limited scale and for small game. The first real progress in bringing bowhunting to the public's attention as a suitable and efficient means of taking all kinds of game came in the 1920s through the efforts of Saxon Pope and Art Young, who were advocates of archery for both recreation and hunting.

The remarkable thing is that the appeal and the romance of archery, which utilizes an essentially primitive shooting system, has not only survived the invention and development of highly sophisticated and efficient firearms but has become the nation's fastest growing shooting sport. From a hunter's standpoint, it's quite obvious that it speaks to the most basic instincts. Saxon Pope, in *Hunting with the Bow and Arrow,* may have explained this apparent paradox best when he wrote:

"Here we have a weapon of beauty and romance. He who shoots with a bow puts his life's energy into it. The force behind the flying shaft must be placed there by the archer. At the moment of greatest strain he must draw every sinew to the utmost; his hand must be steady; his nerves under absolute control; his eye clean and clear. In the hunt he pits his well-trained skill against the instinctive cunning of his quarry. By the most adroit cleverness, he must approach within striking distance, and when he speeds his low-whispering shaft and strikes his game, he has won by the strength of arm and nerve. It is a noble sport."

Many things contribute to the continuing popularity of all forms of archery, but the two most prominent are *opportunity* and *diversity*. In recreational archery, for example, there are many organizations and facilities available. Truly, there are few towns and cities across the nation that don't have some kind of indoor or outdoor shooting range that provides archers a variety of games. Such ranges are listed by state in Appendix C.

Industry has been quick to react to the revolution in archery, and has kept pace with the growing interest by investing heavily in the development of new and more diversified equipment and accessories designed specifically for this market. Many companies have also put professional archers and bowhunters into the field to conduct seminars and instructional sessions to generate even more public interest and enthusiasm. There are many national and regional dealers and publicly attended shows dedicated strictly to archery, and the two most prominent of all dealer shows, the annual Shooting, Hunting Outdoor Trade Show (SHOT) and National Sporting Goods Association Show (NSGA), both held at the beginning of each year, serve as showplaces for all of the new products industry has to offer for archers and bowhunters.

What has generated the most energy and

enthusiasm in recent years has been the huge increase of interest in bowhunting, and especially big game. Where at one time the use of archery tackle for the larger game species was prohibited virtually everywhere in the country (in fact, the first legal bowhunt for deer didn't occur in the U.S. until the late 1930s), today bowhunting for big game is permitted throughout the nation, and in many cases archers have longer hunting seasons than gun hunters—and sometimes larger bag limits.

Finally, the combination of recreational archery and bowhunting further enhances the sport. Many people take up archery with the main purpose of becoming a hunter. If learning required only shooting at bullseye targets to develop skill, recreational archery would soon cease offering challenges. Now, though, with exciting and complex field games that simulate hunting situations, millions of archers are extending their participation to competitive shooting and bowhunting.

This makes the future look very bright, especially for bowhunting. However, it is imperative that this increase in popularity be accompanied by a concerted effort to enlarge and expand the education programs that relate to both hunters and the general public. Remember that hunters of all kinds make up only about 10 percent of the population, and that bowhunters represent only 15 to 20 percent of that number. On the other hand, of the 90 percent of the population that doesn't hunt, about 10 percent are opposed to the sport.

In many cases, this "anti" sentiment is due largely to lack of understanding, so education and information efforts aimed at this group of people can pay significant dividends. Ultimately, though, the major responsibility for maintaining and improving the image of bowhunting lies in the hunters themselves.

Progress is being made. Most states have mandatory Hunter Safety Programs for youths and first-time purchasers of hunting licenses. Interestingly, these sessions are often voluntarily attended by hunters with experience who want to brush up on current rules and safety measures. Seminars conducted by experts and professionals also are very effective means of educating both hunters and the general public. They deal with topics ranging from instructions for beginners to advanced hunting tactics. Individual hunter responsibility is emphasized and encouraged.

Basically stated, it comes down to this: the *tomorrow* of bowhunting will be determined by what bowhunters do *today*.

It's all up to you.

The best way for a beginner to get under way correctly is to consult a salesperson at a sporting-goods store or at a pro shop that specializes in outfitting the archer.

1

Choosing Equipment

In order to get the right start in archery, regardless of what form of the sport is involved—field, target or bowhunting—following some simple first steps will help avoid a lot of frustration and disappointment.

It is important that the novice first gain some knowledge of the fundamentals and realize that archery, like many other skills, requires a "crawl-before-you-walk" approach. One begins with the basics and progresses accordingly. One of the worst mistakes a beginner can make is to go out and buy a bow and some arrows and start practicing. Without any knowledge of what's recommended, it's easy to select the wrong equipment, with the result that often you'll have to unlearn everything and begin all over again. Buying equipment that is too advanced is another error beginners make. The result is similar to trying to learn to drive using a 15-speed tractor trailer truck instead of a car that has an automatic transmission and power steering.

There are several ways to go about learning the ABCs of archery. One of the best is to enlist the help of a friend who is an archer and who can help guide you to right decisions regarding basic needs and choices. Another area of assistance is through some of the excellent instructional videos, tapes and books available. Going to archery or bowhunting meets and tournaments and watching experienced archers shoot can be very helpful, too. At these events there are experts who are usually willing to answer questions and offer assistance to beginners. It's a good idea to get more than one expert's opinion, particularly on equipment items. Experienced shooters have personal preferences that may not be what's best suited for you.

Once familiar with the fundamentals, the next step is the selection of equipment, and this is a point where you can place yourself in jeopardy. No matter how much reading and observing you may have done, it's a mistake to try to personally judge what's best to begin with. Sporting goods stores, department stores and mail-order catalogs feature mind-boggling displays of equipment that can confuse experienced archers, much less beginners. Even at places where equipment can be tried out on the spot, the salesmen sometimes aren't qualified to provide expert advice.

Pro shop experts can tailor equipment precisely for every individual and prevent the small disasters that can occur when a beginner tries the do-it-yourself approach.

The most effective and efficient way to get started right is to go to a pro shop. These places specialize in getting beginners under way properly by determining precisely the best equipment for each individual. This is done by letting the person try many different bows until one is found that feels the most comfortable to handle. Next comes the process of matching the equipment and supplying the necessary accessories. After that, the shop's specialist will monitor your progress and keep adjusting the tackle accordingly. The services of a pro shop cost a little more at the outset, but it's an expense that many experienced archers feel is well worth it in the long run.

If you happen to be in a location where there's no pro shop nearby, some of the major manufacturers of archery equipment will provide the beginner with information and assistance. Supply them with details about yourself—height, weight, age, and the type of archery activity you're interested in—and ask them to make recommendations on the kind of tackle you should purchase to start with, and the names and addresses of either nearby dealers or sales representatives who can lend additional help.

Once you have the right equipment, stick with it. Switching around and experimenting with other tackle can totally confuse and derail the learning process.

FINDING THE MASTER EYE

The first thing a beginner must do before selecting a bow is determine his or her dominant, or "master," eye. Generally speaking, in right-handed persons the right eye is dominant, and vice versa for left-handed persons. However, there are cases where this isn't true, particularly in individuals who happen to be ambidextrous and use both hands with equal ease.

It's important to make this your first step. Occasionally, shooters start out using the wrong hand and eye and then discover later that they have to switch. This means learning all over again, and there's no use doing things the hard way when it can be easily avoided.

There are a couple of simple methods for finding out which eye is dominant. One is to hold the arms straight out and make a triangle with the thumbs and forefingers. Pick an object in the distance and focus on it. Then slowly bring the triangle closer to the face, keeping your eye on the object. The triangular opening will be drawn back to the dominant eye.

Another way is to point your finger at an object with both eyes open. Then close or cover one eye and see if the tip of the finger remains on the point of focus. If it does, the eye you are looking through is dominant. If not, then it is the other eye.

There are instances where the dominant eye is impaired or not functional. This makes it necessary for the person either to learn to shoot with the other hand, or to use a special bow sight with extended pins to compensate for the difference in point of aim.

MODERN BOW CHOICES

Most Americans of a certain age became familiar with bows and arrows by seeing cowboy and Indian movies when they were young, and this inspired a lot of kids to fashion their own versions out of tree limbs and grocer's twine. To say the least, the toy weapons were clumsy and inefficient; but if nothing more, they provided a rudimentary idea of the principles involved. The commercial bow and arrow outfits available for youngsters then (and still available now) had arrows with rubber stoppers on the end that would stick to glass or other flat, smooth surfaces. Often youngsters wore an Indian headdress with brightly colored feathers to complete the look.

It's possible that using these toys may inspire some children to eventually take up the sport of archery. Possible, yes, yet space age weapons seem to be the preference of children today.

The most important media influences on archery in the late 1930s and early 1940s were the popular film *Robin Hood* and the movie shorts showing the fantastic archery skills of the great Howard Hill. Both of these featured the longbow, which provided the sport with a much more attractive and appealing image.

At about the same time, the legendary Fred Bear was generating interest in both recreational archery and bowhunting. His efforts launched archery, and especially bowhunting, on a course that has developed into the fastest growing shooting sport in the nation.

The Longbow

Earlier in this century, when Saxon Pope and Art Young were in search of the best type of

One method of determining the master eye is to extend both arms and form a triangle with the thumbs and forefingers, then draw it closer and the dominant eye will reveal itself.

Another way to find the master eye is to point at an object with both eyes open, then cover one eye and see if the object moves. If it doesn't, the open eye is the dominant one.

The English longbow is the one that American archery pioneers took as their model, and it's still used by those who prefer traditional equipment for hunting or competition.

much more efficient than the Indian bows, so its worth had already been established by the time Pope and Young became active in trying to renew interest in the sport of archery and the attempt to modernize equipment. They added much to the knowledge of longbow construction by experimenting with different kinds of native American wood instead of the traditional English yew. They used Osage orange, mulberry, black walnut, cedar and hickory, and they discovered that Tennessee red cedar backed with hickory was a good substitute for yew. The longbows they made were among the first sophisticated hunting and target bows produced in this country, and their designs became the standard for manufacturing bows for American archers.

equipment to use for target shooting and hunting, they experimented with bows and arrows produced by seventeen different Indian tribes, as well as thirteen others that were created by bowyers in various foreign countries.

The results showed that a 65-pound English yew longbow topped them all, sending an arrow 300 yards. Second was a 70-pound Yaki Indian bow that shot an arrow 210 yards; and third, a 56-pound Nigrito bow propelled an arrow 176 yards. This led Pope to say that this particular English bow was the most powerful artillery of its sort in the world.

Actually, the Thompson brothers mentioned in the Introduction found the English longbow

A trio of shooters with the three types of bows. From front to rear: the typical longbow, recurve and compound bow.

Long after the invention of gunpowder and firearms, African Bushmen were hunting with tiny, poison-tipped arrows.

The Bushmen's arrows were hand-forged from metal and coated with a poison that either killed or incapacitated their prey.

Another great contribution by Pope and Young was Pope's classic books, *Hunting with the Bow and Arrow* and *The Adventurous Bowmen,* published in the 1920s. They chronicled the duo's hunting adventures on the North American and African continents and their various research projects. Both volumes had been out of print for many years until recently reprinted by Wolfe Publishing Company. These books inspired hunters to adopt archery as a sport that offered challenge and satisfaction both as recreation and hunting. Today's gigantic interest in all forms of archery can be largely traced to this beginning.

This classic bow hasn't disappeared from the scene, and is actually experiencing a comeback. Now instead of being a bow for the beginner, it's more often used by veteran shooters who like to return to traditional equipment because of the aesthetics. They're traditional in design, but the current models are made of fiberglass, laminated and impregnated wood, and other modern materials. Many of them, if not most, are custom built and very expensive.

The Recurve Bow

Unlike the longbow, which has straight limbs and an average length of nearly 6 feet, its successor, the recurve bow, is more compact, with elongated S-curved limbs that supply more energy than straight ones, and which results in less recoil.

The modern recurve bow was made famous

A modern recurve bow and accessories.

by Fred Bear in the early 1950s. Bear modified a bow design invented in ancient times by Turkish and Persian warriors, and used modern laminating techniques combining wood and fiberglass to create the fastest and most efficient bows ever built up to that time.

Recurves are graceful in appearance, and this type of bow still has many dedicated users, especially among instinctive shooters. Too, there are some excellent take-down recurve bows available today that are ideal for traveling or storing, and which perform equally as well as the one-piece models.

Today recurves, like longbows, are often used by experienced bowyers who started out with a compound and decided to revert to a more traditional archery form, but there are many hunters who prefer them over a compound bow for various reasons. One is that they're less complicated and are trouble free. Another, just as important, is that with use of modern materials and advanced technology, their performance compares favorably.

This is one of the several styles of custom take-down recurve bows that remain highly popular among bowhunters.

Compound bows come in all sizes and configurations. Here a hunter looks over a high-tech target bow and a mini-bow for young shooters.

The Compound Bow

The appearance of the first compound bows on the market in the late 1960s marked the most radical change in archery design and function in the history of the sport. By traditional standards, they were considered unsightly, but once archers overcame this reaction and began to use them, their advantages quickly became apparent. Today they dominate both the target and bowhunting markets.

The compound bow consists of two limbs made of fiberglass, graphite, foam, wood, or combinations of these materials, and a center or handle section. At each end are brackets that hold eccentric wheels and pulleys and cables that attach to the drawstring. This is a basic description, because from this have evolved some highly complex mechanisms, an immense

A modern compound bow of radical design that is popular with both tournament archers and bowhunters.

variety of bow designs and various high-tech add-on accessories that are described in a later chapter.

What should be considered is that a good-quality compound bow is so easy to handle that it's ideal for a beginner. The main reason is that a person can start out with a bow weight that will continue to be satisfactory for target or hunting purposes as the level of skill increases. No change or upgrade is necessary.

The mechanism just described is what makes this possible. With a longbow or recurve bow, the draw weight increases as the string is pulled back, but with a compound, the weight peaks at mid-draw, then reduces as much as 40 to 65 percent as you reach full draw. It's called "let-off," and it can allow a beginning bowhunter to have a bow that will be capable of bagging

medium-size big-game animals such as whitetail deer and antelope once his or her shooting skills are developed.

Two of the basic considerations in compound bow selection should be what kind of performance you prefer, and to what use it will be put. This is where wheel choice plays a part. The round wheel design has the advantage of providing a smoother draw, as well as being more dependable, efficient and less trouble to tune. Cam wheel bows are faster, but as with many other devices and mechanisms, there's a trade-off involved. These high-speed compounds aren't as quiet as the round wheel types or as rugged. They're also more difficult to keep tuned, which can be a big drawback to hunters in the field or in backcountry.

The most confusing part of bow selection for

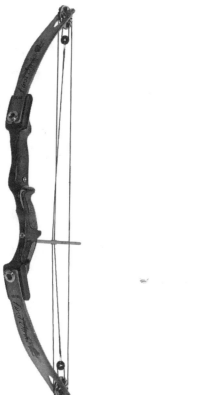

A popular compound hunting bow made by Bear Archery.

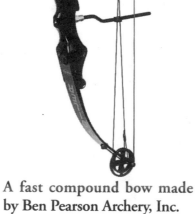

A fast compound bow made by Ben Pearson Archery, Inc.

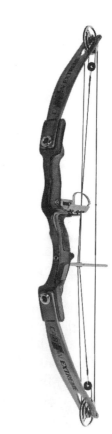

This carbon bow is one of the newer innovations from Bear/Jennings Archery Co.

a beginner is the dizzying array of compound bows on the market that range all the way from basic, functional models to high-tech versions loaded with accessories that resemble something from outer space. Without expert or professional advice and guidance, it's easy to be diverted or influenced by cosmetics or glamour and make a bad judgment at square one.

The Crossbow

Until recently it would not have been logical to include the crossbow in the category of recreational archery, because it was legal as a hunting weapon in only a small handful of states. That situation has changed, magnifying the role of the crossbow and making it a type of equipment that some beginning archers may wish to consider.

This isn't to say that it doesn't remain controversial, and there are many archers, and particularly bowhunters, who vigorously oppose its use. Still, this has been overcome to the point that in 1992 some thirty-five states permitted crossbows for hunting one or more different kinds of game, and further expansion of these privileges is anticipated.

There is a strange attitude regarding the crossbow that suggests that since it was a medieval instrument of war, it is therefore evil. This ignores the fact that the longbow, which has no such stigma attached to it, was in use at the same time. The main reason for looking askance at the crossbow, though, is that the mechanism is different. Traditional archers—as well as many users of compound bows—tend to have a purist attitude. They claim the crossbow is too much like a firearm in both appearance and function.

It's quite natural that the crossbow occupies a separate competitive shooting category, and there are in fact national organizations that include it in their schedule of events.

Crossbows initially followed the longbows and recurves as far as limb design was concerned, but the modern versions use the compound bow system. This makes it possible to bring the string back into the cocked position without the use of a lever. Crossbows are extremely powerful and can be fitted with scopes that make them very accurate within the limits of their range. Incidentally, the shaft delivered by a crossbow is referred to as a bolt rather than an arrow.

As with the other types of equipment, the best source of information on crossbows and accessories will be sporting goods stores or pro shops.

Crossbows are becoming more and more popular. This one is typical of the models available.

The compound bow principle has been added to crossbows, making them easier to cock. With a scope, they perform with great accuracy.

A U-TURN IN EQUIPMENT PREFERENCES

Although plenty of big-game animals had been taken in America by bowhunters before the 1960s, it was about that time that the sport became exceedingly popular. The selection of bows was limited to longbows and recurves, and the offering of accessories was somewhat meager. The fact that the sport posed more of a challenge than gun hunting held off many who were otherwise attracted to it.

That was the situation until the appearance of the compound bow, which immediately created an explosion of interest and participation. Once it began, the zeal to get more people involved in the sport resulted in manufacturers creating all sorts of gadgets intended to make bowhunting so easy that everyone from children to grandparents could participate.

Compound bows allowed millions of people to shoot bows of weights that previously would have been impossible for them to pull back to a full draw. This advanced technology also permitted inexperienced and unskilled hunters to go afield, and this in turn resulted in increased personal injuries and crippled game. In too many instances the basic elements of bowhunting were shunted aside in favor of expediency.

The trend toward simplicity persisted through the 1970s, but at the beginning of the 1980s, a reversal began to occur. Many bowhunters, some of whom had begun with traditional equipment and had moved on to compound bows, did a U-turn and reverted to longbows and recurves.

Principal among their reasons was a desire to rediscover the pleasure and satisfaction they had enjoyed when using their personal skills instead of gadgets. In a sense, it reflected the national attitudes that favored the natural instead of the artificial, as well as a willingness and even a zeal to face challenges.

Whitetail hunters constituted the majority of the "escapees." Gun seasons had become crowded to the point that solitude in the woods was impossible to experience. Early and separate bowhunting seasons offered the opportunity to get out into the woods and enjoy this simple pleasure again. There was also the appeal of a hunter facing nature with only the basics.

The first hunters to re-enter or to choose to enter the traditional fold were those who either possessed or wished to learn the multiple skills required. They liked the idea of becoming *woodsmen* rather than just *shooters*.

Something else became apparent to those who had experienced using all kinds of bows.

Crossbows are very powerful. Each year more states are permitting their use for various kinds of small- and big-game hunting.

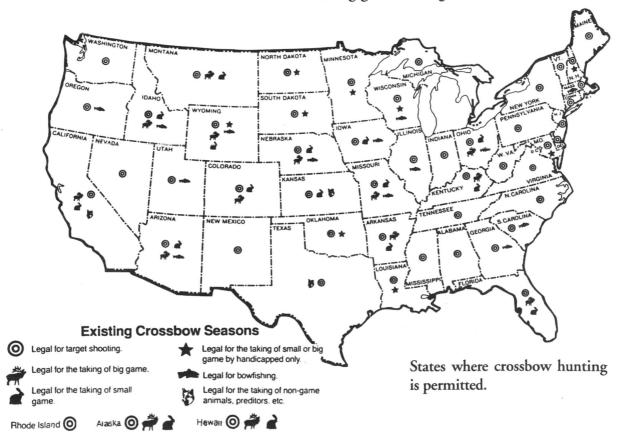

Existing Crossbow Seasons

- ⊚ Legal for target shooting.
- ★ Legal for the taking of small or big game by handicapped only.
- 🦌 Legal for the taking of big game.
- 🏹 Legal for bowfishing.
- 🐇 Legal for the taking of small game.
- 🐺 Legal for the taking of non-game animals, preditors. etc.

Rhode Island ⊚   Alaska ⊚ 🦌 🐇   Hawaii ⊚ 🐗 🐇

States where crossbow hunting is permitted.

They found that when they shot the heavier hunting arrows, quality longbows and recurve bows would do practically everything a compound bow does. The only disadvantage lies in having no breakover or holding weight or the ability to shoot lighter arrows. On the other hand, compound bows upset the rhythm enjoyed when shooting a traditional bow (which is the reason the legendary Fred Bear, the country's most famous bowhunter, never abandoned the recurve).

Evidence of this return to basics is plain to see. In 1980 there were fewer than ten custom "stick bow" builders who advertised; by 1990 the number had climbed to over seventy. This increase gained the attention of the big manufacturers, who began producing more of the kinds of equipment that traditionalists wanted, some of which they'd dropped when the rush to technology was occurring. New longbows and recurves appeared in their catalogs; and as the number of traditional hunters continued to expand, quality rather than quantity became the hallmark.

This isn't a prediction that the pendulum will swing to an opposite position, but it illustrates that as the overall increase in bowhunting continues the ratio of compound bowhunters versus traditional bowhunters is changing.

And as a bonus, some attitudes are changing as well!

BOW SELECTION AND BOW WEIGHT

The term "bow weight" doesn't refer to the *actual* weight of the bow, but rather to the amount of force in pounds that are required to draw an arrow to its full length. For all practical purposes, it's better to think of it as "draw weight."

In the case of longbows and recurve bows, the weight marked on them represents the poundage measured by bringing a 28-inch arrow to full draw. This is the length arrow best suited for the arm span of an average adult male. Obviously, there have to be variations in this system due to age and physical size. A person with a shorter draw length will be pulling less weight, and a longer draw will increase the weight. This is another reason for making certain your equipment is matched. You don't want to start off with a weight that's too great, because this can affect your shooting to the point that you'll likely become discouraged at seeing little progress. Worse still, it could cause you to quit the sport entirely.

Regardless of what type of equipment you choose, make sure you're comfortable with it, not just in draw weight, but also in the general "feel." The best way to determine this is with hands-on experience. Go to several stores and pro shops and try as many bows as you can until you find one that seems right.

Persons preferring to start out with a longbow or recurve bow will begin with a particular weight, then in time they will move up to a higher draw level. Pulling a bow requires the use of certain back muscles that aren't ordinarily given a workout, but with practice, they strengthen and handle more weight. The only problem is that since draw weight on longbows and recurves isn't adjustable, advancing one's skill level means sooner or later buying another bow. In the case of the takedown recurve, however, this means only purchasing another more powerful set of limbs.

Two of the biggest advantages offered by a compound bow are that both the draw length and draw weight are adjustable and can be lessened or increased as needed. This makes it possible to start with one bow and continue to use it from the basic steps in shooting all the way through to hunting big game. A compound bow pulling 45 to 60 pounds can take down most big-game animals on this continent provided the right broadhead is used and its placement is correct. The second plus is the let-off feature, which doesn't require the shooter to hold back the full bow weight at full draw.

This suggests one of the major don'ts in bow selection, which is: don't purchase too heavy a bow at the outset. The idea of being able to draw an 80- to 90-pound bow may bolster the ego, and heavier bows will project an arrow faster and with flatter trajectory. The down side is that it can also be a serious impediment to learning to shoot properly. A heavy bow is hard to hold, and as a result, accuracy suffers. Also, heavier bows are more subject to breakage, and although many companies manufacture them, they will not warranty them beyond a certain poundage.

The best plan to follow is to select a bow that is comfortable to hold and to draw. Get matched arrows and shoot until the procedure becomes almost second nature. Believe in the old saying that "practice makes perfect" and stick with it!

ARROWS

Arrows come in a variety of materials suitable for use in any kind of bow, but they must be carefully matched to the equipment to obtain proper performance. The flight characteristic of an arrow is determined by several factors. One of these is its stiffness, or spine, the degree of which is increased by both draw weight and arrow length. An arrow with too little spine will shatter or fly erratically. Arrow weight is another consideration, since it influences trajectory, accuracy and striking power. The right kind of fletching is needed, too, and this choice has to do with the purpose for which the arrow is intended. Arrowhead weight is important, and when broadheads are used it becomes more critical because of the considerable differences in sizes and design. Finally, proper alignment of the nock and fletching assures better arrow flight. For beginners, this is another project that shouldn't be attempted without expert advice.

The arrow, like a bullet, is a projectile whose flight is launched by the release of stored energy. In the case of a rifle, the energy is in the form of gunpowder contained in the cartridge; in the bow, energy is generated and stored as the string is drawn.

In both cases, the energy is transferred to the projectile in the form of kinetic energy, which is used in its struggle through the air as it flies toward a target. If its shape is blunt, there is more air resistance, causing the velocity to drop rapidly in proportion to the remaining energy. A pointed or streamlined shape is more efficient and retains energy longer. In this sense, "velocity" is simply another method of defining energy and a way to indicate the energy remaining.

For bowhunters in particular, the most important thing is *penetration:* the hunter must make certain the arrow retains sufficient energy to accomplish this satisfactorily. Energy is vital, but the factors of arrow weight, broadhead design, type of fletching and straightness of flight are all involved. All these influence how energy is expended, and there are various trade-offs. For example, since the use of heavy arrows for big game is recommended, adding speed means sacrificing both energy and penetration.

For those who prefer to delve into it further, there is an equation for figuring the kinetic energy of an arrow where V equals velocity:

$$\frac{V^2 \times \text{arrow weight (grains)}}{450{,}240} = \text{foot-pounds of kinetic energy}$$

Gravity and air friction affect anything moving through the atmosphere, and both begin to influence arrow flight the instant it is launched. Contrary to some opinions, arrows leaving the bow do not overcome gravity and "rise." This is an illusion, but one that's easily explained: the actual point of aim is above the spot where the arrow is intended to strike. Basically, the degree of elevation is determined by distance from the target and how the equipment performs.

As far as air friction is concerned, the best way to illustrate its effect in diminishing energy is to think about how much more effort is required of a person walking into a stiff wind.

Some bows are more efficient in transferring energy than others, and each shooter must make a choice based on experience and personal preference. Also, there's a difference between using a mechanical release and using fingers. There is a phenomenon called "archer's paradox" that refers to a bend in the arrow that occurs when it is suddenly thrust forward by the surge of stored energy. This occurs very rapidly and can't be seen by the naked eye, but it has a slight influence on velocity. The bend is more pronounced when using a finger release, since it's impossible to get fingers out of the way. The string rolls off to the right or left, according to which hand you draw with, and it takes slightly longer for the arrow to stabilize and establish a proper flight path. With the mechanical release, you get a perfect release every time, since the string goes in a straight line behind the arrow.

Materials

Matching arrows is much easier now than when wood arrows were the only choice. Wood has inherent problems in regard to weight, density, stiffness and the difficulty in manufacturing shafts with uniform straightness and circumfer-

QUICK REFERENCE EASTON SUPER SLAM XX78 SHAFT SIZE SELECTION CHART							
SIZE SELECTION BASED ON: • COMPOUND BOW WITH ENERGY WHEELS • FINGER RELEASE • 125 GRAIN BROADHEAD OR FIELD POINT							
ARROW LENGTH					SHAFT WEIGHT GROUP AND SIZE		
28"	29"	30"	31"	32"	SuperLite Aluminum	Lite Aluminum	Standard Aluminum
39-44#	34-39#				2114	2016	
44-49#	39-44#	34-39#			2114	2016	2018
49-54#	44-49#	39-44#	34-39#		2213		2018
54-59#	49-54#	44-49#	39-44#	34-39#	2213		2117
59-64#	54-59#	49-54#	44-49#	39-44#	2314	2216	2117
64-70#	59-64#	54-59#	49-54#	44-49#	2314	2216	2219
70-76#	64-70#	59-64#	54-59#	49-54#	2413		2219
76-82#	70-76#	64-70#	59-64#	54-59#	2413		2219
82-88#	76-82#	70-76#	64-70#	59-64#	2514		2317
88-94#	82-88#	76-82#	70-76#	64-70#	2514		2317
94-100#	88-94#	82-88#	76-82#	70-76#	2514		2317

COMPOUND BOW Energy Wheel Peak Bow Weight

ence. Also, wood is porous and can absorb moisture, causing warping and weight increase.

The development of fiberglass, aluminum and carbon shafts has improved the ability to match arrows with much greater accuracy. And while wood is still a choice of archers who use traditional bows, it's mostly because they enjoy the aesthetics and the satisfaction of making their own arrows.

The first alternate to wood was fiberglass arrows. Tougher and stiffer than wood arrows, they could stand more abuse and were proven game-getters. They were also heavier and more expensive. Still, their better qualities won over many archers, particularly the hunters, some of

whom still like them. And fiberglass arrows are acknowledged to be the best for bowfishing.

The innovation of tubular aluminum arrows came next. These quickly became the favorite of both target shooters and bowhunters, and they seem destined to remain so. It's logical, because aluminum shafts can be manufactured to extremely precise diameters, wall thicknesses or gauges, weight and stiffness to fit any condition or situation a shooter can encounter. This allows for more exact matching, and a greater variety of choices. There are other advantages. These arrows are moderately priced, and all but the most badly bent shafts can be put back into service with an inexpensive straightening device.

QUICK REFERENCE EASTON HUNTING SHAFT SIZE SELECTION CHART										
SIZE SELECTION BASED ON:					• COMPOUND BOW WITH ENERGY WHEELS • FINGER RELEASE • 125 GRAIN BROADHEAD OR FIELD POINT					
ARROW LENGTH[1]					SHAFT WEIGHT GROUP & SIZE					
28"	29 "	30"	31"	32"	SuperLite A/C/C	UltraLite Aluminum	SuperLite Aluminum	Lite Aluminum	Standard Aluminum
34-39#					3L-18	2112	2013	1916	
39-44#	34-39#				3-18	2112	2113	2016	
44-49#	39-44#	34-39#			3-28	2212	2114	2115	2018
49-54#	44-49#	39-44#	34-39#		3-28	2212	2213	2115	2018
54-59#	49-54#	44-49#	39-44#	34-39#	3-39	2312	2213	2215	2117
59-64#	54-59#	49-54#	44-49#	39-44#	3-49	2312	2314	2215	2117
64-70#	59-64#	54-59#	49-54#	44-49#	3-49	2312	2314	2216	2219
70-76#	64-70#	59-64#	54-59#	49-54#	3-60	2512	2413	2315	2219
76-82#	70-76#	64-70#	59-64#	54-59#	3-60	2512	2413	2315	2219
82-88#	76-82#	70-76#	64-70#	59-64#	3-71	2512	2514		2317
88-94#	82-88#	76-82#	70-76#	64-70#	3-71		2514		2317
94-100#	88-94#	82-88#	76-82#	70-76#	3-71		2514		2419

COMPOUND BOW - Energy Wheel Peak Bow Weight

ALUMINUM SHAFTS & COMPONENTS

SUPER SLAM XX78, XX75 & EAGLE— SHAFT, POINT & INSERT SPECIFICATIONS

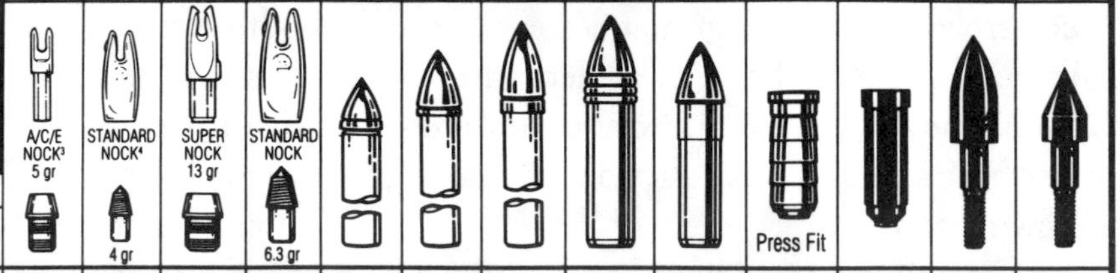

SHAFT SIZE	SHAFT WEIGHT: EAGLE (Grains per Inch)	SHAFT WEIGHT: 75[8] (Grains per Inch)	SHAFT WEIGHT: **SS**[9] (Grains per Inch)	SHAFT LENGTH[7]: EAGLE (Inches)	SHAFT LENGTH[7]: 75[8] **SS**[9] (Inches)	UNI[1] System: BUSHING & NOCK — A/C/E NOCK[3] 5 gr (Grains)	UNI[1] System: EXTENSION[2] — STANDARD NOCK[4] 4 gr (Inches)	SUPER UNI[1] System: BUSHING & NOCK — SUPER NOCK 13 gr (Grains)	SUPER UNI[1] System: EXTENSION — STANDARD NOCK 6.3 gr (Inches)	7% F.O.C. POINT[5] NIBB (Grains)	8% F.O.C. POINT[5] NIBB (Grains)	9% F.O.C. POINT[5] NIBB (Grains)	ONE PC. POINT 125 gr. Bullet (Grains)	ONE PC. POINT Bullet (Grains)	RPS[6] INSERT Alum. Press Fit (Grains)	RPS[6] INSERT Carbon (Grains)	RPS[6] POINT 125 gr. Bullet (Inches)	RPS[6] POINT Chisel (In.-Grains)
1413	—	5.92	5.98	—	26	—	7/32	—	—	41.1	—	—	—	30.0[13]	—	—	—	—
1416	—	7.15	7.22	—	27	—	7/32	—	—	46.1	—	—	—	52.0	—	—	—	—
1511	—	5.62	5.64	—	26 1/2	4.2	7/32,1/4	—	—	—	48.6	55.0	—	—	—	—	—	—
1512	—	5.78	5.84	—	27	4.8	7/32,1/4	—	—	—	49.1	56.0	—	—	—	—	—	—
1516	7.51	7.34	7.41	26	27 1/2	—	7/32, 1/4	—	—	48.0	—	60.3	—	54.0	—	—	—	—
1611	—	5.97	6.03	—	27 1/2	5.5	1/4	—	—	—	53.6	—	—	—	—	—	—	—
1612	—	6.21	6.27	—	28	6.8	1/4	—	—	—	54.8	—	—	—	—	—	—	—
1616	8.73	8.35	8.43	27	28 1/2	—	1/4	—	—	55.7	—	70.0	—	63.0	12.8[12]	—	—	—
1711	—	6.45	6.52	—	28	6.1	1/4	—	—	—	61.1	—	—	—	—	—	—	—
1712	—	6.64	6.71	—	28 1/2	6.3	1/4	—	—	—	62.3	—	—	—	—	—	—	—
1713	—	7.42	7.49	—	29	—	1/4	—	—	53.5	—	66.6	—	—	17.2[12]	—	—	—
1716	9.42	9.03	9.12	28 1/2	29	—	1/4	—	—	60.2	—	76.1	—	68.0	16.0[12]	—	—	—
1811	—	6.96	7.02	—	29	7.1	1/4, 9/32	—	—	—	64.9	—	—	—	—	—	—	—
1812	—	7.24	7.31	—	29 1/2	7.7	1/4, 9/32	—	—	—	67.1	—	—	—	—	—	—	—
1813	—	7.86	7.94	—	30	—	1/4	—	—	56.3	—	70.7	125	—	23.5[12]	7.1	—	9/32-61
1816	9.89	9.27	9.36	29	30	—	1/4[10]	—	—	62.9	—	79.7	—	74.0	13.0[11]	7.3	—	9/32-61
1912	—	7.54	7.62	—	30	8.1	9/32	—	—	—	70.0	—	—	—	—	—	—	—
1913	—	8.34	8.42	—	31	—	9/32	—	—	63.7	—	79.9	125	—	18.0[11]	9.0	5/16	5/16-76
1916	10.29	10.05	10.15	30	31	—	9/32	—	—	72.0	—	91.0	—	82.0	16.0[11]	8.8	5/16	5/16-76
2012	—	7.93	8.01	—	31 1/2	8.6	5/16	5.2	5/16	—	82.5	—	125	—	22.1	11.2	5/16	5/16-76
2013	—	9.01	9.10	—	32 1/2	—	9/32	—	—	68.2	—	85.9	125	—	21.0[11]	11.2	5/16	5/16-76
2016	—	10.56	10.67	—	32	—	9/32[10]	4.6	5/16	80.0	—	100.7	125	90.0	20.0[11]	10.9	5/16	5/16-76
2018	12.00	12.28	12.40	30 1/2	32 1/2	—	5/16	4.1	5/16	89.0	—	—	—	—	18.0[11]	10.3	5/16	5/16-76
2112	—	8.34	8.42	—	31 1/2	9.1	5/16	7.2	5/16	—	88.0	—	125	—	25.8	14.4	11/32	11/32-91
2113	—	9.30	9.39	—	32 1/2	—	5/16	—	—	78.2	—	98.2	125	—	24.0[11]	13.5	11/32	11/32-91
2114	—	9.86	9.96	—	33	—	5/16	7.7	5/16	78.2	—	98.2	125	—	24.0[11]	13.5	11/32	11/32-91
2115	—	10.75	10.86	—	33	—	5/16	—	—	83.1	—	104.7	125	—	24.0[11]	13.5	11/32	11/32-91
2117	13.00	12.02	12.14	32	33 1/2	—	5/16	7.7	5/16	96.7	—	122.0	125	—	24.0[11]	13.5	11/32	11/32-91
2212	—	8.76	8.85	—	32 1/2	10.3	11/32	9.5	11/32	—	102.0	—	125	—	30.0	15.9	11/32	11/32-91
2213	—	9.83	9.93	—	33 1/2	—	5/16[10]	8.9	11/32	88.0	—	106.5	125	—	29.0[11]	15.9	11/32	11/32-91
2215	—	10.67	10.78	—	33	—	5/16[10]	—	—	95.0	—	—	125	—	29.0[11]	15.9	11/32	11/32-91
2216	—	12.02	12.14	—	34	—	5/16[10]	8.7	11/32	98.0	—	122.0	125	—	28.0[11]	15.2	11/32	11/32-91
2219	13.50	13.77	13.91	32	34	—	11/32	8.0	11/32	106.6	—	135.0	—	—	26.0[11]	14.4	11/32	11/32-91
2312	—	9.39	9.48	—	33 1/2	11.9	11/32	10.6	11/32	—	—	109.0	125	—	50.0	19.0	11/32	11/32-91
2314	—	10.67	10.78	—	34	—	11/32	11.6	11/32	—	—	—	125	—	44.0	18.0	11/32	11/32-91
2315	—	11.66	11.78	—	34 1/2	—	11/32	—	—	—	—	—	—	—	48.0	18.0	11/32	11/32-91
2317	—	13.26	13.39	—	34 1/2	—	11/32	12.7	11/32	—	—	—	—	—	48.0	18.0	11/32	11/32-91
2413	—	10.40	10.50	—	34	—	11/32	13.4	11/32	110.0	—	—	125	—	51.0	19.0	11/32	11/32-91
2419	—	14.55	14.70	—	34 1/2	—	11/32	—	—	—	—	—	—	—	48.0	18.0	11/32	11/32-91
2512	—	10 18	10.28	—	34 1/2	13.7	11/32	14.5	11/32	—	—	114.0	125	—	64.0	23.0	11/32	11/32-91
2514	—	11.33	11.44	—	34 1/2	—	11/32	14.2	11/32	—	—	—	125	—	58.0	22.0	11/32	11/32-91

EASTON X7— SHAFT & POINT SPECIFICATIONS

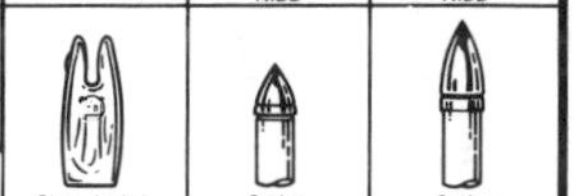

SIZE	WEIGHT Gr. per In.	LENGTH[7] Inches	NOCK Size - Inches	7% F.O.C.[5] NIBB Grains	9% F.O.C.[5] NIBB Grains
1516	7.39	27	7/32	48.5	60.9
1614	7.73	28	1/4	50.9	66.6
1616	8.38	28 1/2	1/4	56.2	70.7
1714	8.07	29	1/4	55.9	70.3
1716	9.03	29 1/2	1/4	60.7	76.7
1814	8.57	30	1/4	59.5	75.9
1816	9.53	30 1/2	1/4	64.3	81.8
1914	9.28	30 1/2	1/4	64.1	85.8
1916	10.10	31	9/32	72.4	91.6
2014	9.56	31 1/2	9/32	71.2	89.8
2114	9.78	32 1/2	5/16	78.2	98.2
2115	10.77	32 1/2	5/16	83.1	104.7

— Indicates not available
1 UNI—Universal Nock Installation System
2 UNI Extension also available in plastic - 3.0 grains
3 G Series Nock also available - 6.5 grains
4 Nock size for standard swaged nock taper, UNI Extension, and Super UNI Extension
5 F.O.C. is Front-of-Center balance position on the arrow shaft for the most commonly used length of each shaft size.
6 RPS = Replaceable Point System with 8-32 AMO Standard thread
7 Length is approximate stock shaft length for each size.
8 XX75, Easton 75, GameGetter, GameGetter II
9 **XX78 Super Slam in bold type**
10 GameGetter, GameGetter II, and Eagle Hunter are produced without reduced diameter taper and require the next largest nock size.
11 6-32 insert also available
12 6-32 insert only
13 Chisel

Carbon arrows, while controversial, are used more in target shooting than in bowhunting, although there's evidence that this may change in time. Carbon has great stiffness and can be used to make slimmer, lighter arrows that can achieve exceptional speed.

Tournament shooters like these qualities, since when propelled from a powerful bow with an overdraw, the trajectory is flattened significantly. The objections many bowhunters raise are that these arrows are too light and are not suitable for big-game hunting. They can shatter on impact, resulting in carbon fibers being imbedded in the meat. Even worse, they increase the possibility of crippling. The expense is also prohibitive, so there's little chance carbon will replace aluminum as the most suitable and practical material for manufacturing arrows.

Fletching

Fletching is the arrow's guidance system, providing it with drag to maintain stability and rotation to keep it on course. Without fletching, the arrow is like a ship without a rudder, even though the shaft itself may be straight and true.

Throughout previous centuries and on into the present one, feathers have been the standard fletching material. They still occupy a major place, although the alternative of plastic vanes has become extremely popular among both target archers and bowhunters—particularly those using compound bows. The centershot handles don't require the flexibility of feathers, since the fletching doesn't touch as the arrow is shot. From the hunter's standpoint, plastic vanes are more durable and less noisy than feathers. Too,

There are various kinds of fletching for different types of hunting and target shooting. These are a few examples of fletchings made with feathers, the standard material for centuries.

they perform well in all kinds of weather conditions. This is especially important to hunters, because feathers can flatten when wet, rendering the arrow either useless or highly unpredictable in flight.

Because of the heavier shaft and broadhead, fletching on hunting arrows must be longer in order to provide stability. Plastic fletching is heavier than feathers, but the weight difference is small. Feather-fletched arrows leave the bow faster than ones with plastic, but they also slow down more rapidly. Ultimately it's a sort of trade-off, and shooters can decide for themselves.

Whatever the material, fletching not only stabilizes the arrow, but it also determines how fast and how far it will travel, and several factors are involved when it comes to the purpose or result that's desired. If long range is the goal, one type will be best. If speed is the objective, there's a different formula. And let's not overlook the important aspect of plain old cosmetics. When it comes to that, it's hard to beat the kind of effects that can be created with bright colored and barred or spotted feathers. Or natural-colored ones, for that matter.

Straight fletching was once the rule, but today shooters have a variety of configurations from which to choose—standard, left and right wing helical (spiral), and straight offset. The type chosen by individual shooters is really a matter of preference, since tests have shown that there's very little difference in the flight characteristics of the various kinds. The length of the fletching depends upon arrow length and weight and type of point used.

There are what can be called "specialty arrows" designed for specific purposes. Flu-flu fletching, for example, causes an arrow to have very limited range and a rapid loss of speed in flight. There are a number of different styles, but all are virtual balls of feathers at the terminal end of the shaft. Flu-flu arrows are used principally for wing-shooting birds.

There are also arrows fletched specifically for bowfishing and frog hunting which have either plastic or rubber vanes.

Most shooters prefer arrows with three vanes, with one feather or vane set on the shaft at right angles to the slot of the nock. This is referred to as the "cock feather," and is often of a different color. The others are called "hen feathers" or "vanes." The use of four vanes isn't uncommon, and by comparison, the performance is about the same. However, in the excitement of hunting situations it's easy to incorrectly nock four-vane arrows, and perhaps that single disadvantage is enough to tip the scales in favor of the three-vane kind.

Making Your Own Arrows

As shooters gain experience many start making their own arrows. The components for this kind of endeavor are easily obtainable. The major aluminum arrow maker offers a selection of blanks for every target or hunting need, and there is a kaleidoscopic array of fletching material to choose from, as well as different styles of nocks. Tools for every aspect of home arrow manufacture are sold, including fletching jigs, nock locators, alignment devices, straighteners, scales and other accessories. It's truly high-tech compared to the old days when almost everything was done from scratch!

Economy plays a part in this, but it isn't the key factor. Archers, particularly those who use traditional equipment, find great pleasure in being personally involved in as many aspects of shooting as possible. They can customize the arrows to whatever degree they wish, and producing their own arrows adds another measure of pride and self-satisfaction.

Points for Practice and Small Game

The type of activity in which an archer is going to be involved determines what kind of point or head will be used on the arrow, and there are

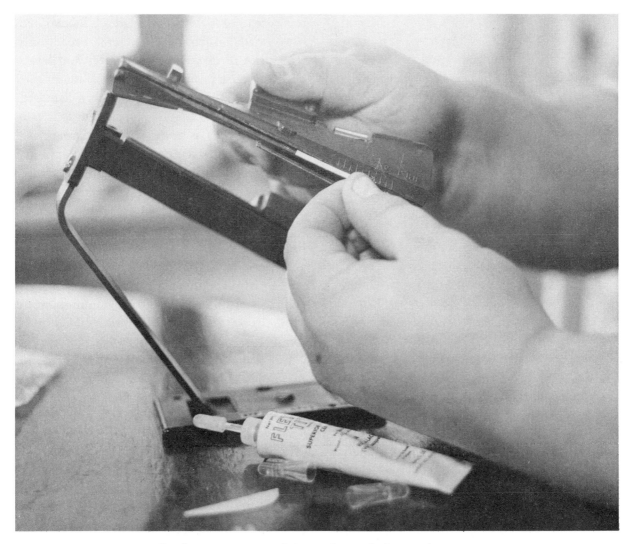

A fletching jig is one of the tools needed to make arrows.

oncs designed for every target and bowhunting purpose.

Beginning shooters will generally start with field points with some form of blunt and graduate to other types as their skills increase. In the past, when wood or fiberglass arrows were used, points had to be affixed to the shaft with glue. With the development of tubular aluminum shafts, an insert placed in the end of the arrow allows the shooter to choose the kind of point needed for the activity involved. This makes it possible to purchase a set of arrows at the start and continue to shoot with them in many kinds of target or field situations as long as the proper balance is maintained.

Blunt points are not only for practice, but they're also useful for hunting small game where shock rather than penetration is all that's required. There are several varieties available.

Field points are used in practice, also, and they are intended to simulate both the weight and the flight characteristics of hunting arrows. This same kind of point is sometimes used for target shooting, but there are special target points that provide less weight and a greater degree of accuracy. Their design makes them

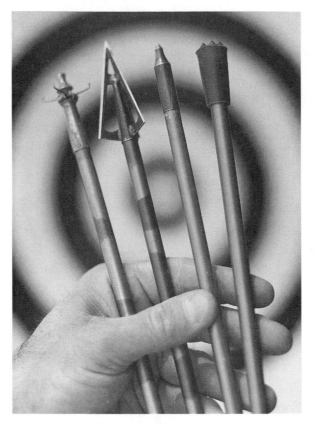

Four kinds of commonly used arrows for target practice and for small game and birds.

easier to remove from targets, also.

There are specialty points made for bowfishing. Some are much like harpoons in design, and others—called judo points or "grabbers," with wire arms of various dimensions—are very practical for use on small game and birds, and they also help stop arrows short and keep them from being lost under leaves and undergrowth.

Broadheads for Bowhunting Big Game

The selection of broadheads available is extensive. New versions pop up regularly in an already broadhead-inundated market.

It is in the area of bladed hunting points that the greatest amount of diversity occurs, with dozens of designs and configurations available. The earliest models were relatively simple: solid,

one-piece heads with two blades that required occasional sharpening. Next came broadheads with three blades; and shortly afterward heads with three or four pre-sharpened, removable blades that could be either replaced if damaged or resharpened and used again. There were also innovations such as blades with cutouts or vents that help improve accuracy; points with retractable blades that open up after penetration; heads with corkscrew or serrated blades; and among these, blades so badly designed that they had poor flight capabilities. Some broadheads have cutting edges all the way to the tip and others have blades set back from the nose cone. There are three versions: the plain nose cone, the cutting nose and the pyramid point.

The basic decision on hunting broadheads relates to what you want to accomplish. If you're hunting thick-skinned or dangerous animals, put penetration at the top of the list (and this usually means a two-bladed head). On thin-skinned species like whitetail deer or antelope, you want to punch a big hole clear through with a multi-blade broadhead and do a lot of tissue damage so there's either a quick end or a good blood trail. Within the myriad kinds of three- and four-blade heads there are many types of blades and blade configurations.

Most of the "ready-to-use" points are of the puncture type, with a nose cone which has to punch through an animal's tough hide before it becomes effective. As can be readily seen, this resistance diminishes both velocity and energy. Tests have shown that it takes as much as five times the pressure in pounds of thrust to push a puncture-type broadhead through a piece of leather as that required by the cutting nose or pyramid points most commonly used by hunters who prefer the fixed-blade heads. These slice through hide cleanly and provide a much better chance of the arrow passing entirely through the animal. More internal damage is done and an exit hole assures a good blood trail.

Three-blade heads are good, but four blades

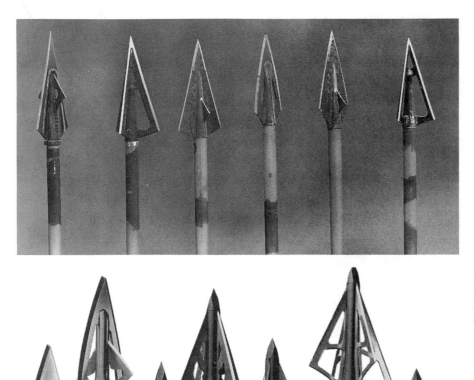

Six of the many kinds of hunting broadheads.

Some of the broadheads made by Bear Archery Company.

are even better, since the purpose is to create a large, lethal arrow path into and hopefully through the animal. Common sense shows that having one more cutting edge offers a distinct advantage.

Since the major goal in hunting big game should be to accomplish a clean, quick kill, using the most effective broadhead is one way to help assure it.

How to select the best broadhead? This is something that requires an intelligent and prudent approach. Conscientious hunters don't experiment on game in the field; rather, they practice with life-size, three-dimensional targets that are made of material that closely approximates animal flesh in terms of density and resistance. Seeking the advice of other big-game

bowhunters can help, also, since you can use their experiences to narrow the field of choices. Finally, when you find a broadhead that works well for you, stick with it and no matter how highly touted new versions may be, resist the temptation to switch until you learn more about them. Remember, you're dealing with living creatures, and there's no excuse for reckless "testing."

Think of it this way: When hunting big game, even the largest kind, your shots are going to be—or should be—within thirty yards. Light arrows with more speed and a flatter trajectory aren't critical. What you want is a heavy arrow that will deliver the most pounds of energy possible for attaining maximum penetration.

One thing that sets hunting broadheads apart

It's essential to keep hunting broadheads razor-sharp. This hunter is using a handy sharpener in the field.

from most of the other points is that they must have razor-sharp edges. There are options where this is concerned. The factory-sharpened kind offers the easiest way to go about it, because otherwise the hunter must put the razor edge on the points. Sharpening is a process that requires time and skill, yet serious bowyers prefer to do this themselves. It's satisfying, but it also gives them additional confidence in this vital piece of equipment and makes a clean kill on big game even more meaningful.

Of course, even those who use the pre-sharpened blades must realize that they're not completely immune from this task. All blades lose their fine edge between hunts, regardless of how they're stored or how carefully they're handled.

Moisture in the air causes oxidation, which dulls the blade, however minutely. Because of this, blades must be touched up before each hunt. The simplest way to do this is with one of the several kinds of sharpening devices available. Cross sticks are popular, as are sharpeners with wheels and the box-type diamond models. Many hunters, especially those who sharpen their blades initially, use a medium-grade, single-cut mill file.

Matching to Draw Length

There are do-it-yourself methods of matching arrows to draw length, but visiting an archery pro shop to accomplish this and the other aspects of getting prepared is the most reliable way to get a satisfactory result.

For one thing, the standard formula for making this determination with longbows and recurve bows doesn't work with compound bows. The bow weight on the traditional bows has been marked on the basis of a 28-inch draw length, and while this works as a general rule, it isn't always accurate. Another method for making this determination is to measure an individual's arm spread and match it with a chart that indicates the length of arrow to be used. This formula covers differences in arm spread from 57 to 77 inches, and arrow lengths from 22 to 32 inches. Like other "formula" methods, this isn't a dependable technique. Even what seems to be the simplest of them all—drawing a long blank arrow in a lightweight bow to the anchor point and having someone mark the spot where the arrow crosses the leading edge of the bow—can't be trusted.

When it comes to compound bows, there are no established rules of thumb or formulas, because the draw length varies due to many factors, some related to the individual and others to the particular equipment being used.

Again, ask for professional help, at least in the beginning.

BASIC ACCESSORIES

Beginning archers will get their basic training on targets, and even if this will occur on a range, it can be helpful to have a backyard target for additional practice.

Initially, the bullseye-type targets are the best for the beginner. They provide a specific spot for the eye to concentrate on, and this is the type used at most training facilities. For alternate practice away from the range, there's an inexpensive model mounted on a stand which has a series of flip-over targets that feature the standard bullseye and a variety of birds and animals. The latter selection is appealing to those archers who want to hunt game eventually. Several steps up from these flip-over targets are life-size, three-dimensional targets that are as close to the real thing as a shooter can find, even in terms of the density of the material used in the forms.

Wherever targets are set up, special attention should be paid to what's behind them so that arrows that pass through or miss can't do any harm. A good backstop usually will handle this best, but if you're shooting in an open field, make sure there's nothing beyond the target within maximum arrow range that might be hit.

Arm guards worn on the inside of the forearm that holds the bow are essential in any shooting situation with any kind of bow, since they not only prevent painful abrasions from the bowstring, but also keep loose sleeves out of the way. There are many versions of arm guards available, most of which are quite inexpensive. And until you get clothes designed for shooting, a chest guard is a device that's worth having.

No matter whether you use a traditional or a compound bow, you should include either a shooting glove or a tab as a necessary accessory. Both protect the fingers on the drawing hand and help assure a cleaner release.

Finger shooting was formerly the preferred method for teaching beginners, but the development of mechanical releases brought them into the forefront for both target shooters and

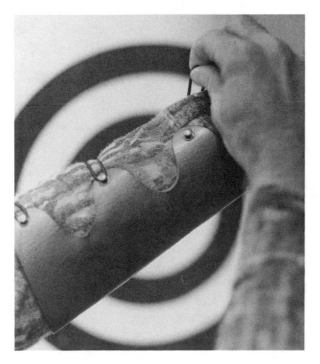

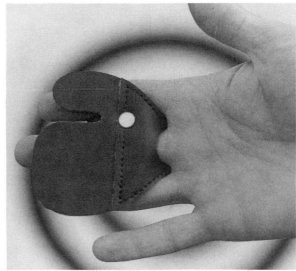

An arm guard (left) is a vital accessory to prevent painful abrasions. Some shooters using the finger release prefer tabs to shooting gloves.

Four types of mechanical releases that aid in assuring a smooth and silent let-off.

bowhunters. There's wide diversity in the design and function of the mechanical releases, and it requires experimenting with many types to find the most suitable one with which to begin.

A quiver is another basic accessory, and even though a beginning shooter may be using only arrows with practice points, it's important that they be kept enclosed in a quiver at all times. Target shooters usually wear holster-type quivers that attach to the belt or around the waist, or the kind that fits over the shoulder on a strap. Field shooters or bowhunters usually have quiv-

One type of string silencer that is very popular with hunters.

Puff string silencer is supposed to be the most effective for sound reduction.

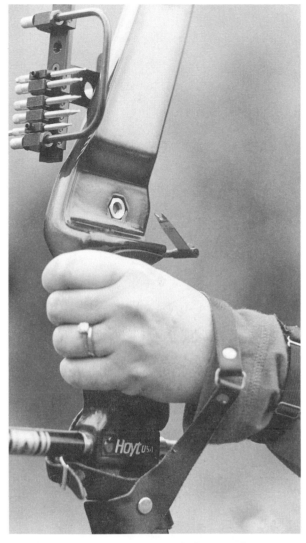

A wrist strap increases stability and ensures that the bow won't be inadvertently dropped at the shot.

ers that are attached to the bow with clips that hold the arrows firmly in place, and with hoods to cover points and fletching.

Other Accessories

A good bow case is an important accessory, because it protects equipment that is being transported or stored. Soft cases with padding are suitable for local events or trips into the field when the equipment is under your personal supervi-

sion. Hard cases are best when equipment is being shipped, because they offer more protection. Also, some of the larger aluminum or plastic models are large enough to hold a lot more than just the basic tackle, including extra parts and even clothing items.

Those using longbows or recurve bows should have a good cord bowstringer (to aid in safe and easy stringing and to keep from damaging the bow), a stringkeeper (to maintain the

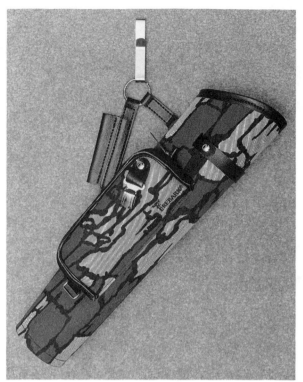

A quiver is an important accessory. Here are three kinds that are popular with both field archers and bowhunters.

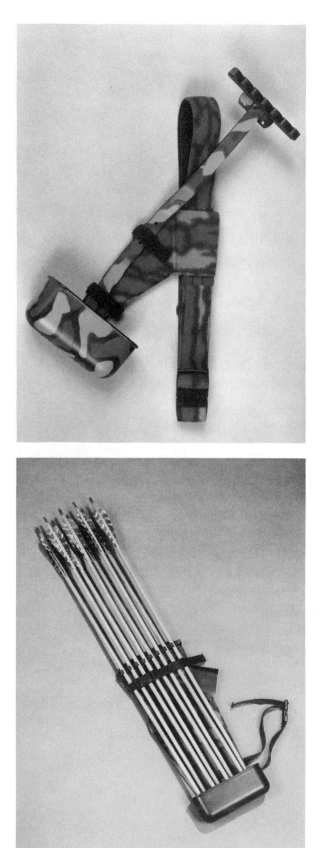

proper brace height of the string and protect the lower limb tip when the bow is unstrung), and a bow square. According to the type of equipment, having a few other items along is helpful: extra nocking points, bowstrings, a small repair kit. As your skills progress and you begin to diversify, your accessory list will expand.

EQUIPMENT AND INSTRUCTION FOR YOUNGSTERS

The compound bow has made getting into archery more attractive to youngsters because they can begin with tackle that can be used for practice on standard ranges instead of just back-yard targets. Previously, a youth had to begin with a particular draw weight and bow length

A metal bowcase is valuable for storing equipment and transporting it safely.

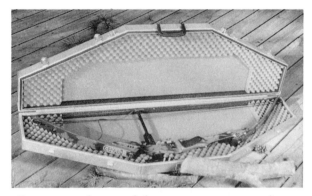

Contoured metal bowcases are made to accommodate width of compound bows.

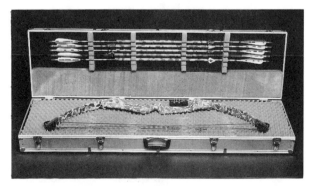

Rectangular cases handle all types of bows.

which during the learning—and growing—process, had to be periodically upgraded or altered. The compound bow's adjustable weight and let-off features permit an experienced shooter or pro shop specialist to start a youngster of practically any age with gear of professional caliber. There are mini-bows that perform remarkably well, yet which even small children can draw easily.

Just as important as equipment selection is the next step, which is thorough and competent instruction in the fundamentals of shooting and all of the vital safety factors. Most archery clubs welcome young shooters to participate and provide assistance and encouragement. Also, the majority of states throughout the nation have hunter safety courses administered by the game and fish agencies. Successful completion of the course is a requirement for obtaining a hunting license. There is also an excellent manual produced by the National Bowhunter Education Foundation which contains a wealth of information from the basics of the sport to the preparation of game for the table. The NBEF address is listed in Appendix A

All of the training shouldn't be left up to clubs or agencies. Parents or friends can supervise beginners, and in the case of children, should keep a close eye on them at all times when they have archery equipment in their hands. It's easy for youngsters to get a little irresponsible and shoot at things other than the target, or shoot arrows into the air to see how far they will fly. They must come down, of course, and a descending arrow can inflict serious injury or damage property. Shooting at a lower angle into an open field is a better idea. And just as with firearms, the cardinal rule applies: "Never aim at anything you don't intend to shoot!"

Rules of safety must be constantly kept in mind, not only in regard to your own conduct but in awareness of what others are doing, like driving in a car defensively. Being confident of your own ability doesn't make you immune from becoming a casualty.

2

Learning to Shoot

It's necessary to learn the fundamentals of the bow and its function before actually attempting to start shooting. Some of the steps relating to this are required only with the longbow and recurve bow, but they are important for these kinds of equipment.

BRACING THE BOW

There are a variety of methods of stringing bows safely and properly. For example, there is a wood device that works well for backyard shooting or indoor and outdoor ranges. It's not handy to carry around, though, so the pocket-size cord stringer is much more widely used. This is a length of nylon cord with leather pockets at each end. You place one pocket on the lower nock and slip the other over the opposite end, then stand on it and pull up at the handle. This creates the necessary curve that allows the upper bowstring to be slipped into place. This technique works for both longbows and recurves.

To string by hand, use what's known as the "step-across" method. Frankly, you're well advised to have it explained and demonstrated by a proficient archer than to try to do it yourself by following written instructions. The late Fred Bear described this procedure many years ago, and his instructions prove this point:

"First, the string loop should be in place on the lower bow nock and held in place by a rubber band or bow tip protector. Holding the other string loop in the left hand, step across the bow with the right leg so that the bow handle lies against the back of the thigh as high up as possible. Your right leg is between the bow and the bowstring. The pressure of the thigh must be against the bow handle to avoid bending one limb more than the other. Hold the upper bow limb just under the recurve in your right hand and place the lower recurve over the instep of your left foot, being careful not to let the bow tip touch the floor or ground. (Some archers use a leather harness slipped on over the shoe to hold the bow tip in the right position.) Now apply pressure backward with your thigh on the bow by leaning forward from the waist and applying pressure with the right hand. The string loop held in the left hand can then be

It's important to string a bow carefully, and that's most easily done with a bowstringer. Here an archer is stringing a classic longbow.

slipped into place in the upper nock. Before releasing pressure, make sure the string loops are firmly seated in the bow nocks."

This isn't all, but it's enough to boggle any beginner's mind and inspire gratitude for compound bows. And to give credit where it's due, Fred Bear's final comment on the subject was that it is best to get a bowstringing device.

BRACE HEIGHT

For longbows, this refers to the distance between the bow handle and the string. Normally this was about six inches. The brace height of modern bows is measured at right angles with a bow square from the string to the deepest cut on the handle. Because of the variety of handle designs and configurations on today's bows, the brace height is usually recommended by the manufacturer, and the commercially made bowstrings they supply with each bow will ordinarily provide the right brace height or be very close to it. The correct height keeps noise, vibration and wrist slap to a minimum and influences arrow flight. New bowstrings will stretch, but when they reach their final length, the proper height can be adjusted by twisting the string a few turns in the direction that tightens the serving, the bound portions of the string in the center and at the ends.

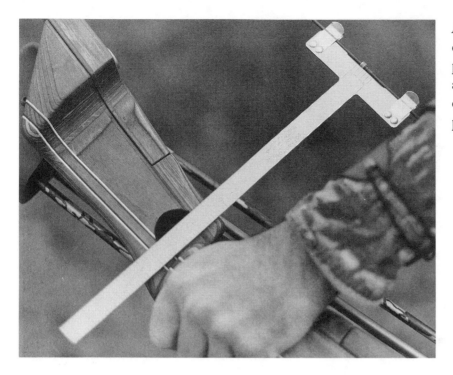

A bow square is useful in determining the nocking point and brace height on a regular bow and making other adjustments on compound bows.

For compound bows, each manufacturer has a recommended brace height for each model. This can be increased or decreased by turning the limb bolts to change the angle, or "tiller," of the limbs.

NOCKING POINT

The nocking point on a bowstring is an indicator that ensures correct placement of the arrow, and there are various ways archers mark its posi-

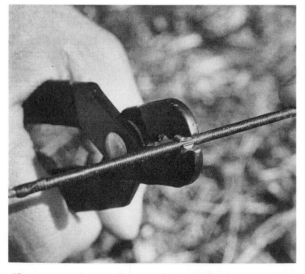

Slip-on nock can be easily installed in proper position with nocking pliers.

The arrow nock should be brought snugly into place directly under the nock point.

tion. The simplest is a few wraps of thread coated with cement, but just as easy to install are the metal slip-on or heat-shrink type.

A bow square is the best tool for quickly determining the exact place for the nocking point. It should be 1/8 to 3/16 inch above the arrow rest. Once in place, the nocking point indicates exactly where the nock of the arrow should be placed. When nocked, the arrow can look peculiar because of the downward angle. But this is the best alignment for smoothly launching the arrow.

Differences in shooting styles and whether or not the shooter uses a mechanical release or fingers will determine the exact nock placement.

SIX STEPS TO SHOOTING SKILL

Shooting skill can be accomplished only by following the six commandments basic to the learning process: Standing, Nocking, Drawing, Holding and Aiming, Releasing, and Follow-through. Practice each step of the program until you have mastered it.

Stance

You can establish a comfortable stance without

Best shooting stance is with the feet about parallel to the target and the legs spread to maintain a comfortable balance.

The hand should be relaxed when holding the bow handle, with the pressure on the web between the thumb and forefinger.

Here's a good example of a relaxed hand position on the bow handle.

Gripping the bow handle tightly can create torque and an erratic arrow flight.

equipment in hand. The feet should be placed apart far enough for good balance, with the toes approximately at a 90-degree angle to the target. Some shooters come to prefer a precise square stance, while others find they shoot better with an open stance. The latter positions the body so that there is less chance of the bowstring colliding with the chest or forearm.

With your head erect, turn it toward the target, and hold it steady. After doing this a few times, you can quite naturally assume the proper stance, at which time you add the bow and begin the additional sequences of instruction and practice.

By the time you first bring the bow into the picture, chances are that you'll have tried it out at the pro shop and handled it enough so that it feels comfortable in your hand. Don't grip the handle; instead, let it lie easily in the V between the thumb and forefinger. The pressure when drawing must come at this point, not at the heel or palm of the hand, and it's vital that the wrist is held straight and not bent, and that the handle *never* be gripped hard. This would create improper alignment and cause the string to strike the forearm or wrist. It would also seriously reduce accuracy.

Nocking

The bow should be held in a horizontal position while the arrow is nocked by grasping the arrow between thumb and forefinger with the cock feather or vane up. The nock should be slid into position snugly against the nocking point. For a finger release, hook the first three fingers of the hand over the string with the arrow between the

first and second fingers. A glove should always be worn for protection. With a mechanical release, the procedure is different.

Drawing

The draw is where many beginning shooters experience their most nagging problems, because it involves some of the most critical aspects of shooting. Once the bow is raised to a vertical position the draw should be a smooth, uninterrupted movement that includes pushing forward with the arm that holds the bow and pulling back with the hand that controls the string until it reaches the side of the face. The drawing arm should be held on a level with the shoulder so it is in line with the arrow at full draw.

The shoulder muscles provide most of the

Establishing an anchor point is important, because it will ensure consistent arrow flight.

power for the draw. Since some of these muscles are not normally used, the draw weight may at first seem a little too great, but as the muscles tone up and become conditioned it will begin to feel comfortable. A bit of patience is required, but this is true of any learning procedure.

Some of the problems encountered by beginners in the past, such as arrows falling off just before release, have been eliminated with the development of new kinds of arrow rests and other equipment advancements. The compound bow and mechanical releases have been the most significant in this respect.

One of the most important aspects of the draw is that it allows an anchor point to be determined. This is the point to which the index or middle finger is brought on the draw. Experiment with this until you find the one that feels most natural and comfortable. Once you have established this, use it consistently. Be aware, though, that different shooting methods may require that you vary the anchor point; nevertheless, this isn't always the case.

Holding and Aiming

The slight pause, or hold, that occurs at the completion of the draw in order to aim has been given extended life, so to speak, by the let-off system of the compound bow. With longbows or recurve bows, the maximum draw weight is being felt at this moment, so there's a quite limited amount of time the position can be maintained. Not only that, but with these bows additional pressure must be applied during the pause. Otherwise, the arrow will creep forward, adversely affecting its flight and accuracy.

It's important that the target be the focus of attention when aiming, because if everything else is in order, where the arrow is going to strike is the major concern. It's good to practice concentrating on the target and getting the feel of

Holding and aiming is much easier with a compound bow because of the let-off system that reduces the weight being drawn.

the equipment, because no matter what kind of bow you're using, this helps to develop an instinct for the entire process. Once this is accomplished, most archers can actually shoot reasonably well with only the most basic equipment.

Release and Follow-through

Mechanical releases have been gaining in popularity, and justifiably so. For one thing, the finger release creates slightly more torque than a mechanical release and sometimes makes more noise. Too, mechanical releases are easier to use. Yet whatever method is used, the moment of release is extremely critical both in competition and in hunting. With all else in place, a clean, crisp release is what can assure that the arrow will fly truly and properly.

The next second (or part of a second) after release—the follow-through—has to be classed as just as vital. Failing to perform this properly can spoil all previous efforts.

Anchors using a finger release ordinarily employ a grip on the string with one finger over the nock and two fingers under.

Follow-through involves keeping the bow arm perfectly still and rigid as the arrow is released and as it goes on its way to the target.

Correct follow-through ensures that the arrow will fly true, so it's important to stay in position until the arrow hits the target.

Any movement at the moment the arrow is launched will affect its flight, so the best rule is to remain statue-like until it strikes the mark. Follow-through is also essential to good performance in golf, skeet shooting and tennis. The difference is that in those sports players have to continue a motion rather than hold in place.

AIMING AIDS

Archers who either use traditional bows by choice or compete on ranges in the classes that ban any kind of aiming aids still use some of the techniques once considered as standard shooting practices. All of these are effective, but a beginner is much better served by using a bow sight, which will help produce satisfactory results more quickly. One reason a sight seems natural is because most people have already shot or pointed a gun when they first pick up a bow and are accustomed to using a sight.

Before the invention of the bowsight, the various methods prescribed for learning to aim were primarily point-of-aim, instinctive, gap shooting, three fingers under, and string walking. Each requires guesswork to a large degree,

---

LEARNING TO HIT YOUR TARGET

By Harold Knight
Cadiz, Kentucky

One of the main things to learn in hitting your target is how to judge distance, and one of the best ways to learn is simply by practicing while you're out scouting or hunting. For example, first estimate the distance, then actually step it off. You'll soon become quite adept at judging distance. There is no good substitute for practice.

It's important to shoot bow equipment that you can handle. Don't make the mistake, as many people do, of overweighting your bow. I prefer the equipment of today over the kind I used when I began to hunt thirty-five years ago. Back then, the arrows were made of wood and feathers, and a great deal of time was spent sharpening the broadhead. Also, it was not unusual to have to go through fifty shafts before finding six straight ones. Today the broadhead is presharpened to a razor edge for a good, clean, quick kill.

The sight system introduced on bows has been a tremendous help in hitting the target. It gives the ability to select a specific part of the animal instead of simply aiming at the entire animal and hoping you'll hit a critical area.

Another welcome improvement in recent years is in the area of tree stands. They are more comfortable and safer, enabling one to stay in the tree longer while hunting. Clothing also has improved; it's much warmer and drier.

Bowhunting has always been a favorite sport of mine. I like the challenge it offers. I think one of the most difficult things to do in North America is to harvest a whitetail trophy buck with bow and arrow!

Harold Knight is a consummate outdoorsman who is thoroughly versed in all aspects of woods lore. With this background, it is natural that he is the inventor of many game calls, including the Tube Turkey Call and the Double-Grunt Deer Call. They are manufactured by his company, Knight/Hale Game Calls. Harold conducts many seminars throughout the U.S. on various aspects of hunting, and hunting deer and elk with a bow is at the very top of his preference list.

either from the standpoint of distance to the target or the trajectory the arrow will follow. Also, by comparison with learning with a bowsight, these procedures are cumbersome and often extremely confusing.

Point-of-aim required the archer to aim over the point of the arrow at a spot between the shooter and the target and not look up at the target until after the arrow was released. It's a method that can be considered obsolete.

Instinctive shooting is still practiced, but it's definitely a kind of skill not every archer has the ability to master. This method requires an archer to aim and shoot automatically, and many people don't possess this ability. It's much like picking up a stone and hurling it at an object without any consideration of distance, size or its speed in motion. Those who can perform in this way are fortunate, and it can be greatly satisfying to bowhunters who are able to instantly let an arrow fly and feel confident of hitting the target. However, it's a skill that isn't suitable for tournament shooting.

Gap shooting is closely linked to instinctive shooting, because with this method the shooter concentrates strictly on the target, yet remains conscious of the distance so that the point of the arrow can be adjusted accordingly. In rifle shooting, gap shooting would be classed as a form of "Kentucky windage" that requires guesswork based on a lot of experience.

Both three fingers under and string walking are ways to bring the arrow closer to the eye. With three fingers under, the anchor point is often moved from the corner of the mouth to the cheekbone to get a sort of down-the-gun-barrel view of the arrow, which is especially useful when aiming at close ranges. In string walking, the drawing fingers move farther down the string. The lower the fingers, the closer the arrow is to the eye.

Many traditional archers continue to use these methods, and even though most of today's beginners learn with a compound bow equipped with

The three-fingers-under position on the string makes it possible to change the position of the arrow in relation to the shooter's eye, as is demonstrated in these two pictures.

a sight, almost all eventually experiment with other kinds of equipment and shooting methods. This can add pleasure and a better appreciation of the sport. Also, discovering one has a talent for instinctive shooting, or the ability to learn it, can be quite a confidence booster.

Kinds of Sights

A beginner's bowsight can be as basic as a single pin that is backed up with a bowstring peep sight, enabling easier alignment with the target.

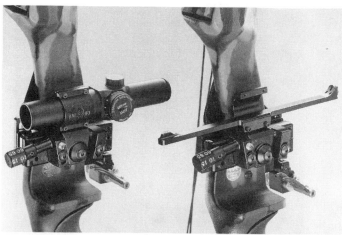

One of the more recent additions to archery has been the use of scopes. There are various kinds that can be used on some of the mounts.

Bowsights with pins are favored by most archers, and particularly by bowhunters.

Here are three types of bowsights (from top): crosshair, pin and lighted crosshair with pin models.

With a pin properly placed for a particular yardage, the shooter learns how to achieve dependable accuracy. It's then a simple matter to use multiple pins set for different distances and arrow variations.

Many types of bowsights are available. They range from the conventional to the exotic in both design and function. Some bowsights have multiple pins. Others have a crosshair system, and still others have lighted pins for low light conditions. There are pendulum sights for use in tree stands, basic telescopic

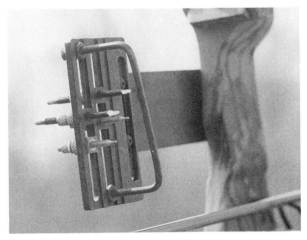

This is a pendulum sight developed for bowhunters shooting from tree stands. It automatically adjusts for range and angle.

Some bowsights have intricate adjustment systems and lighted dots. They are used principally by bowhunters, for obvious reasons.

sights, and scopes with laser-like lighted dots. And there are many more.

IMPROVING YOUR AIM

The next step in preparing for hitting live targets is to use various tactics for improving your aim at different distances.

Pick a comfortable range and keep working at the target until you can consistently place a group of arrows within two or three inches. Stay with that range until it feels natural to you, then move back about five yards and work at that distance. Keep increasing your distance from the target five yards at a time until you are get-ting tight groups of arrows from about forty yards, then begin varying your distance from session to session to retain control at all ranges.

At each range, practice shooting from various positions: standing, kneeling, sitting, leaning around a bush or even lying prone on the ground. Try different angles, such as high shots from stands or a ladder.

Practice in different lighting conditions such as you would encounter in the field. The more you duplicate field conditions and become familiar with them, the better you will be prepared for your first venture into the field. More advanced types of practice include various games, which are described in Chapter 14.

3

When Things Go Wrong

All archers encounter problems of one sort or another as time passes, some caused by human error and others by either faulty or mismatched equipment. The main thing is to recognize that something is wrong and to correct it as quickly as possible. The longer you allow a problem to linger, the more detrimental the effect can be on your shooting ability, confidence and progress as a shooter.

The initial step is determining what's causing the difficulty—for example, inaccurate arrow flight. The best way to determine what's causing this is to have an experienced archer watch you shoot, because chances are that the culprit is you rather than your equipment.

Bad habits that are sometimes unnoticed by the unsupervised shooter are easy to develop, but they will sooner or later begin to affect accuracy and consistency. Yet they're very easy to see by a qualified person looking over your shoulder. Erratic arrow flight is almost always due to errors in stance, draw, aiming, release or something similar, and once spotted, usually only small adjustments are needed to get things back on track.

If the problem is in the equipment, it's often easy to spot. Examine your arrows carefully for damage, and check for cracked or broken nocks. A cracked or misaligned nock can cause erratic and even dangerous arrow flight or a "dry-fire"—where the arrow separates from the bowstring before release (essentially, as if there had been no arrow in place)—which can harm the bow.

If there seems to be no problem with the arrow, it's best to have the bow checked out by professionals to be sure all of the components are matched and balanced. Regardless of where it was purchased, the best move is to take it to a pro shop where the trouble can be expertly diagnosed. If the equipment isn't functioning properly, manufacturers are usually happy to replace it at no cost and offer any additional assistance they can in making sure everything gets back in proper order.

SAFETY IN THE FIELD

Safety on the range and in the field is of paramount importance, and even though accidents will occur no matter how careful the shooter may be, paying particular attention to likely causes can reduce their incidence.

This responsibility begins with the basics—equipment—because without proper care, maintenance and handling these items provide potential danger. Consider a few of them:

•Bowstrings that are too heavy, too light, frayed or weak can cause an array of problems: equipment damage, injury to the shooter, or erratic arrow flight.

• Arrows, especially razor-sharp broadheads, are hazardous when in flight, of course, but they can just as easily inflict injury or cause death through carelessness or mishandling. As such, arrows should be regularly inspected for flaws in fletching and straightness. All arrows should be carried in a quiver, but those with broadheads should be contained in the kind that has a hard shield covering the points.

• When hunting from an elevated stand, the hunter should always leave the shooting equipment on the ground and, only after getting in place, pull it up. Also, be sure to lower it *before* you descend.

• *Always* use a safety belt when ascending a tree, and keep it on all of the time you are in the stand.

• Make certain to inform a companion with you in the field or someone at home where you're going to be hunting. That way, if something goes wrong and you're injured or incapacitated, they'll know where to look for you.

• Bowhunters must follow the same primary rules of safety they learned in target or range shooting, but there are additional elements to be considered. Shooters must be certain that there is a clear path between their positions and where the target is likely to be. If this isn't the case, one must simply refrain from releasing an arrow.

• Most vital is that the hunter be *absolutely sure* of the target before shooting. One of the best pieces of advice ever given on this matter is in *Woodcraft*, a book written in 1888 by a writer who used the pen name "Nessmuk." In it he said: "In still-hunting, swear yourself black in the face never to shoot at a dim, moving object in the woods for a deer, unless you have seen that it is a deer. In these days there are quite as many hunters as deer in the woods; and it is a heavy, wearisome job to pack a dead or wounded man ten or twelve miles out to a clearing, let alone that it spoils all the pleasure of the hunt and is apt to raise hard feelings among his relations."

Anticipate conditions that you may encounter in the field and be prepared for them. Having an emergency kit is wise, and a knowledge of how to give first aid treatment is essential.

Some of the items that should be considered for inclusion: first aid kit, ace bandage, canteen, trail food, waterproof match box, multi-bladed Swiss army knife or one of the sturdy folding devices that includes an array of tools, battery-powered strobe blinker, flashlight and extra batteries, extra midget flashlight, signal mirror, whistle, compass, map, emergency blanket, long-life candle, length of rope, plastic bags, a small roll of duct tape, water purification tablets and topo map of the area you're hunting.

You can add or delete from this list, but the main thing is to be sure the most vital elements are always included.

If you become lost or disoriented, stop and determine the direction you plan to take. Mark a spot with surveyor's tape or a strip of cloth, then keep repeating this at about 50-yard intervals. This can serve two purposes: First, it will give someone searching for you a trail to follow; and second, if you decide you've made the wrong choice you can easily backtrack, collecting the markers as you go to be used on your next attempt to solve the dilemma.

When you haven't found your way out, plan to make a signal fire (if you're in an area where fires are allowed). Smoke signals by day or a bright glow at night may bring rescuers to your site.

Weather can be a menace, particularly in the high country of the West where dramatic changes can occur very quickly. Go prepared for this kind of eventuality with what it takes to survive for several days.

You may find natural shelter from the elements under a rock overhang or other protective feature. Snow provides insulation, and a bed of dry brush or leaves in your shelter will help keep you warm on very cold nights.

One of the most common dangers encountered in the field is hypothermia. Its early stages have few warning signs, so when it strikes the effects are far advanced and can be lethal. Because of this, *precaution* is just as important as *treatment*.

Hypothermia results from what could be called a "deep chill" in which the temperature of the internal organs drops gradually by slow

---

BACKCOUNTRY BOWHUNTING

By Dwight Schuh
Nampa, Idaho

If one fact explains my bowhunting success, it's hunting undisturbed animals. They're less wary than heavily hunted game, and they follow normal daily patterns. To find these kinds of animals, I either hunt off-road as far as possible or seek out places no one else has thought to hunt. To find undisturbed pockets, I study maps, analyzing the country for roadless or rough terrain, blocks cut off by private land, or places so obvious they are overlooked by everyone else.

A daypack may be the most important backcountry hunting tool. The pack eliminates fear and lets you hunt most efficiently. My pack has a lightweight frame and padded hip belt, which allows me to carry weight more comfortably than does a rucksack or fanny pack. In addition to hunting items—knife, game bags, and the like—my pack always contains topographic maps, compass, flashlight (with extra batteries and bulb), fire starter, emergency shelter, plastic flagging, first aid kit and warm jacket. With these items I feel comfortable to hunt anywhere, knowing that even if I get lost or hurt, I'll survive comfortably. That knowledge means efficient backcountry hunting.

The frame pack allows me to pack meat easily. I can load it with 70 or 80 pounds of meat on the spot and carry my game back to camp, without returning to camp for a "meat" frame. To retrieve animals from the back country, I bone them out and carry nothing but pure meat. I'd rather carry a deer on my back five miles than drag it 100 yards.

Even if I'm camping near a road, I go prepared to hunt off-road. In addition to my small frame pack, my gear always includes a lightweight sleeping bag, backpack stove and cookware, freeze-dried foods and lightweight shelter. Then if I discover some good animals more than a day's hike off-road, I can bivouac within easy hunting distance of the animals.

These tips help me to hunt undisturbed backcountry animals. I think they'll work for you, too.

Dwight Schuh is bow and arrows editor for Sports Afield *and as a free-lance writer has been a contributor to all the major bowhunting magazines. He has been bowhunting for 20 years and considers backcountry bowhunting for deer and elk a specialty. Dwight has taken several Pope and Young record book animals.*

WHEN THINGS GO WRONG   55

cooling. Frigid conditions can certainly be a cause, as one would logically suspect, yet people often succumb to hypothermia in temperatures as mild as 40 to 50°F when wind, wetness or a combination of both make it impossible for the body to ward off the chill.

Dressing properly is important, but this alone can't prevent falling into the water or being disabled in bad weather situations. That's why it's vital to carry survival equipment at all times. The "musts" for cool weather are fire-starting kits, an emergency blanket, a pocket-size emergency sleeping bag, and extra dry clothes. Other life savers can be a small stove or heat tabs and instant soup or other beverage. Getting something warm inside can be extremely helpful. And when you have these articles with you, it's often better to wait it out rather than to strike out on your own at the mercy of the elements.

When emergency situations involve accidents, a thoroughly prepared bowhunter will have the knowledge and training necessary to handle even serious ones. Many things that can (and do) happen in the field require more than just band aids and antibiotic creme.

Typical are the many falls hunters suffer while climbing trees, alone or with a stand, or from the stand itself once they are in position. Tumbling from a height of 15-20 feet can inflict a lot of physical damage, and it isn't uncommon to have broken bones, concussions and other injuries as a result.

You should also know how to treat bleeding and have actual practice in "pressure dressing" a wound. There are different treatments for chest wounds, abdominal injuries, and bleeding from extremities. In case of injury, panic is an enemy. You will want to act quickly, but knowing exactly what to do and what not to do will give you confidence and help you to remain calm.

Knowing what to do can also mean the difference between life and death. Because of this, it can be extremely valuable to take an advanced first aid course that teaches the emergency setting of fractures, treatment of head injuries, CPR, and other resuscitation procedures.

Nor is having this kind of training just for the benefit of the other person. There's always the possibility that someday you will find it advantageous to use the expertise on yourself. Nobody is excluded from the probability of accidents.

Thoughts of this sort make a good point for use of the "buddy system," because regardless of a person's knowledge of how to respond to emergencies, a lone individual can be incapacitated and unable to function.

The Boy Scout motto, "Be Prepared," is good to remember. Even better for bowhunters in the field, though, might be to insert one more word ("Well"), placed right in the middle!

4

Ethics

There is no way to overstate the importance of ethics in bowhunting. The acceptance or rejection of the sport in the eyes of the public, or in those of other hunters, is greatly affected by the kind of conduct and responsibility displayed by the participants.

Webster defines *ethics* as "the study of standards of conduct and moral judgment," deriving from Latin and Greek words referring to "character, custom." What is considered ethical, then, is what conforms to the actions deemed acceptable by a given group. To bring the question home, consider how the decisions each bowhunter personally makes and how the kind of behavior that results squares with the prevailing "acceptable" standards. The buck stops with the individual.

It's no secret that bowhunters come under closer scrutiny than other members of the hunting community, and some of the reasons for this can be traced directly to a variety of unethical practices. It isn't a question of whether or not this scrutiny is warranted; the point is that everyone should make a special effort to help reduce the criticism and improve the sport's image.

Today virtually all bowhunting organizations place the ethics question high on their list of important issues. It is a subject given great emphasis in seminars conducted by organizations and by individuals, where the question is not only the individual's role but the overall image of bowhunting. Sometimes, an entire seminar is devoted to bowhunting ethics. Most experts consider these points to be imperative:

WHAT TO DO

Know Your Equipment: This is a basic step in the area of personal responsibility, and it has to do with both the individual's safety as well as that of other hunters. It's necessary to be totally familiar with all of your equipment and hunting gear, certain that it's in good condition and fully functional, and confident in your ability to use it.

Know Yourself: Every hunter should be fully aware of his or her capabilities, and that means an honest self-evaluation to establish boundaries and make certain you don't exceed them. For instance, there's a big difference between shooting at a target range and drawing on a big buck.

In a hunting situation the elements of excitement and anticipation can override skills and judgment. It's better to be too conservative in making decisions than too bold.

Keep Practicing: Bowhunters, like concert pianists, ballet dancers and high wire performers can't maintain their level of proficiency without constant, year-round practice. Some sports don't require this kind of dedication, but bowhunting does. Most bowhunters enjoy practicing and look forward to it, so it's not regarded as a chore.

Accuracy: Clean, quick kills are the goal of every bowhunter. Achieving them requires both the ability to place arrows accurately and a thorough knowledge of the anatomy of the animal being hunted. The kill zones aren't the same, particularly in big-game species, so doing some homework on this subject is important. There are plenty of good references available in sporting goods stores and books on big-game hunting. What usually isn't included are the places to plant arrows when the animal is at angles other than broadside. This is where practice on 3-D targets can be very helpful.

Follow-up: The recovery of wounded game is a task all bowhunters should feel morally obligated to perform to the very best of their ability, regardless of the time or effort involved. Disregarding this responsibility and leaving a crippled animal to suffer or die is inexcusable. There are many ways to avoid losing wounded animals, including game trackers attached to the arrow, arrows equipped with sonic devices, infrared game finders, and chemicals that make blood trails more visible.

Go by the Rules: All bowhunters should be fully knowledgeable of the current hunting rules and regulations in their home state or wherever else they may be afield. Breaking the law is a serious personal mistake, yet it also reflects on other participants in the sport. A few bad apples can have an enormous impact. Something else: bowhunters who care for the sport shouldn't be reluctant to report violations. It's their responsibility to do so if they wish to preserve the idea of good sportsmanship.

Respect Landowners' Rights: No one has the privilege of trespassing on private land without permission, yet this is one of the most common examples of bad behavior displayed by hunters. Those who ignore "No Hunting" signs create ill will among property owners and cause more lands to be posted. Such actions also help generate more anti-hunting sentiment among the general public. Many states have laws that require a hunter to have the written consent of a landowner, and in most places this is strictly enforced. Basically, though, it comes down to the matter of hunter behavior.

Respect for Others: This is where application of the Golden Rule would be quite enough, because simple politeness is the main point. By nature, hunting is somewhat of a competitive sport, but this should be a contest between hunter and quarry, not hunter versus hunter. Don't intrude on other hunters' territory by setting up a stand nearer than 100 yards from their position, and if you are on the move give them a wide berth so as not to spook game that may be in the vicinity. Crowding results in the loss of opportunity for all parties. Also, you can win yourself a star by offering to assist a fellow bowhunter drag a big-game animal out of the woods.

Know the Issues: Bowhunters should make sure they're up to date on current problems and issues relating to the sport and are able to talk about them in an intelligent and calm manner to critics or other hunters. Knowledgeable hunters make favorable impressions and improve relations with others; ignorant or hotheaded individuals don't. It isn't difficult to become well informed and remain so, since there's a constant flow of information on these subjects in newspapers, magazines, and on television and radio.

Boost the Sport: All hunters share the spotlight of attention that's focused on them by the general public, and rather than shrink from it, they should use the opportunity to boost the sport. It must be remembered that all non-hunters aren't anti-hunters, and sometimes they're more curious than critical. Most laymen don't understand wildlife management and the need for balanced game populations. They also often aren't aware of the fact that hunters' dollars are what fund the conservation programs responsible for maintaining and perpetuating not only the species that are hunted but nongame species as well. The public needs to recognize that the majority of bowhunters are conscientious and proficient, and that the sport is wholesome and safe.

WHAT NOT TO DO

Anyone with experience in the field is aware of the things that some hunters do—or fail to do—that are bad for bowhunting. They're all correctable by using a little common sense.

Presenting a Negative Image: The media sometimes depicts hunters as slobs, and those who go afield unshaven and dressed sloppily help to validate this caricature in the minds of many people. Viewing a hunting trip as relaxing is okay, but personal appearance shouldn't be neglected in the process of "unwinding." After all, you're almost certain to be seen, and neither the public nor other hunters will react favorably.

Acting in an Offensive Manner: Nothing damages the image of hunting more than those who drink in public and use loud and offensive language. Everyone knows that alcohol and lethal weapons don't mix, and this kind of behavior sends out far-reaching ripples of criticism that are impossible to counter. Nearly as harmful are hunters who boast of "sticking" animals and losing them, or who like to portray themselves and bowhunting as "macho" through their actions and the display of repulsive slogans on hats, bumper stickers and T-shirts.

Bad Taste in Displaying Game: At one time it was acceptable to drape a big-game kill over the hood of a car and triumphantly exhibit it on the trip home. That's no longer the case. The display of dead animals isn't appreciated by the public nor, for that matter, by most hunters. The same applies to photographs of harvested game. They can be posed in a tasteful and attractive manner without showing bullet wounds or open body cavities. Pride in a trophy is justified, but it should be demonstrated tactfully.

COURTESY TOWARD LANDOWNERS

Bowhunting often takes place on lands owned by other individuals, or by corporations or government agencies. Being considerate of the property owner should be the aim of every hunter. Some simple rules of thumb are widely accepted, for obvious reasons.

First, be sure you have permission before you hunt on someone else's property, and find out what restrictions the owner requires. For example, building a permanent tree stand may not be allowed, or the owner may not be willing for you to start a campfire on the property.

Be careful not to damage trees or crops. Do not drive off-road without permission or block trails with your vehicle. It is a good idea to leave a sign on your vehicle showing your name, address and phone number.

Be sure to remove all evidence of your visit—the carcass and all organs, as well as any garbage that remains. Heavy trash bags are useful for this purpose. In fact, leave everything the way you found it.

Small, quiet groups work better than large, noisy ones when bowhunting. Silent drives with just a few hunters protect the environment for others who may want to hunt the same location the next day.

By showing consideration for the property owner, you are enhancing the perception of bowhunters as responsible people and creating a positive image not only for yourself but for your fellow hunters.

The popularity of the ethics question and its widespread discussion in seminars and training courses are having a significant effect. Virtually every new bowhunter has been indoctrinated in ethical behavior, and hunters violating these rules are coming under increasing pressure to change their ways. The impact of these education efforts will ultimately assure more conscientious bowhunters and a public that is better informed.

5

Big-Game Animals

The North American continent offers probably the greatest "menu" of big-game species of any region except Africa. At one time, nearly all of these species were sought exclusively with rifles, but during the past several decades, the bow has been gaining popularity as an alternate tool for taking large animals.

More than any other single factor, the resurgence of the whitetail deer in North America has been responsible for the phenomenal growth in the number of people who have become active big-game hunters. Some individuals have taken up the bow and arrow as their initial hunting venture; some added it as another skill they wished to master; and still others are hunters who abandoned the gun in favor of the challenges bowhunting offers.

What's also significant is that once the door was opened for bowhunters to seek these animals, the acceptance of the bow as a legitimate and suitable hunting tool for all types of big game spread like wildfire, not only throughout North America but to other parts of the world as well. Today, there's almost no large game animal species that can't be hunted with a bow

anywhere on this continent, and that includes everything from the innocuous species to those that can—and will—literally eat you alive!

One word of caution: With all that's available, it's easy to "get too big for your britches," as the old saying goes, and tackle things beyond your capabilities. A wise bowhunter will progress in an A-B-C manner when it comes to expanding his or her horizons, moving ahead only when sufficient experience and knowledge have been gained. That's the sensible and ethical way to go about it, and it pays off in terms of success and personal satisfaction.

But back to whitetails and the bonuses that bowhunters enjoy, which attract more participants every year. One of these is the increased amount of hunting opportunity the sport provides.

WHITETAIL DEER

Whitetail deer are the most widely distributed big-game species in North America. They're found throughout southern Canada, throughout the forty-eight contiguous states except in the far Southwest, everywhere in Mexico except the Baja Peninsula, and also in Central America. (Whitetails are also native to South America, and they have been introduced into New Zealand, the West Indies and Europe.)

The whitetails in North America include: northwestern whitetail, northeastern whitetail, southeastern whitetail, Texas whitetail, Coues whitetail, Mexican whitetail, and Central American whitetail. There is also the tiny Key whitetail, which is endangered and fully protected.

Before the various management programs were begun shortly after the turn of the century, the nation's whitetail population was at about 500,000. Today, they number close to 13 million, with an annual sport hunting harvest of over 2 million. And both the range and numbers of the animals continue to increase.

In the United States there are seasons for bowhunters that begin as early as August and extend through January. Bowyers are permitted in the field well in advance of the gun seasons, and these early-bird segments are usually of the either-sex sort. Archery equipment can also be used during the regular gun seasons, with the exception of some special hunts. Having an extra period gives bowhunters the chance to bag more animals. In some places this may be a single buck or doe, but there are a few states with extremely generous limits that allow many more to be legally harvested. One, for example, allows a deer a day, and another has no limit whatsoever.

That aspect certainly is appealing, but just as important to dedicated bowhunters is the luxury of being in the field without the noise and

Whitetail Deer

Mule Deer

clamor that is generally associated with the gun season. All of the learned skills can be practiced without interruption, and the aesthetics of silence and solitude can be enjoyed to the fullest.

One final point about bowhunting the whitetail is that the interest in this species has broadened now to include many other big-game animals that were once almost exclusively sought with firearms.

MULE DEER, BLACKTAIL DEER

While their ranges are much less extensive than the whitetail, mule deer and blacktail deer also offer bowhunters a great deal of opportunity, since collectively they occupy almost all of the western states. There are four species, with Rocky Mountain mule deer the most numerous. They are found in all or parts of twenty-two states and southwestern Canada. The desert

mule deer's range includes extreme southern California, parts of Arizona, New Mexico and Texas, and Baja California, northern Sonora, northern Chihuahua and northwestern Coahuila.

The Columbia blacktail deer occupies a narrow range along the Pacific Coast that extends from Bella Bella, British Columbia, in the north, including Vancouver Island and other offshore islands, to Monterey County, California, in the south. They have also been introduced on Kauai Island in Hawaii.

The Sitka blacktail deer occupies the most limited range of all, most of it along the coastal region of southwestern Alaska and British Columbia. They are also found on some offshore islands including the Queen Charlotte Islands, and have been introduced in some other islands in Prince William Sound, as well as Afognak and Kodiak islands. In the case of these species, bowhunters usually get advantages

Sitka Blacktail Deer

in the way of earlier seasons and bag limits. In some places, the ranges of the whitetail deer, mule deer and blacktail deer overlap, and there are only a couple of small spots in the West where none of them are present.

ELK

A bull elk is a trophy that practically every bowhunter in the country covets, and the numbers trying to get permits from the various western states that have hunts increases by leaps and bounds annually. Again, bowhunters get an early chance ahead of gun hunters, and it is usually during the peak bugling period when a good caller can bring an urgent bull to within easy bow range.

Elk were at one time found from the Atlantic to the Pacific coasts, and from the Mexican border northward almost to the Arctic. Today, their range is spotty and vastly more limited, yet these trophy animals are the second most sought by American bowhunters.

There are four recognized species: Roosevelt elk, Tule elk, Rocky Mountain elk and Manitoba elk. Of these, the Rocky Mountain elk occupy by far the largest range, which includes the Rocky Mountain region of southeastern British Columbia and southwestern Alberta; eastern Washington and Oregon; Idaho; western Montana; Wyoming, southwestern South Dakota; northwestern Nebraska; northeastern Nevada; Utah, western Colorado; Arizona and New Mexico. Limited introductions have been

Elk

made in eleven eastern and western states, most of which offer no hunting opportunity.

Manitoba elk once occupied most of the prairie regions of Alberta to Manitoba, but they now are found at various locations in eastern Alberta and southern Saskatchewan and Manitoba, mainly in national and provincial park areas. Hunting opportunity for this species is very limited.

Tule elk are found only in California, where they once occupied large areas in the coastal and central parts of the state. Now, only several small herds exist within the original range. A transplanted herd in the Owens Valley provides the only Tule elk hunting opportunity, and this is by drawings for a limited number of permits issued annually.

The Roosevelt elk is the largest of them all, with bulls of up to 1,100 pounds having been taken. The range of this species is Vancouver Island in Canada, coastal Washington and Oregon, northwestern California, and an intro-

duced population on Afognak and Raspberry islands in Alaska. Some of the largest specimens are taken in the rain forests of Washington's Olympic Peninsula, which also offers some of the toughest hunting conditions.

Hunting tactics for elk are considerably different from those for whitetails, and there's also a greater challenge where shooting skills are concerned. Elk are big-bodied, and while they're as vulnerable as any other animals to arrows in the kill zone, a powerful bow, multi-bladed broadheads and pinpoint accuracy are important to success. Bowhunters score best during the bugling season, and since this begins fairly early in the fall, archery seasons often occur at the most ideal period.

The use of pack horses or four-wheel-drive vehicles in conjunction with elk hunts is highly desirable. Packing out a big bull is an extremely tough chore, yet the reward is great, since many people consider elk to be one of the most flavorful of all game meats.

CARIBOU

In recent years, bowhunting for caribou has taken a giant leap forward in terms of popularity. Not only are these large-racked animals very abundant all across Canada, but in some places overpopulation has caused provincial governments to increase the bag limit to two caribou per hunter. Also, once aware of the great number of American archers who were seeking new adventures, numerous outfitters created bowhunting-only camps to allow them exclusive havens. It has been a boon for both parties.

Caribou are distributed throughout most of Alaska and Canada, and small fingers of range extend into northeastern Washington, northern Idaho and northwestern Montana.

There are six recognized caribou species, although some record keepers prefer to place them into three regional categories. Yet since there are some fairly major differences among them, it's worthwhile to have information on all six.

The Alaskan-Yukon Barren Ground caribou, found throughout most of Alaska, the Yukon, and part of the Northwest Territories is the most widely hunted of all the varieties. The migrating herds of animals sometimes number as many as 100,000. Visiting hunters take large numbers, but these animals are also a major source of food for natives, who depend on them for subsistence during the winter months.

The Central Canada Barren Ground caribou has a broad range that includes most of the Northwest Territories and parts of King William, Southhampton and Baffin islands; and far northern Saskatchewan and Alberta. This species is a smaller race with simple antlers. The principal herds are the Baffin Island, Bathhurst, Beverly and Kaminuriak.

At one time, the Arctic Islands caribou was called Peary caribou, named after the arctic explorer Admiral Robert F. Peary. This is the smallest of the caribou, and its range is the arctic islands of the Northwest Territories, mainly Banks, Victoria, Prince of Wales and Somerset. Herds are small and tend to be mainly residential, and hunting them in these remote areas can offer some very severe conditions.

Caribou

Mountain caribou are the largest species, weighing up to 600 pounds, and their heavy antler configuration makes them the favorite of many hunters. Their range includes the southern part of Yukon Territory; the southeastern part of the Northwest Territories; most of the eastern half of British Columbia, extending into Alberta; northern Alberta; and to a small extent into northeastern Washington, northern Idaho and northwestern Montana. Because of their preference for mountainous terrain, they're the most difficult to hunt.

Most of Quebec and Labrador have the species named for the region—Quebec-Labrador caribou—with the Ungava herd by far the largest. This race draws a lot of attention, since it is the one most accessible to hunters in the eastern U.S. Too, chances of success are very high, because their numbers have grown dramatically during the past ten years. Due to the increased competition for food, the herd is highly migratory, on the move most of the time throughout the year. This country is laced with lakes and waterways, and the principal hunting method is to locate cross-ings and intercept the animals. There are many outfitters in the Quebec-Labrador region that have camps restricted to archery only which attract huge numbers of bowhunters annually. The bag limit of two caribou per hunter is an added incentive. Quebec-Labrador caribou sometimes have spectacular racks.

Another species popular with eastern hunters is the woodland caribou. Found in small numbers in central Saskatchewan and Manitoba, a major herd is found in northern and central Ontario. There may also be small herds on the Gaspé Peninsula in Quebec and in New Brunswick and Nova Scotia. The best opportunity is on Newfoundland Island, but this is hunting on foot instead of by canoe, and it can be tough going.

BEARS

"Once upon a time," as the bear story begins, these animals occupied almost all of Canada and the United States, and in the case of some kinds, their distribution is still fairly extensive.

Black Bear

Agriculture and deforestation have been the principal enemies of some bruins, while over-hunting has definitely played the primary role in reducing the numbers of other kinds.

There are three major bear species: the American black bear, the brown-grizzly bear and the polar bear. Collectively, they are among the top three kinds of big-game animals sought by American hunters.

American Black Bear

With the exception of the whitetail deer, the black bear has the most extensive range of the North American big-game animals. It also has the largest population of any bear species in the world. Because of this, it's logical that it is also the bear that gets the most attention from hunters, many of whom don't have to venture out of their home state.

Black bears inhabit all of Alaska and Canada other than the extreme northern regions; the greater part of the western U.S. and into Mexico; the states around the Great Lakes; and the Ozarks, Appalachians, Florida and a narrow band of territory along the Gulf Coast that includes parts of Louisiana, Mississippi and Alabama.

This species has become a favorite of bowhunters, particularly in places where baiting is legal, since this provides an ideal situation for hunting from elevated stands. Outfitters have become acutely aware of this, and there are many camps that are strictly archery-only operations. Other methods—hunting with dogs or stillhunting—aren't as popular or productive.

Alaskan Brown Bear

No hunter who hasn't stood looking up at a standing mount of an Alaskan brown bear can fully appreciate how intimidating this animal can be, or what a challenge this species poses for bowhunters. Considered one of the top North American trophies, these big bruins are still sufficiently numerous to provide adequate opportunity. However, brown bear hunts are very expensive, and hunting conditions can be quite strenuous.

The range of this species is restricted to a narrow band of territory along the Alaskan coast and on adjacent islands where salmon runs occur.

Brown Bear

While this isn't its only food source, it is the most important one overall. Like all bears, it is omnivorous and feeds on whatever vegetable or animal matter is available, including carrion.

Grizzly Bear

The grizzly is the bear of legend, and its Latin name, *Ursus arctos horribilis,* seems especially appropriate. While perhaps no more dangerous or aggressive than either the Alaskan brown or the polar bear, its wider distribution and larger populations have always gained it more attention. Many tales of the Old West contained hair-raising accounts of humans in face-to-face encounters with ferocious grizzlies, and outdoor magazines once used these situations regularly for cover illustrations. Even today occasional encounters by campers or hikers are reported in the news.

In those pioneer days the range of this species was much larger, extending throughout all of western North America from Alaska to northern Mexico, and from the coast eastward to the Great Plains. Presently, the larger populations are in Canada and Alaska, with small pockets of grizzlies still remaining in Montana, Wyoming, Idaho and in Yellowstone National Park.

From a bowhunter's standpoint, next to the black bear, the grizzly offers the best prospects. This is because there is such a large range for hunting them. They can be sought in British Columbia, Saskatchewan, Yukon Territory, Northwest Territories and Alaska.

Polar Bear

The most fearsome of all the bear species is the polar bear, which lives in an icy desert where food is scarce and anything that moves is

Grizzly Bears

Polar Bear

regarded as a potential meal. A polar bear has no preference between a seal and a person, and unlike some other animals, it isn't deterred by the scent of man.

Some veteran hunters who have faced dangerous game animals in all parts of the world regard the white bear as the most ferocious and dangerous of them all. It is as large as the Alaskan brown, attaining weights of 800 to 1,000 pounds, but it vastly surpasses it in cunning and aggressiveness. These bears pose an enormous challenge to gun hunters but an even greater one to bowhunters. It took pioneer bowhunter Fred Bear three trips to the Arctic before he managed to take a polar bear with only his bow. He had put arrows into bears on two earlier trips, but each had to be finished off with a rifle to avoid lethal consequences.

There is actually double jeopardy in this kind of sport: one from the treacherous bears and the other from the weather, which can be equally deadly.

PRONGHORN ANTELOPE

These small, graceful animals offer bowhunters the chance to test many of their acquired skills, including stalking, the use of camouflage, and most of all, the ability to judge range and shoot accurately. Pronghorns are most often found in wide open country with near-tabletop terrain, and they don't take cover. They're wary, though, so the matter of getting close enough is the problem.

The good news is that they're very plentiful, and in most places it's possible to conduct stalk

Pronghorn Antelope

after stalk until finally one pays off. Less widespread than in the past, their range is still very large, encompassing all or parts of Alberta, Saskatchewan, Oregon, Idaho, Nevada, California, Montana, Wyoming, Colorado, Arizona, New Mexico, North Dakota, Nebraska and Texas. The largest concentrations are in Wyoming.

Bowhunters should remember that the pronghorn is the fastest of the big-game animals. It can hit 60 mph in spurts and hold at well over 40 mph for long distances. Running shots are not recommended.

NORTH AMERICAN SHEEP

There are two kinds of sheep on the North American continent: the American thinhorn sheep and the bighorn sheep, each of which has two species. In the thinhorn category are the Dall sheep and Stone sheep; in the bighorn category are the Rocky Mountain bighorn sheep and the desert bighorn sheep.

Many American hunters see wild sheep as the ultimate trophy, and collecting all four species for a "grand slam" is a feat every sheep fancier aspires to accomplish. It is extremely difficult for a gun hunter to do it and an even greater challenge for a bowhunter. It is also a very expensive trophy for both types of hunters.

What makes this sport so tough is that in almost all instances sheep live in mountain country that's rugged, intimidating and physically demanding beyond what many hunters care to endure. Stalking at close ranges is very difficult and often dangerous.

WILD BOAR

These animals, also referred to as European wild boar or Russian wild boar, were first introduced into America in New York State in the 1880s. Later they were introduced into many more states, including North Carolina, Tennessee, West Virginia, Florida, California, Texas, New Hampshire and several coastal islands. However, interbreeding with domestic and feral hog stocks has destroyed all purebred stock except some held on a preserve on an island off Nova Scotia.

FERAL BOAR

The feral boar preceded the appearance of the wild boar in America by many years. These hogs were brought into the country by Hernando de Soto as food sources for his exploration parties, and ones that escaped created the nucleus of the free-roaming feral hog population that's present today from coast to coast in no less than eighteen states.

These animals are particularly popular with hunters, since the abundance provides ample hunting opportunities. Many states consider these animals pests and have year-round open seasons on them with no limits. Other states class them as game and have special hunts where they can be hunted with dogs. There are also many commercial hunting preserves which operate on a year-round basis which are very popular with bowhunters, because they provide the chance for the thrill of hunting an animal that is tough, wily and dangerous in close quarters when wounded or cornered because of its sharp tusks. It also can add an impressive trophy to a collection.

AFRICAN GAME ANIMALS

No place on earth is as intriguing and compelling to hunters as Africa, and with a constant progression of nations opening their doors to bowhunters, the potential continues to broaden. The acceptance of archery equipment has been accelerated as it becomes known that a bow in the hands of an accomplished hunter is a viable weapon for African game. The economic benefits no doubt also have persuasive powers.

The first significant bowhunting venture in modern times occurred in 1925 when Saxon Pope and Arthur Young made an expedition to what was then called Tanganyika. Until that time, the Dark Continent, as it was once called, had been ignored by bowyers from other countries since ancient times. Pope's classic book, *The Adventurous Bowmen,* tells of this:

> In the past other men have pursued African game with the bow and arrow. Every great Egyptian ruler seems to have on his tomb a record of his hunting exploits. There we see birds, jackals, gazelles and lions pierced by arrows. The Assyrian kings hunted lions in northern Syria; Assur Nasir-Pal shows us in bas-relief a picture of his hunting expeditions. He shoots from a racing chariot; beaters drive lions out of the jungle; arrow slain beasts lie on the ground about him; it is a royal hunt.

> Other rock engravings depict the king grasping a lion by the throat and stabbing him with a short sword. The beast is full of arrows and this is probably the death stroke. We have no reason to doubt the courage of the king, but there is a suggestion of dramatic license here.

> At least there is every evidence to prove that archers had invaded Africa long before our day. And, of course, we know there are millions of natives who use the bow and arrow in the wild of Ethiopia today as they have for thousands of years in the past.

> But since the epoch of the Crusades, no archers shooting the English long bow and the broadhead arrow have been in the country, and never to our knowledge has any representative of Robin Hood's Merrie Men ever loosed a flying shaft in that continent of mighty beasts. It was therefore with a pro-

found feeling of the romantic significance of the event that we planned to carry the legend of the long bow into the jungles of Africa. We were to journey to the last stronghold of big game; we were to make a holy pilgrimage to the Mecca of all mighty hunters; we had set ourselves the task of vindicating the honor of the arms of our English forefathers with the yew bow and the broadhead arrow.

The Pope and Young expedition, although exciting and successful, had only minor impact outside a small group of archery buffs. Thirty years later, when interest in bowhunting had been revived and was rapidly gaining popularity, Africa was again visited. This time it was by Fred Bear, and on this first trip in 1955, and two subsequent ones in 1964 and 1965, he collected a broad array of game animals, including elephant, Cape buffalo, lion, kudu and many other kinds of antelope. His success in taking even the biggest and toughest animals was inspirational to bowyers.

Such exotic ventures may seem intimidating, but in truth, even bowhunters with no big-game experience beyond whitetails needn't be discouraged from thinking about an African hunt. The broad gamut of game species available includes everything from the tiny blue duikers that weigh only about 8 pounds to the gigantic bull elephants that top 6 tons. With this kind of selection, it's simply a matter of choosing the size game one feels qualified to go after. You can learn big-game hunting as easily on African game as on what's available in the U.S., the difference being the cost in both time and money. Just the same, when it's considered that a reasonably priced safari can result in a hunter collecting a half-dozen or more small to medium-sized animals in a single trip, the experience is not so difficult to justify.

OTHER BIG-GAME OPPORTUNITIES

Africa is only one of the many places outside North America where there are excellent big-game opportunities available to bowhunters. South America has four native species and seven others that have been introduced. There are a dozen trophy animals in Europe that are indigenous, and three exotics. The continent of Asia has more than two dozen big-game animals, and with the greater access hunters now have to both Russia and China, an immense amount of previously off-limits territory has been opened up. A number of places in the South Pacific, Australia and New Zealand in particular, have good offerings of both medium-sized and large animals.

6

Hunting Big Game

Big-game hunting is something that places a great responsibility on the bowhunter, and it should not be undertaken until one possesses the confidence and skill necessary for effectively dealing with and killing the animals being sought.

A lot more than just the basics is required, and a serious bowhunter should undergo a rigorous training schedule before taking on big game. There is nothing more critical than the individual knowing *positively* what his or her maximum range is when it comes to placing shots. Some of the most heated and justified criticism of bowhunters—some of which is generated by bowhunters themselves—is the high incidence of hunters shooting at animals that are too far away. This can't be justified, and a truly conscientious bowhunter will avoid taking a long shot, no matter how tempting it may be.

The main thing is to recognize that everyone has limits, and these limits can increase with time and practice. However, the hunter's known capability at the time of the hunt is what must be considered. An easy way to determine the maximum range at which *dependable* accuracy can be achieved is to set up targets at various distances—20, 25, 30, 35 and 40 yards—and shoot five arrows at each. Then see which group is the tightest. Repeat this a few times and the answer will be evidenced in the results. Be sure your "test results" are current when you schedule a hunt.

Unlike some other sports where occasional handling of the equipment is sufficient to stay in top shape, bowhunters must practice constantly. There's no "off-season." A consistent regimen also pays off in improving accuracy, the ability to judge range and dexterity.

Shooting on ranges where authentic hunting conditions are duplicated permits hunters to broaden their skills and try new things. Some of the important skills: the ability to shoot well from all kinds of unusual positions, including prone; the ability to assess distances quickly and accurately; the ability to shoot through small openings in cover; and the ability to shoot accurately at moving targets.

SHOOT TO KILL

Range judgment and shooting accuracy are important skills for hunting big game, but just as important is shot placement.

It's generally known and accepted that a hit in the heart/lung area will effect the quickest and cleanest kill. Of the two organs, the lungs are the best target to keep in mind. They occupy a much greater part of the rib cage than the heart, and when punctured by a broadhead there's always profuse bleeding. This is because the lungs are laced with a network of blood vessels, and when these are severed the lungs quickly fill and the animal or would it severely.

Striking the heart will always kill the animal, but it presents a much smaller target. Also, in different species, the location differs slightly. The best plan is to aim for the area low on the chest and just behind the foreleg. That's easy on a broadside shot, but if the animal is standing in any other position, it's a different matter. Sometimes a heart/lung shot isn't possible, and an alternate must be decided upon.

The liver, lying to the rear of the lungs and forward of the stomach, can bring an animal down very quickly if the large arteries serving it are cut. If not, even though the wound will eventually be fatal, the animal may move for some distance before succumbing.

Those three—heart, lungs and liver—offer the spots that are the most vital in all big game. Some lucky hits, such as ones to the brain or spine, will usually bring about either an instant or relatively quick end. But they're not shots that should be attempted unless one is very certain of exact arrow placement.

Shots that sever any of the major arteries will result in death, although in some cases the animal may be able to put a lot of distance between itself and the hunter before collapsing. There are five of these large blood channels. The carotid travels up through the neck; the pyloric through the stomach; the renal-cavel to the liver; the aortic down the back;

and the femoral down each of the back legs. However, they're slim vessels and can't be dependably targeted.

Hits at other places result in crippling the animal, and what occurs after this happens is determined by two things: the severity of the wound, and the hunter's reaction.

In almost every case, no matter where you think the arrow hit, simply sit tight and watch the animal to determine the line of flight. Listen carefully, too, because sometimes it will die and come crashing down within earshot.

After a little time has passed, it's okay to walk to where the animal was when you shot it and look for hair and blood. If your arrow passed through, there will definitely be evidence of both. If it didn't, the blood trail may not begin to show up at the site. Walk slowly along the path the animal took when fleeing, scrutinizing every inch of ground along the way. Sometimes blood sign may be no larger than a pinhead, and in some cases this may be all you have to go on for a considerable distance. Don't concentrate only on the ground, but look on shrubs and other vegetation where contact with the animal may have occurred.

There are telltale signs of where an arrow hit and what parts of the anatomy were damaged. Lung shots produce light red, frothy blood, as do shots to the carotid artery. Bright red blood indicates arterial bleeding, and dark red blood is from the liver or the renal artery. Finally, blood mixed with greenish or yellowish matter means a stomach shot, and while not always a lethal shot, the presence of blood increases the chances of recovering the animal.

In the case of deer, elk and similar animals, another clue is the kind of hair that's found. Shots low on the animal will shear light, short hair; medium brown hair will have come from the middle part of the body; and darker, coarser hair from higher on the animal.

The waiting period before following up wounded game should be at least twenty minutes, and the pursuit should be slow. If the blood trail is scanty or sporadic, it's a good idea to mark each new spot so that if you can't find another in the line you're traveling, you'll have a point of reference to which you can return and try again.

One exception to this wait-and-follow-slowly tactic is when you know the animal is hit in the leg or other spot where little bleeding will result. At such times a slow but steady pursuit should be initiated right away, traveling just fast enough to keep the animal on the move. If the blood doesn't coagulate, the animal may eventually weaken and go down.

FIELD DRESSING GAME

No matter what kind of weather conditions or temperatures exist, it's important to field dress game soon after it is killed.

Unless you plan to hang the animal before field dressing it, you will need only a good, sharp hunting knife for the basic procedures. Only when it comes to quartering will a hatchet, axe or meat saw be needed. Other necessary accessories are some cloth and a plastic bag; and rubber surgeon's gloves for the cleaning process.

The first step is to make an incision around the anal vent, then pull it free and out until you can either tie it in a knot or tie it off with a string. This prevents fecal matter from getting into the body cavity when the intestinal tract is removed.

Next, with the animal on its back, open the entire cavity by making a cut from between the legs all the way to the base of the neck. Keep the cutting edge of the blade pointed upward, and use two fingers to guide the blade and hold the skin up to keep from puncturing the internal organs. Sever the windpipe where the cut ends.

At this point, try to locate the broadhead (if it hasn't exited) and remove it so as to avoid injury while field dressing, or problems later when the meat is cut up.

Once the cavity is open, roll the animal on its side and roll the contents out onto the ground. A cut will have to be made around the diaphragm that separates the stomach and intestines from the heart and liver. Pull them out and store them in the plastic bag. They're especially good to eat, and they will provide the first rewards to appear on the table.

The animal should then be rolled over and allowed to drain. When this has been completed, wipe the body cavity dry with a cloth.

Cooling the meat quickly is important. Hanging it is one of the best ways to do this, and if it can't be transported back to camp and hung right away, the body cavity should be propped open as wide as possible with sticks. In some cases it may be wise to skin and quarter the animal to expedite cooling. Many hunters carry cheesecloth in which to wrap meat and protect it from insects. The quarters can be hung up or laid out in cool, shady places.

Care of game meat from field dressing to the freezer makes a big difference in how it will fare on the table, so every step of the process should be conducted with this in mind. Delays in field dressing can be ruinous, and under some conditions bloating and spoilage may begin within an hour. Make sure all damaged tissue is trimmed off, and that all wound channels are free of bone splinters and hair.

USING GAME MEAT

Game meat has always been considered a delicacy by many people who prefer it over domestically produced kind for reasons of taste alone. In addition, it's more nutritious and healthier, since it doesn't contain any chemical additives. This factor alone has been responsible for more people discovering the benefits and pleasures of game meat. And there are many families in North America that still rely on game as their primary food source. Looking back in America's history, there was a point when almost everyone did!

Paradoxically, today there are many people in the U.S. who don't hunt at all yet who benefit greatly from hunters' success. Because of the constantly growing whitetail deer herd and the need to manage it by allowing hunters more generous bag limits, there is a huge amount of venison harvested annually. Most hunters can't utilize as much as they can kill, so rather than waste animals, they stop hunting well short of their legal limits.

This doesn't have to happen anymore. Throughout the country various groups and organizations dedicated to feeding the homeless and hungry urge hunters to donate game meat to their organizations. The programs are very successful, and hunters have eagerly responded to the requests. It's an ideal plan, because it gives hunters both the incentive and a sound reason to harvest more game, plus the reward of knowing they have contributed to a very worthy cause. There's no trouble in finding out how to go about this. All that's required is a call to the state wildlife agency or its local representative.

ACCESSORIES

Trying to identify all of the accessories available to the bowhunter would be an almost impossible task, because it seems the list of items grows almost daily. Many are essential, some are useful or needed only in certain situations, and others are of minimal value.

Certain things used with the hunting bow are small and incidental in appearance, yet being without them can spell the difference between success and failure. To name a few, there are string, cable, whisker and muff silencers that help prevent an animal from "jumping the string" at the moment the arrow is released. Also important are such accessories as camouflage suits, scents and calls.

Mechanical releases are preferred by many bowhunters because they eliminate the torque that invariably results from the finger release. There are a large number of variations and models, some using triggers and others levers or buttons to free the bowstring. Some veteran bowhunters shun releases because of the possibility of mechanical failure under certain conditions, but the majority of both target shooters and hunters now employ them.

An **arrow rest** assures that the released arrow begins its flight properly. In the old days (and possibly still used by some traditional longbow fans) a crooked finger or notch cut in the bow served this purpose. Today's bowhunter can choose from a variety of devices that are much more suitable and convenient. There are two basic types: the launcher rests of the flipper/plunger design used by those who prefer the mechanical release; and the side-support rests favored by shooters using the finger release. Because there is a wide array of selections in both categories that can be confusing to a beginning bowhunter, it's best to choose a model recommended by an experienced archer or a pro shop.

Stabilizers are another way of dampening or eliminating torque and vibration by adding weight forward of the bow on the end of a metal rod. The weights vary from 6 to 16 ounces according to the shooter's needs. Target shooters use stabilizers that are up to 3 feet long, but stabilizers of less than one foot in length are

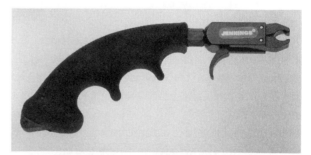

This type of mechanical release features a caliper system that allows the arrow to have a more torque-free departure from the string.

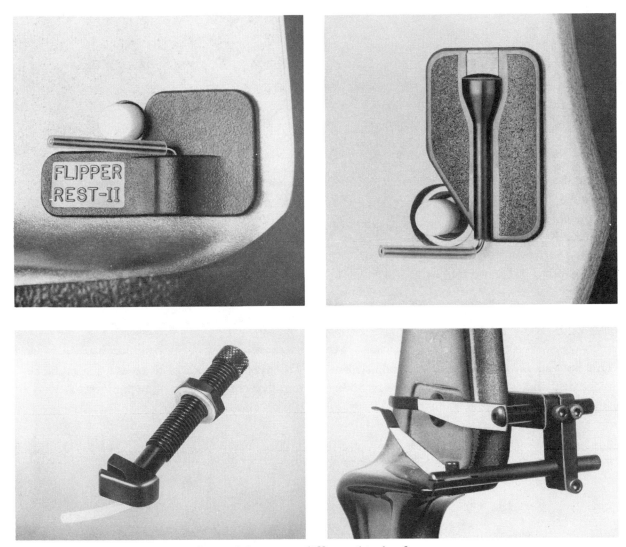

A sampling of the many different kinds of arrow rests.

preferred by bowhunters. Longer ones are cumbersome in field conditions.

Hunters operating from tree stands always leave their shooting equipment on the ground to avoid accidents while ascending. A **bow hoist** is handy for this purpose, because it can be attached to either the hunter's belt or the stand. The stout nylon twine is attached to the equipment, and as it is raised, the spring-loaded reel stores the line to prevent tangling and snagging.

Bowhunters who also hunt with rifles are often more comfortable and confident using **peep sights** because of the similarity to the gun sight system. The peep, mounted in the bowstring, is much like the rear sight of a rifle and gives the shooter assurance of identical alignment with the eye to the bow sight each time.

Binoculars can be one of a bowhunter's best friends in the field, not only for scanning for game, but also for scrutinizing shooting lanes for any obstacles not visible to the unaided eye. There are numerous small, compact models that can be tucked into a shirt or jacket pocket. The best of these have good light-gathering qualities for dawn or dusk viewing. Binoculars serve another purpose, too, which is to provide

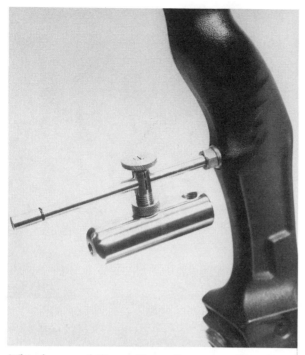

This bow stabilizer allows for easy adjustment in the field and extremely delicate bow balance.

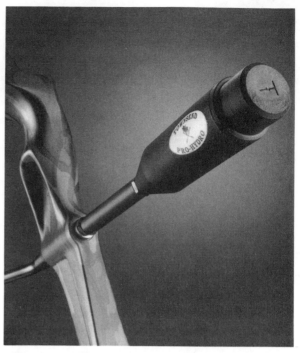

This type of stabilizer features a hydraulic system that controls a free-flowing internal piston.

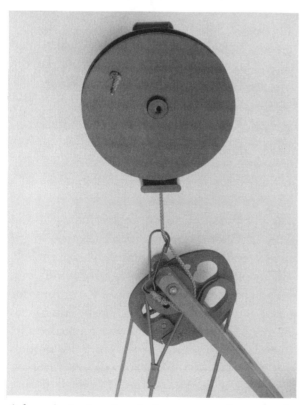

A bow hoist is a handy item to use in a stand, since once the equipment is raised, the cord retracts into the reel body and is out of the way.

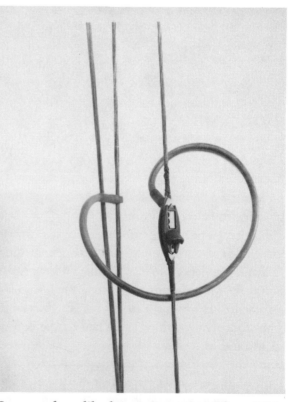

Some archers like bowstring peep sights. This model has interchangeable apertures to fit every shooting style or condition.

Binoculars are vital for bowhunters, particularly ones like this pair that are designed to give maximum visibility in low light conditions.

Compact range-finding devices like this shirt-pocket-size model can aid in determining distance to the target with great accuracy.

A spotting scope can permit a bowhunter to watch game or check out new territory.

Here's a bowhunter checking the range to a crossing where he expects to see game.

enjoyment and pleasure by being able to observe wildlife activities that otherwise might be overlooked.

Rangefinders can be very valuable, also, since this form of optics permits the accurate measurement of distance from the bowhunter to the target or to other objects near a stand that can serve as yardage markers. One of these devices developed especially for bowhunters is only 2¼" x 2¼" x ½" in size, and 2 ounces in

weight. Another is only slightly larger and weighs 5 ounces.

Whether you're hunting from a stand or the ground, a light **folding saw** will make clearing shooting lanes or trimming branches for climbing stands a lot easier. They don't take up much room in a jacket or day pack, and they're well worth the space.

A **flashlight** is an essential for hunters, since most often they're going out or coming back in the dark. When units powered by a couple of D or C batteries were all that were available, it was a somewhat cumbersome accessory. Not so anymore. Due to space age technology, there are tiny units with krypton bulbs using AA and AAA batteries that produce much more illumination than their much larger predecessors. And that's all the more reason to carry a couple along just in case one is lost or malfunctions.

Choosing the right **knife** depends mainly on how you will use it. Sometimes the best idea is to have more than one as standard equipment. A fairly small folder is adequate for field dressing most small game, and it sometimes is sufficient to handle medium-size animals such as whitetail deer or antelope. However, if either the pelvic or breast areas need to be opened, an alternate saw-tooth blade is necessary to do the job well.

For big animals like elk or caribou or bears,

BOWHUNTING *BIG* BIG GAME

By M. R. James
Kalispell, Montana

Sooner or later most experienced deer hunters start dreaming of a hunt for big-antlered bull elk, moose or caribou. And what veteran black bear hunter hasn't imagined drawing an arrow on a big-bodied grizzly or brown bear? Modern-day bowhunters venture as far as Alaska and Africa to tag the biggest and baddest of the world's big-game animals. Here are some time-tested tips:

Shoot the heaviest pulling bow you can shoot accurately, but don't overbow yourself. A well-placed arrow from a 65- or 70-pound bow is better than a bad hit—or complete miss—with a bow pulling 90 or more pounds. Proper arrow placement is the key.

Always aim for the animal's heart/lung area. A double-lung hit is a bowhunter's most deadly shot. Wait to release until the animal is broadside or quartering slightly away. Never rush your shot.

"Pick a spot" is advice worth repeating to all bowhunters drawing down on bigger animals. It seems that the bigger the target the easier it is to forget this commonsense rule. Aiming at the entire animal is the surest way to miss. Think small to score big.

Never use a broadhead that isn't shaving-sharp. Look to sturdy, well-constructed heads that fly true from your hunting bow. Well ahead of the actual hunt, practice shooting with broadheads only.

Learn your effective shooting range and take all shots within the self-imposed yardage limitations. Always resist the temptation to take an iffy shot. Patience pays.

Finally, realize that most big-game animals—whether a 200-pound mule-deer buck or a 1,400-pound bull moose—are taken by bowhunters at ranges of thirty yards or less. Always work to get as close as possible to your quarry, unseen and unheard, then make that first shot count.

M. R. James is editor/publisher of Bowhunter Magazine *and is an award-winning writer and public speaker (with the PBS and OWAA Speakers' Bureau) who's been bowhunting for more than thirty years. He took his first Pope & Young animal in 1963 and has several in the P&Y record book. He has written several books and hundreds of magazine articles. He is currently first vice president, senior member and official measurer of the Pope & Young Club; and he is director of the National Bowhunter Education Foundation, and of Bowhunters of America.*

nothing beats a big, broad-bladed, one-piece knife and a good whetstone for the occasional sharpening required when working with thick, tough skin. And the companion tool should be one of the compact **heavy-duty saws** that hunters use for many different camp tasks. An alternative is a holstered **knife/hatchet combination.**

A cold or wet "behind" hampers a hunter's powers of concentration, not to mention being downright uncomfortable. That's why it's a good idea to carry along a light **cushion.** There is a wide variety, some that are solid, others filled with shredded materials, and one that is a cloth-covered innertube that can be inflated to whatever degree of firmness the hunter prefers.

It's smart and sometimes necessary to mark trails that have to be followed into stands or other pre-selected spots in darkness. Some hunters carry a roll of **red** or **blaze orange survey tape** for this purpose, and although it's effective, it also points the way for other hunters to your "honey hole." Another method is the use of the little **thumbtacks** that can be pushed into a tree. They glow brightly in a flashlight beam, but unlike the tape, they're very unobtrusive in the daytime.

Sophisticated **sound amplifiers** have been developed in recent years that can help a hunter hear sounds in the woods long before they would otherwise be audible. This can help identify the direction from which an animal or bird is approaching or determine if it's something other than what's being sought. This is an outgrowth, or new application, of the devices that have long been used to listen to and record bird songs.

Position in this list of accessories doesn't have anything to do with order of importance. If it did, the suggestion that the use of a **game tracker** for whitetail deer, black bear and wild turkey would have appeared earlier. The device is a cylinder that mounts on the bow and which holds up to 2,500 feet of 17-pound-test nylon

Sound-amplification devices can give hunters an edge in the woods. This hands-free model that fits on a cap is a practical choice.

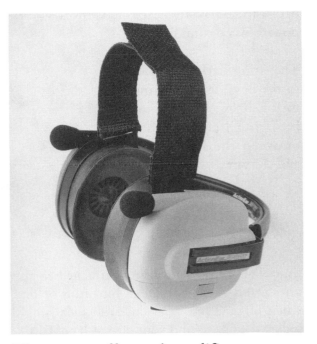

These ear-muff sound amplifiers are very sophisticated, with features for volume control and radio reception.

A string tracker makes an animal's escape route visible, especially in thick underbrush or dim light.

The string tracker attaches to the bow, and the string to the arrow, by a clip or by being held in place between the broadhead and the insert.

line. The end of the line is attached to the arrow, and if the animal or bird runs or flies when hit, the line pays out. You then simply follow the line to find your quarry. It's of particular value near dark when you can't see your arrow or when rain washes out a blood trail. Some outfitters insist that all clients use this device as a way to reduce losses, and some even refer to it as a "game saver."

Night tracking can be greatly assisted with a **high-powered light** that generates up to 500,000 units of candlepower. An alternate to bright illumination (which can cause too much disturbance in the field) is a less-bright light with a red lens that doesn't frighten game. And a substance is now available that turns blood on a game trail florescent, so it has utility in both daytime and nocturnal situations.

The threat of Lyme disease has made hunters acutely aware of the dangers ticks pose, so at times of the year when these pests are present, it's important to carry along the right **repellent**. There's also a compact kit on the market that has the items needed for safe tick removal. As far as other insect repellents are concerned, some big-game hunters shun them because of their odor, but one company has developed one with an earth scent that is supposed to be undetectable. Of course, the odor factor has no bearing whatsoever on many kinds of game sought by bowhunters. Wild turkeys are a good example, and the thought of hunting them in the spring in many parts of the South without repellent makes one cringe! The same goes for spring bear hunting in blackfly country, or seeking caribou on the tundra in early season when both blackflies and mosquitoes are still swarming everywhere.

USING SCENTS AND OTHER TIPS

By Wayne Pearson
Naylor, Georgia

Over the past few years, I've harvested several Boone & Crockett and Pope & Young record-book animals. There are many ingredients for success. You have to hunt an area which holds big bucks. Pre-scouting is a must, and you must get to know your area well.

Keep wind intensity and direction in mind, and place your stand according to the prevailing winds. Allow ample time for the deer to become accustomed to your stand. Generally, the higher you are, the better. I like to get at least sixteen feet up the tree. Be sure to always use a safety belt.

Approach your stand early in the day, allowing time for the woods to settle. Pack a lunch so you can hunt all day. You may only have one opportunity for that really big buck, so I suggest wearing rubber boots to help eliminate odors. I use a scent product called B-Scent Free Spray from Johnson Labs. It actually eliminates human odor by neutralizing odor-causing bacteria.

Also, I wash my hunting clothes in baking soda, and I use unscented soaps and deodorants. Keep your hair smoke-free and your body clean.

I have harvested a lot of nice bucks by rattling and using grunt tubes, but for a record-book-class buck I leave my horns and tubes at home. A trophy buck didn't get that big by being stupid, and you can't afford to alert him in any way.

So, remember: clean clothes, clean body, proper stand placement, wind direction, good scouting, good coverup (B-Scent or comparable), rubber boots, and plenty of dedication. Use these tips, hunt long and hard, and you will be successful.

Good luck with your hunting.

Wayne Pearson is widely known as the host of "Ultimate Outdoor Experiences with Wayne Pearson" on ESPN. Responding to viewer requests for an outdoor club, the Lancaster/Outdoor Trail Sportsman Club was formed. Members receive a quarterly publication and are eligible to win free hunting and fishing trips. Wayne is a lifelong outdoorsman who has several Boone & Crockett and Pope & Young animals—deer and antelope—to his credit. He is proudest of his Double Grand Slam on wild turkeys (two each of four separate species in one season).

An emergency kit can be a true lifesaver at times, and while particular components are necessary in all cases, the kit can be tailored for specific areas or hunting situations.

There's an element of danger present whenever a hunter is afield, and every bowhunter should carry a basic **tool kit** with the items necessary for replacement or repair, but in addition, having a basic **emergency kit** can be extremely important.

Camouflage

It would be impossible for most hunters to imagine going afield without camouflage, because it has become such a vital element in so many types of big-game, small-game and waterfowl hunting throughout the country. It's even used in some situations where it offers no advantage other than making the individual feel more a part of the environment.

Prior to World War II, commercially produced camouflage was unknown to hunters. They wore clothes of the color that best matched or blended with whatever situation they were in, and they used natural materials to further enhance their efforts to be unseen. The big change came when war surplus outlets offered clothing, netting and other items in military camouflage patterns. This was a veritable boon for hunters, and it created an appetite that has become insatiable. Today, there's hardly any hunting item that isn't available in camouflage, including camouflaged toilet paper and a host of other products that border on being little more than gimmicks.

There's also some question of judgment when considering how far the camouflage concept should be carried. Little things like mini-flashlights, diaphragm turkey call holders, pens and pencils are very hard to spot if lost or dropped in the woods, and in these cases it seems logical

Camouflage can be an important asset to a bowhunter, especially when the right pattern is selected for the setting.

that blaze orange or some other highly visible color should be used.

Several factors have contributed to the enormous growth of the camouflage industry, one of which has been the huge expansion of whitetail and turkey populations that has provided hunters with vastly more opportunity. Since camouflage is regarded as vital for pursuing both species, the demand has increased correspondingly.

There has also been a continuing insistence for innovations and improvements in both equipment and clothing, and it is in this area that bowhunters have played a significant role. Bowhunters have a greater dependency on

excellence in things that contribute to their ability to be stealthy and well concealed, since they must approach game closely in order to be successful. They're particularly discriminating in selecting equipment and accessories, and their constantly growing impact on the economy of the outdoor industry has given manufacturers additional impetus to develop materials and designs suited for their needs.

The advancements have been notable. Once manufacturers departed from the military camouflage concept, new ideas emerged. One of the first was a design simulating tree bark that was very suitable for hunting in deciduous forests. That opened a flood gate of both imitators and

Using a natural object like a stump to break up your outline enhances the effect of camouflage.

innovators, and what emerged has been a succession of new patterns too numerous to list. You name it, and there's almost certainly a type to fit the situation, not only in appearance, but also in suitable weight for whatever climate condition exists. Snow? No trouble. Dry, arid desert? Sure. Marsh grass, bottomland hardwood timber, pine forests or whatever? No problem. Additionally, many kinds are offered in color variations that key in with seasonal foliage changes.

There's been another very notable advance, and one for which bowhunters can take a great deal of credit: the development of hunting clothes made of soft fabrics that make moving in the woods vastly more quiet than when wearing garments of the traditional textiles. To bowhunters, silence is indeed golden, and no

other breed of hunters has to depend upon it so heavily.

Dozens of choices in camouflaged boots and hats are on the market, so this becomes a matter of individual preferences and the situations or conditions in which they will be used. Other things that assist in the bowhunter's quest for invisibility are those which hide the face, the hands, and all equipment items that are visible. There's even a treatment for clothing that allegedly makes it impossible for deer to see the ultraviolet light that is supposed to cause a hunter's clothing to glow. (Identifying this claim as controversial is at the least an understatement.)

Hiding the face and hands is essential, and there are two main ways to go about this. Head nets and face masks are popular. Some fit loosely over the face and others made of tightly

The ultimate in camouflage is the three-dimensional kind that can effectively alter a hunter's body form.

woven material fit skin tight. The alternative is camouflage greasepaint that allows a hunter to create patterns for each situation and alter them in the field as the situation may warrant. As for the hands, gloves can be used, but many bowhunters prefer greasepaint, since it doesn't impair the delicate feel for the bowstring they need when shooting. However, tight-fitting, fingerlike gloves work well and are especially desirable in cold weather.

Most hunting bows, arrows and quivers are now offered in camouflage, and those that aren't can be easily disguised with either spray paint or tape.

And just to prove that there's almost no limit to how far the camouflage concept can be carried, "breath camouflage" can be obtained in both liquid and chewing-gum form.

Scent

Long before it became a major part of either the

Camouflaging the face and hands can be easily accomplished by choosing from the broad selection of greasepaints and spray paints available for the purpose.

gun hunting or bowhunting scene, scent was understood and utilized by trappers, and it was from this base of accumulated information that the industry and individuals got a head start on putting it to other uses.

Basically, there are two kinds of scents: those that attract or lure, and those that mask or cover odors. Deer and some other big-game animals find human odor frightening, and encountering a human scent causes them to avoid the source. It's also understood that some odors are attractive to these animals, especially those that relate to creatures of the opposite sex at certain times of the year.

Bowhunters have more at stake where scents are concerned because they must get close to game, so they go the extra mile to be sure that what they select works.

Those scents that attract animals can be ones related to food types, which are useful at any time during the season. During the rut period, sex or musk scents work the best. This entails the use of one or more of the substances and materials for this purpose. There are many, but the most common are: doe in heat, tarsal gland, fresh trail, mock scrape, deer pellets, estrus and things that combine more than one of these elements.

Even when using these kinds of scents, it's still advisable to use cover scents, too, because if human odor is present, it can override the other types of scents and affect the animal.

There's no limit to how far some hunters will go to be sure everything's camouflaged—even their breath!

There are scents for both attracting animals or covering human scent, and dozens of each are available. Here's a typical display rack.

Cover scents can be odors that smell natural to the animal, or even a neutral odor that isn't identifiable. The effectiveness of any kind of scent can be much improved by bathing the night before with a non-perfumed, anti-bacterial soap and wearing clean clothing washed in one of the soaps available in sporting goods stores that leave no detectable odor. Effective, also, are scent-eliminator sprays that can be applied in the field as an additional assurance of non-smell.

Cover scents can be applied to clothing, boots or the skin, and this is usually done before entering the woods in order to prevent leaving an odor trail. Attractants should never be used in this manner. They should be applied at the site, but distant from the stand so the deer's delicate nose can't pinpoint the hunter's exact location. Wind direction and other factors will determine where the scent should be located. For additional insurance, cover scents can be also placed in the vicinity of the stand.

Remember that when stalking or stillhunting you must be aware of your odor. A scent that masks it is effective when you're on the move. The ones to use are what works best for you, and there are some very successful hunters who concoct their own formulas with natural materials and don't rely on any of the commercial products.

Horn rattling is a very productive method of calling in bucks, especially during the season of the rut.

Calls

Attracting big-game animals with sounds of various sorts isn't anything new to hunters. Elk and moose calls are traditional, and in some parts of the country, rattling for mule and whitetail deer has in the last few years gained great popularity and a large following as an effective tactic for luring in big bucks during the mating season.

However, the increased attention now being paid to deer vocalization, primarily in whitetails, has caused hunters to regard a deer call as essential and one of their top priorities. It's been adequately proven that the use of these devices

---

GRUNT AND RATTLE TECHNIQUES

By Eddie Salter
Brewton, Alabama

I never go into the woods without a grunt call. Early in the season I adjust the call to make the soft sound of a doe rather than the rough sound of a big buck. I get in the tree stand early when there is enough light and give three to four notes of subtle grunts, which I repeat every fifteen minutes. Don't overuse the grunt. When you are in the stand you can't see behind you to know if a curious deer is approaching, and when a deer is in sight your call will cause it to look up out of curiosity. But if you see a deer start to wander away, a grunt may detain it.

Later in the year, a doe may make a more aggressive call with a deeper-feeling sound, and about seven to ten times in sequence.

When the deer are in rut, the dominant deer will tend to be more aggressive to protect their territory. Adjust the grunt tube to sound rough and bad, like the biggest buck in the woods. Make a series of three to four notes in fifteen-minute intervals, repeating this all day while you're in the tree stand. This is a natural sound and will not scare the deer off.

When you know the rut is at its peak, pick a more aggressive, quicker note. Again, use it just to get the deer's attention, but don't overdo it.

Rattling can be enormously successful, though some areas of the country are better than others. For instance, where there are good buck-to-doe ratios, the bucks will be more aggressive and responsive. Often, after being quiet in a tree stand for three or four hours with nothing happening, I start thinking about getting down and rattling. This can cause a nearby buck to investigate.

I've found that early to mid-morning is the best time. First, I find an area where a big buck has been. Scrapings, hooking of trees, and pawing of the ground are clues. Get close to the area, but check the wind direction. I start by pounding the ground and raking the leaves with both antlers. After that, clang them together and twist and turn them. Then, come out of this position. Pause, listen. You may want to let out a long, aggressive grunt instead of locking antlers again.

Basically, I do three series of these twisting and locking maneuvers, then move on to another area. Fifteen minutes later, I start again.

All these sounds are part of a deer's everyday routines, and some day a P&Y buck may come along to reward you. Above all, don't give up. If you go out and successfully grunt or rattle just one trophy buck, it is worth all the time and effort.

Eddie Salter is a world-champion caller and maker of Eddie Salter Calls. He has hunted extensively in Texas, Alabama, Ohio and a number of other states. Eddie is spokesman for Bear Archery and McPherson Archery.

Rattling bags (above) containing wood or ceramic sticks are handier to carry than a set of antlers, and they often produce equally good results. The grunt call (right) has become very popular as a way of imitating various kinds of deer vocalization.

can provide a big advantage in that they lure deer into closer range, and this has given bowhunters special reason to want to learn to use them.

In all calls, the signals sent consist of everything from greetings to challenges, and from invitations to play around to cries of distress or injury. Sometimes, they are successful by doing nothing more than arousing the animal's curiosity and causing it to investigate what's going on.

There are numerous mechanisms for producing the various sounds deer use to communicate, but the ones that have been found to be the most effective calls are the reed-type "grunt calls" that provide the most authentic reproductions of "deer talk."

7

Tree Stands

The idea of hunting game from an elevated position isn't anything new, because early man found tree limbs ideal spots from which to drop big rocks or hurl spears at animals passing underneath. Since some of the creatures they sought were dangerous, the method proved to be safe as well.

Using this tactic of staying out of harm's way while hunting became more sophisticated over the centuries. Instead of simply perching on a limb, hunters built structures in which to sit that provided both better concealment and a larger degree of comfort. In Africa and India they were used mainly when seeking lions and tigers, but they also began to appear in parts of Europe where red stag and various kinds of deer were hunted.

The European models were usually towerlike wooden platforms that either stood independently or were built in or against trees. More often than not, they were built to accommodate from two to four people. The advantage wasn't safety, but increased visibility.

Some of the early stands used in America followed this pattern, but just as common were very simple structures that sometimes consisted of little more than a couple of planks nailed across parallel limbs and a series of spikes or wooden crosspieces to climb to the perch.

With the appearance of portable stands, the use of wooden structures began to diminish. For one thing, they were permanently attached and in time could deteriorate and become unsafe. Also they weren't aesthetically pleasing. But more important, they did damage to trees. Because of this, they were declared illegal on federal lands, as well as on many state and timber company holdings.

Portable stands are extremely popular among big-game hunters in different parts of the country, but especially so in the eastern United States where whitetail deer are the principal species sought. They're particularly favored by bowhunters, and to say that perhaps 80 percent use them would be a conservative estimate. This is because being situated well above ground level allows a bowhunter to be more effective in a number of ways. It allows the hunter to be less obtrusive and improves the chances of game coming into closer proximity. Too, certain loca-

A securely fastened stand and a safety belt make shooting from elevation much less hazardous.

tions will offer better shooting lanes than can be obtained by removing a few limbs or branches, so deciding where and how to place a stand should be given careful consideration.

Deer don't always look up, so the odds favor bowhunters seeking this species, but when it comes to wild turkeys, which look everywhere, you're sometimes just as well off in a ground blind.

There are enough kinds of stands on the market today to offer the bowhunter every kind of option imaginable, and in virtually every price range. Some of the basic types are little more than metal frames that strap to a tree and cost only a few dollars. On the other end of the line are big, comfortable stands with padded seats and other special features that are quite expensive. However, with the intense focus of attention on safety, almost all manufacturers use high-tech materials and the best designs to address this concern. It should be

Always ascend the stand without the shooting equipment, then bring it up once you're in place with safety belt attached.

remembered, though, that anytime one is situated high above the ground there is a danger factor, and avoiding accidents is the individual hunter's responsibility.

CLIMBING STANDS

One of the first commercial models to be introduced was the two-piece climbing stand, which operates on a sort of inch-worm principle. Both sections are attached around the trunk, with a sharp or serrated blade that will bite into the bark when pressure is placed on it. The hunter stands on the lower part, raises the upper part with the arms and puts it solidly in position, then repeats the process with the lower unit. A safety belt is a must for this or any other kind of climbing operation.

Until quite recently, these stands required trees with straight trunks and no limbs to interfere with the climb. If some were present between the ground and the height the hunter wished to attain, they had to first be removed. However, one company has developed a revolutionary type of climber with separate units for each foot that permits a hunter to simply climb around and past limbs.

Because the original climbing stands, as well as some still currently available, can do damage to trees, they are illegal to use in many forest areas. This ban has caused significant changes in design, and many of these modified climbers no longer present a hazard to the resource and are environmentally acceptable.

STRAP-ON STANDS

Strap-on and chain-on stands have advantages over the climbers because they can be placed almost anywhere on the trunk, and there is one model that can be set up like a stool on horizontal limbs. They also don't draw fire from the game agencies and timber companies, since the methods of attachment aren't

Today's tree stands are designed to make them comfortable to sit in for long periods of time.

Here's an example of a hunter ascending a tree with a climbing stand.

This compact climbing stand is especially designed for bowhunters.

detrimental to the trees. What has caused problems are the procedures used to climb the trees to put the stands in place. One popular way is with metal screw-in steps, which are sturdy and safe. Still, they also do tree damage, and this has led to their being outlawed in many places. Again, industry responded quickly and satisfactorily with strap-on steps that use only nylon webbing to hold them in place. They're easier and quicker to attach than the metal ones, and if a hunter wants to add a measure of protection, they can be quickly removed upon departure, leaving no access to the stand.

Another practical device to use in conjunction with these kinds of stands is a lightweight, sectional metal tube with steps that can be strapped to a tree to erect the stand, and to use getting in and out. As with the strap-on steps, it can be taken down each day after the hunt and either carried out or hidden nearby.

LADDER STANDS

Ladder stands are one of the most convenient of all, because they are simple to erect, don't require any steps to be put in place, and can be quickly and easily moved from one location to another. They're also safe and comfortable, and most manufactured models have sectional legs that allow them to be erected at whatever level

---

TREE STANDS

By Noel Feather
Sterling, Illinois

I hunted with a bow for a long time before using stands and before they really got popular. I killed some deer, of course, but when we switched to stands I started having real success.

Deer have no natural enemies from above, and so at first I could make noise and they very seldom looked up. Now they're getting more used to being attacked from trees.

In most of the places I hunt, I prefer a lock-on type of stand. That's one where I can just climb up using the limbs, find a spot that's clear of limbs, hang the stand and lock it on the tree. Usually this type of stand has a safety belt and is pretty safe. I use them a lot because in Illinois we have a lot of oak, hickory and ash that have limbs close to the ground and so can be used this way.

In the South, where there is a lot of pine, climbing tree stands seem to be popular. In those trees, the first limb may be thirty to fifty feet from the ground. I do believe they are a little more dangerous, though some types seem safe. Some of these are the strap-on type of stands, and in some places you have to use them so as not to damage the tree.

The strap-ons have not given me a problem, but I like the climbing sticks much better. They have four-foot sections, and one goes inside the other, allowing you to go up to the height you want and then hang the stand on.

The company whose products I use makes a climbing stand, the lock-on type, and a ladder stand. I prefer a ladder stand if I can go in with a 4-wheeler and don't have to carry it far. They are a little more bulky than some of the other types and are heavier to carry than the lock-on type I regularly use.

Rattling is a technique I use often, and probably 90 percent of my rattling is done from a tree stand. I feel the advantage of being in a tree stand is significant. When you're in a stand, you're up above most of the brush and you can see so much better. You can spot that buck coming, and you have time to stop rattling, get rid of the horns, and get your bow ready. That's half the battle. If you have the horns in your hand when the buck is on the ground looking up at you, you won't get that shot.

One thing that is extremely important in bowhunting (or any hunting, for that matter) is to pay attention to the ethics of the sport. I push that idea in my seminars, and I also stress practice.

Noel Feather has been bowhunting since the mid-sixties. He is a championship antler rattler who has rattled in and taken three whitetail deer that qualify for the Boone & Crockett record book (two were taken with a bow). He is a member of the Pope & Young Club, with twenty-eight big-game animals representing many species in the P&Y record book, and in 1981 and 1982 was Bowhunter of the Year.

Noel is a hunting consultant and booking agent for pronghorn and black bear, conducts seminars, has made many media appearances, and is an advisor to industry.

This type of stand design allows a hunter to use horizontal or angling limbs as the base.

It took this bowhunter less than five minutes to put his stand in place using the strap-on ladder.

A bowhunter attaching a strap-on type stand. Note that the safety belt is in place.

Attaching a strap-on ladder. It does not damage trees and is legal on all hunting lands.

Strap-on steps are now mandatory in many places because they don't damage trees.

is desired. Some commercial deer hunting operations use ladder stands made of wood that serve the same purpose, but which aren't as portable.

These kinds of stands run the gamut from the simple to the fancy, and some on the high end of the spectrum have camouflaged skirts around the platform to hide the hunter and even umbrellas to protect him from the rain.

TRIPOD STANDS

The three-legged tripod stand can be very important in providing bowhunters with an elevated position at clear cuts or other locations where there are no trees present. They're not as easily moved around as other stands, but if placed in an area where there will be deer activity throughout the season, this isn't necessary, anyway.

Ladder stands like this one are very popular and easy to put in place or move from one spot to another.

SCOUTING AND STAND PLACEMENT

By Bill Jordan
Columbus, Georgia

Scouting before bow season begins, often and regularly, helps you put the deer puzzle pieces together, especially those relating to trophy bucks. Ideally, you should start within a month after a season has ended to scout for the next season. By then, whitetails will return to their normal movement patterns, so you can check for the most heavily used trails and locations you missed during the open season.

Before the season is also a time to pick up shed racks. Finding a huge set of deer antlers tells you that a trophy buck has made it through, and you can't help getting excited about the upcoming season!

I make it a point to get out forty-five to sixty days before the season, looking for main trails going between bedding and feeding areas. Scouting right after a rain allows you to scrutinize deer tracks. I make notes recalling when and where I locate outsize hoof marks. I also check out the acorn crop in trees overhead and note the sunny hillsides that will be loaded with mast by opening day. The easiest way to zero in on any deer before the rut is to identify their food sources.

This is when I place many deer stands, often setting them on these trails very close to the feed sources. I work hard to find where two or three trails converge or crisscross. For bow hunting I like to set up fifteen to thirty-five yards from the trail, depending on the thickness of the surrounding trees and vegetation, and I place the stand fifteen to nineteen feet above the ground. I prefer the lock-on type for most situations, though it takes some time to erect them and lock

them firmly and safely in place. Having multiple stands allows me to alter my game plan each day during the season, adjusting to the wind direction and other factors.

Once each stand is in place, a great deal more effort goes into cutting out shooting lanes of the right size. I cut out as many shooting lanes as is practical, then I put out markers at twenty, thirty and forty yards. The markers can be ribbons, string or colored clothespins attached to branches two to three feet off the ground. With my bow I shoot pins sighted in to each of those distances, so when a shot is presented I know which sight pin to select. There's no guesswork.

Camouflage is very important. I pick my Realtree Grey-Leaf or Brown-Leaf according to the tree I choose to hunt from. And I like to place my stand in and around foliage.

Bill Jordan has been an avid bowhunter since 1968, has harvested many trophy whitetails—six 10-pointers, two each 11- and 12-pointers, one each 13- and 14-pointer—four of which made the Pope and Young record book. He has placed at or next to the top in four Buckmaster Classics (once first, three times runner-up). Bill is president of Spartan-Realtree Products, Inc., and designer of the company's popular trademarked Realtree camouflage patterns. His specialty, he says, is "shooting straight with a compound bow."

The swivel seats on these stands give a hunter 360-degree visual and shooting potential, and it's possible to shoot from either a sitting or standing position. Most tripod stands have

either a standard or optional metal bar surrounding the hunter to which camouflaged skirts can be added.

Telescoping legs make it possible to adjust

Tripod stands are very practical and useful in places where there's no other way to gain elevation.

these stands on uneven ground, but it's wise to consider them as somewhat unstable under any conditions. An abrupt movement by the hunter or gust of wind is sometimes enough to tip them over. To safeguard against this, drive a wood or metal stake at the base of each leg and secure the two together with rope. That eliminates the threat of falling and guarantees peace of mind.

Because elevated stands cause the major part of injuries hunters suffer in the field, many hunting camp operators take extra precautions regarding their use. They have the welfare of their clients at heart, and aside from personal feelings, there's the matter of liability claims that could be leveled against them.

One way some operators reduce the chance of such accidents is by having their guides assist getting hunters in place and making sure their safety belts are properly attached. The hunters

are supposed to remain in the stand until the guide returns. That covers two-thirds of the potentially dangerous period, and the rest is up to the individual hunter.

The matter of liability is a subject that causes manufacturers of stands to cringe, since many lawsuits of this sort have been brought against them. As a result, some companies have been driven out of business and others have been financially crippled. In some instances manufacturers have been at fault, while in others hunter error has been the bigger factor.

One good result has been a concerted effort on the part of manufacturers to make stands as safe and sound as possible. Plenty of progress has been made through the use of high-tech materials and innovative engineering. Still, the responsibility for stand selection and its proper use remains with the hunter.

8

Stalking

Other than being able to shoot well, there is no skill more important to becoming a fully qualified, all-round bowhunter than being able to stalk, or as some refer to it, stillhunt.

This is the ability to seek out game instead of waiting for it to come to you, and to match wits with the animal on a one-on-one basis. It's an especially rewarding kind of hunting that creates an immense sense of self-satisfaction. There's a special thrill and feeling of accomplishment when you are standing over a nice buck you've bagged by being able to get within shooting range, or an antelope that has required a long, slow, inch-by-inch approach over open country.

For the bowhunter who plans to seek several kinds of game, a talent for stalking is an absolute necessity. There are many animals, large and small, that you have to go after. They can't be collected by sitting in a stand or a blind.

MOVING QUIETLY

Silence is truly of great importance when it comes to moving on the ground, and if there is any term that best describes how to do it, it is "catlike."

Think of it for a moment and you'll see why. You've no doubt seen a cat stalking a mouse or a bird, and noticed the way it behaves in the process.

First of all, it approaches its prey very slowly, instantly freezing in place if the prey looks in its direction. Second, it places its paws down softly and carefully in order to avoid making any sound. And all the while it is concentrating completely on the creature it is stalking.

Remember how, as a kid, you liked to sneak up on playmates and surprise them. The main difference in hunting is that animals are more alert and harder to slip up on than humans. Also, conditions in the woods like dry leaves, twigs or thick understory growth make moving silently a great deal more difficult. More often than not, it's a one-step-at-a-time process, studying every spot before putting a foot down on it. Progress can be agonizingly slow at times, but there's no alternate way to success.

Looking at it from another perspective, sounds aren't always a nemesis, because there are some that don't alarm animals and which you can use as an advantage. Things like planes passing over, the buzz of a chain saw, a train whistle, barking dogs, crows calling or other noises provide a mask for any sounds you may make as you move. Some creatures create their

This bowhunter has quietly stalked within shooting distance of a buck. Stealth is the key to this hunting tactic.

own baffles against outside sounds. When squirrels are cutting nuts, they can't hear much except their own endeavors. The same applies to gobbling turkeys or bugling elk. By acting quickly when such opportunities present themselves, you can gain a few extra yards, which at times can be very precious!

A basic formula for stalking is to take three or four slow, careful steps, then stop for at least a full minute, scanning everything around and listening intently. If you're serious about learning this technique, you must remember there are no shortcuts, and time shouldn't be of consequence.

Concentration is required throughout, of course, but like the cat, you must always have your "eye on the sparrow," whether or not it's in

sight. If you can see the quarry, then you will be zeroed in on it every second, constantly shaping your strategy according to what it is doing, and trying to anticipate what it might do next. If you haven't seen it yet, then it's imperative that everything in front of you be minutely examined before each forward step.

Finally, becoming an accomplished stillhunter doesn't happen overnight, and the only way to attain any degree of proficiency is to practice. One of the best ways for beginners to learn is to go squirrel hunting. Stalking bushytails involves all of the elements needed for hunting virtually any kind of game, large or small. You don't even have to shoot: just see if you can get to where you could if you wanted to.

Good camouflage, patience and slow and careful movement are the elements most important to the hunter who stalks.

USING THE WIND

Perhaps the most quixotic element a hunter stalking big game has to contend with is the wind. Even though the basic rule is to hunt facing into it, this isn't always possible. Animal trails or animals within view may go in any direction, and sometimes terrain features create problems. To overcome them, a hunter has to make decisions that may require either taking lengthy detours to avoid getting into a following wind, or if a cover scent is being used, staying on the same course and hoping for the best.

The worst scenario is a shifting wind that is constantly changing and seems at times to be coming from all directions at once. No matter what tactics are used, the odds are stacked against a stillhunt, but some hunters don't mind long odds.

Animals are also confused by a shifting wind and tend to stay in one place rather than move about. The downside is that without being able to depend on their noses, they're nervous and looking around everywhere for possible danger.

BAD WEATHER

Stalking bowhunters have their best chances of getting close to deer and other big game during periods of extreme cold, rain or snowstorms. At such times the animals move into cover and bed down. They're less alert because they're relaxed and sometimes asleep, and a stealthy hunter can quite often get to within a few yards of them fairly easily.

This means going out in some really tough weather conditions, but for bowhunters who are looking for new experiences, it represents both an exciting challenge and a chance to take a big-game animal in a different kind of circumstance.

CLOTHING

The choice of clothing is very important, too, especially when you're passing through shrubs, branches and briars. With garments made of fabrics like brushed cotton, chamois or fleece, you can move more quietly than in those with harder finishes. The sound of a bramble sawing across the surface of a regular hunting jacket can be heard for a remarkable distance, and it's one that rings an alarm bell in an animal's mind.

The demand by bowhunters was a principal force in convincing the outdoor industry to create "quiet clothing" that has enhanced the ability to move through cover almost noiselessly. Not surprisingly, it has become extremely popular with gun hunters for the same reasons, so everyone has benefited.

Footwear is another item that deserves consideration. If a poll were to be taken among bowhunters to determine their favorite kind, the rubber-bottomed pacs exemplified in the venerable and famous L.L. Bean Maine Hunting Shoe would no doubt be their top choice by an overwhelming margin. It's understandable why. This type of boot is light, flexible, waterproof and suitable for use in practically all sorts of terrain. Too, in the opinion of most hunters, they're the quietest footwear available. Pacs are made in noninsulated and insulated versions, so they can be worn in all seasons. There are also models with a variety of inserts to match whatever conditions exist.

Some bowhunters add insurance for extra footwear silence by wearing socks over the boots or shoes.

To grant traditional bowhunters their due, it's well to note they believe that Indian moccasins are the quietest footwear in the woods. If that's so, then maybe bare feet are even better!

KNOWING THE TERRAIN

Knowing what you're doing when stillhunting is one thing, but knowing *where* is quite another, so having as thorough knowledge as possible of the area you'll be stalking is a way to increase your chances of success.

Remember that you're seeking animals on their own turf, so to speak, and within it they have intimate knowledge of all its features. This includes normal travel routes, seasonal feeding and watering locations, places to seek sunshine and warmth on cold days, dense cover for either safety or protection from the weather, the best points from which to observe the most territory, escape routes and all other things that have to do with daily routines and survival.

Your responsibility as a stillhunter is to learn as much about all of these things as you can in order to be able to compete and sometimes to second-guess or anticipate what your adversary is going to do.

There is more than one way to go about gaining this knowledge, the best being to spend as much time as possible scouting the area prior to the season. Preferably, you should do this at different times of the year in order to get a better idea of what the animals are doing seasonally and how their habits vary.

Your scouting forays will familiarize you with the terrain, the animals that live there, where their food is located, where they sleep and the routes of their trails.

You can begin by studying topographic maps and talking with people who know the area. Once you have permission from the landowner your scouting can begin in earnest. Look for open fields, areas of cover, any structures or natural barriers, and water supplies. Pinpointing these features on your map will refresh your memory later.

With the aid of binoculars or a spotting scope, you can study the open fields during early morning and late evening from a distance. Inside the cover, look for trails leading to the fields, heavily traveled trails, and bedding areas.

The ability to read game sign is an important skill that will enable you to identify the places just mentioned. For example, if your quarry is deer, from their tracks you can determine the size of the game, the number of game animals passing through the location, and the direction of their movement.

STALKING OPEN-COUNTRY GAME

By Judd Cooney

Pagosa Springs, Colorado

Mule deer, elk, whitetails and antelope are all animals that originally spent much of their time in open country, but as the population increased, they were forced to adapt to areas of heavier cover and rugged terrain in order to survive.

A bowhunter today often encounters one of these critters that doesn't play according to the rules. Instead, it spends much of its time out in the open where getting within arrow range can seem impossible.

Patience is the bowhunter's greatest asset in open-country stalking. A good set of binoculars is the second most important item in your stalking arsenal, allowing you to study the animal and its surroundings.

I prefer to let the animal come to me if at all possible, or at worst make it a fifty-fifty proposition: I'm stalking toward it while it is moving toward me. Seldom will stalking along behind an animal put you within bow range. Spend time with your binoculars, determining what the animal is doing and where it is going, and then try to anticipate a course that will put you in front of it and in the best cover possible. This may be a small gully, a single small bush, or a rock outcropping. Avoid large, obvious ambush sites! These animals will walk within a few feet of an unlikely place, but they always seem to stay just out of arrow range of the more obvious places.

The bigger the trophy, the sharper the animal.

Always keep the wind in your face and the sun at your back or side, if possible. Animals dislike looking directly into the sun—and if you can stay in a shadowed area, so much the better.

You're probably going to get just one chance to stalk that particular animal in that area. When there is simply no feasible way to approach the animal in open terrain, you must recognize this fact and simply back off and wait for another time.

Stalking to within bow range and making a clean kill on a big-game animal in open country has to be the epitome of the bowhunting experience and the supreme challenge for all bowhunters.

Expert bowhunter Judd Cooney has been hunting with a bow since 1956. He is a full-time freelance writer/photographer who covers all outdoor subjects, specializing in large-game hunting with bow and gun. He is also an outfitter for Colorado big-game. He holds several Pope and Young record-book animals, and until 1990 was tied for the P&Y World Record Antelope.

Stalking is a form of hunting where woodsmanship plays a vital role. Here a hunter has spotted a shed deer antler.

Fresh rubs show that there's a rutting buck somewhere in the vicinity. Both fresh and old rubs mean the area is well traveled.

When you see a rub, or an area of a tree or bush that has been rubbed repeatedly, you can be sure of the presence of a buck in the area. There may be a series of rubs going between a bedding area and a feeding area. If some rubs are new and others much older, the area is well traveled, and chances are even better that you may see a buck.

Another indicator of both bucks and does is the scrape, and exposed area on the ground that results from pawing. These are made during the breeding season and are usually located under low branches that have been broken by the chewing and rubbing of bucks who want to get the attention of the does.

During most bow seasons the deer are usually very busy eating. They like tender tips of plants, or browse, and a close look will tell you if the plant tips have been torn off. Acorns are a favorite deer food, but many types of field crops and wild plants complete their diet.

A fresh deer scrape during the rut means that there's a buck making regular rounds in the territory and trying to attract does.

You can also learn much by studying the droppings. Different sizes indicate different sizes of animals, and where you see both old and new droppings the area is in use throughout a period of time.

Bedding, or resting, areas are identified by leaves or other ground cover that are matted down. They indicate an area in which the deer will rest. In cold weather they will likely be found in sunny, southern exposures with a minimum of cover.

Finally, look for hair on obstructions along deer trails, such as fences or large fallen logs.

Once you determine the presence of deer and the composition of the population, plan your strategy according to the information you have gained. You may want to ambush a big buck in a bedding area, and so you will become very familiar with the location in order to get on stand while it is still dark. You will also need to identify the trails and the deer's direction of movement. An intersection of trails is also a potential hot location for a stand.

Some of the most successful hunters visit an area many times during the course of a year to observe changes in food sources, population movements, and onset of breeding activity.

While nothing beats this kind of personal investigation and exploration, sometimes you're going on a hunt in a location you haven't visited before. In this kind of situation, having a topographical map well in advance of the trip will give you essential information. Make notes on how the land lies and of some of the features like old logging roads, openings and prominent landmarks that can be used to your benefit.

And don't forget that when hunting in unknown territory, particularly when a large expanse is involved, it's wise to use a compass to plot your course. At the least, getting lost in the woods is embarrassing; at worst, it can be extremely dangerous, especially in adverse weather conditions. The little time it takes to prepare yourself this way will make you feel more confident and comfortable and remove the possibility of such things happening.

9

Driving

Driving is a tactic that is very useful in hunting some kinds of game, particularly deer, and one that often will get results when other methods fail. Driving often works when the animals aren't on the move or are in dense cover that's impossible to stalk successfully; or when weather conditions make other forms of hunting impractical or unproductive. What's more, it's also a useful strategy to consider as an added attraction following a normal morning's hunt in the woods, since it can be a way to put some more venison on the camp meat pole.

Bowhunters conduct drives differently than gun hunters do. The latter generally like to make noise to startle the animals and run them out of their refuges. In bowhunting, the idea is to move slowly and quietly, making the animals aware of the drivers' presence, but not attempting to put them on the run. The reason for this is that a deer that isn't alarmed won't bolt, but instead will try to slip along ahead of the hunter. This way the standers, those at the end of the woodlot or whatever cover is being driven, don't have to anticipate trying to hit a target that's running wide open.

Successful drives can be organized with as few as two hunters, with one walking through the cover and the other waiting at the end. Four work a lot better, with two driving and two standing. Of course, this can be enlarged to any number desired. Part of this depends upon the size of the area that's going to be driven.

Whatever number of drivers are involved, it's important for them to remain close enough so a deer can't reverse its direction and come back between them. Being within sight of each other is the best rule of thumb to determine this distance.

On short drives it usually isn't necessary to have standers along the flanks, but on long ones there's the distinct possibility that the deer will attempt to make lateral moves to escape. That's one reason why they shouldn't be attempted by a small group of hunters. If there are only two to four involved, pick out spots that can be properly handled.

At times it may be preferable to have the standers actually in elevated stands, since this provides greater visibility and an additional safety measure. Missed shots from stands send

In driving, it's important that the standers be extremely careful to keep an eye on the position of the drivers at all times.

arrows into the ground instead of sailing out through the woods.

Driving involves stalking, or stillhunting, skills. The difference is in what you're trying to accomplish. The chances of a driver getting a good shot at a deer are not very good, but sometimes it can happen, as when a deer tries to sneak back through the "enemy lines." Because of this, the hunter has to be prepared, but also fully aware of where both his driving partner and the standers are located. In some cases, the drivers go unarmed, and there's merit in that kind of thinking. Another very sensible suggestion is that drivers all wear some kind of blaze orange, whether it be a vest or a cap.

Something deer hunters sometimes overlook

is that both whitetails and blacktails are animals that are likely to be found in small woodlots or other forms of cover close to areas of human habitation, or even near interstate highways where noise is a constant factor. These are places that are particularly well suited for drives,

---

DRIVING DEER

By Paul Butski
Niagara Falls, New York

I've been driving deer for a number of years while bowhunting. It's a good activity around midday when you've been sitting in a tree stand all morning, and it's when the deer will be bedding down. A few hunters can get together, put on some "silent drives" and often have good success.

If there are just a few guys, you should look for small patchy woods or good bedding areas where you can hunt effectively. I like to have some good funneling areas for the guys that will be on post. Deer don't like to break out in open areas, so in narrow strips of woods where there are fields outside, they will funnel toward the end. Deer also like to break across a road or on the end of a little draw or in a creek bottom. It takes a bit of scouting to find these escape routes.

To be more successful, learn to read signs in the woods. Improving your woodsmanship will help you to determine those areas deer are moving through.

Bigger bucks like to double back when driven. If there are enough hunters, some can serve as posters, some as drivers, and others as followers 75 to 100 yards behind the drivers to bag those big bucks that double back. A lot of bucks will be off the paths somewhat, so keep your eyes open for deer that try to sneak through that way.

Posters need to get into position quickly and quietly, without being seen by the deer. Otherwise, the animals will move out even before the drivers get there.

Wind is probably the single most important factor in driving deer, whose keenest sense is smell. The drivers should be downwind. There are three basic driving styles: silent drives, noisy drives, and circle drives. In a circle drive, every-body is a driver. The drivers form a circle around a small patch of woods, for example, and then converge at a slow pace. Deer are likely to break toward somebody.

Cornfields are also good places for driving. Drivers can string across the field and work the rows, and often you will see deer standing or lying in there.

I like silent drives best. First, everybody has a chance at getting a deer. Deer can run into the poster or back into the driver, even circle back. The drivers can string out fifty to seventy-five yards apart and just walk and stop, walk and stop, quietly. The deer may bolt a little, stop, and then start moving again. There are many different driving patterns: criss-crosses, loops, and the like—all of which can work effectively.

Noisy drives are not recommended for bowhunters, because it's next to impossible to get anything but a running shot.

One final point: Don't put on a drive if you expect to hunt the same area later that evening. The human scent you bring in will scare the deer away. They'll be back, of course, but maybe not that night.

Paul Butski, a national turkey-calling champion, is considered one of the top whitetail and turkey hunters in the U.S. In conjunction with his business partner, Billy Macoy, he has produced several highly rated hunting videos. He owns a company that manufactures a variety of game calls.

mainly because they are usually ignored by still-hunters or standhunters. Some others with good potential are wooded areas along stream or river banks, grown-up thickets in sinkholes or stands of planted pines.

Big-game animals other than deer can be driven, but not as dependably or as successfully, and the methods differ considerably.

Antelope can be manipulated in this fashion to some degree by having a hunter or hunters walk slowly toward them with the hope of causing them to run in the direction of companions already in position and hidden. This can sometimes work with caribou, too, and occasionally with elk, but in each of these cases it's a long-shot proposition and highly unpredictable. Ordinarily there's too much open territory involved and the animals have too many choices of escape routes. Frankly, it's better to hunt them in more traditional ways.

10

Small Game

Bowhunters sometimes get caught up in thinking about big game, but they shouldn't lose sight of the pure fun and satisfaction that hunting small game can provide. It's a form of the sport in which individuals of all ages and levels of experience can participate, and not infrequently the hunt can begin as close as your own backyard. Too, licenses for small-game hunting are less expensive than those that include big game. Some states even allow certain small-game species to be hunted without any license requirements at all.

There's another big advantage, which is that the accuracy required to bring down small targets makes this activity very beneficial, providing an excellent way to hone shooting skills. It is an ideal training ground for young bowhunters, and it is an extremely important activity for veteran shooters.

There are many kinds of small animals to choose from, but the favorite by far is the rabbit. One or more kinds of rabbits are found all over North America. There are more than a dozen species, but the most common are the cottontails—eastern, swamp, marsh, mountain and desert—and the whitetail and blacktail jackrabbits.

Bowhunters also like to hunt snowshoe hares. They're found throughout Canada and Alaska, but in the U.S. they're limited mainly to New England, the Northwest, the Rockies and some midwestern states bordering Canada.

Hunting rabbits with a bow is a stalking game, and while it can be done solo, it's something in which several people can be involved. Three or four hunters conducting rabbit drives through cover patches can usually come up with some tasty game dinners.

Keen eyesight is a bowhunter's best advantage when hunting rabbits, because spotting them before they bolt permits a chance for a shot at a stationary target. Once a rabbit is flushed and on the move, the chances of hitting it are sharply diminished. One key is to look for the rabbit's eye rather than the entire form. It's the only part of its body that isn't camouflaged, and once you develop this skill, it can make a big difference in what you bring home.

This kind of hunting allows the hunter to use a light bow. Shots will be at close range, and

Small-game hunting can offer bowhunters a lot of fun as well as a challenge in shooting at small targets. Here a couple of hunters move through a field looking for cottontail rabbits.

only minimal weight is required. Most cottontails can be successfully taken with blunts that deliver sufficient shocking power to knock them down. For the larger swamp and snowshoe rabbits, though, broadheads are a better choice. The same goes for the big, tough jackrabbits.

There are myriad kinds of both tree and ground squirrels in North America, the majority of which provide the bowhunter only with small, challenging targets. However, the eastern gray squirrel and the eastern fox squirrel are prized for their table qualities as well. Both species occupy almost every state from the Great Plains to the Atlantic Ocean, the excep-

tion being that the fox squirrel isn't found in upper New England.

Gray and fox squirrels have traditionally been the favorite quarry of small-game hunters, and in earlier days they were an important source of food for rural families. Almost every farm boy had an all-purpose dog that would tree squirrels or go after any other kind of game. In those days a single-shot .22 rifle was the standard weapon, but now there is a new generation of hunters who enjoy the challenge of seeking these sly and elusive animals with a bow.

As mentioned in an earlier section, stalking skill is essential for success in squirrel hunting,

SMALL-GAME HUNTING

By Richard "Rick" Sapp
Gainesville, Florida

Small-game hunting is the undiscovered country of archery: squirrel, rabbit, hare, pheasant, groundhogs, prairie dogs, raccoon, red fox, rough fish and more. Not an endless list, but it is long and the populations are generally healthy from coast to coast.

Hunting small game with the bow and arrow does not require an investment in clothing or gear beyond what you have acquired for hunting deer. You may wish to alter your shooting style, however, to shoot quicker at smaller, faster targets:

• by lightening the draw weight of your compound bow or even switching to a recurve,

• by dismounting your sights and shooting instinctively,

• by shooting with fingers rather than a release aid.

Although your basic deer hunting equipment will serve your needs very adequately for small game, you may wish to acquire a few additional accessories:

• small-game heads such as blunts or Judo Points for your arrows,

• flu-flu arrows with wide, fluffy fletching to reduce their flight distance;

• heavy-duty brush trousers or leggings, since you may often find yourself moving through thick ground cover (and in certain areas of the country, leggings to prevent snake bite are advisable),

• a variety of game calls for squirrels, fox, crows, coyotes or turkeys,

• a belt bow carrier which will leave your hands free for binoculars, when moving through cover, or when you need to assist your children in some way,

• bowfishing reels, arrows and harpoon heads;

• a backpack and canteen for a long, beautiful day wandering afield (and it's a place to carry your small game trophies, too).

Richard Sapp, director of advertising for Bear Archery, Inc., has been bowhunting since the mid-1970s. He has hunted caribou, pronghorn antelope and black bear and has several antelope and bear in the Pope & Young record book.

but so is the bowhunter's ability to shoot accurately. Squirrels are lean and long and present a pretty small target, regardless of the range. That makes getting as close as possible very important. A light bow and either blunt or field points are the best combination.

One species that can be both exciting and sometimes a bit risky is the javelina, or peccary, of the Southwest. These little wild pigs have nasty tempers and tough hides, and they're formidable adversaries for bowhunters. They ordinarily run in packs and aren't easily intimi-

dated. On many occasions hunters have been charged and put up trees by the ornery critters. This is an animal that should be hunted with a bow in the 45- to 60-pound range, and with razor-sharp broadheads.

If a bowhunter wants to do a little night shooting, raccoons and opossums can offer some fun and excitement. Hunting with dogs is the best and surest way of locating and treeing these animals, although in the fall opossums can often be found easily by visiting some persimmon trees and spotting them with a flashlight.

Raccoons are good small-game targets, since they're quick and are usually hunted at night.

For some hunters, bagging these animals is all that counts, but others like to eat them.

Speaking of nocturnal activities, the sport of hunting bullfrogs shouldn't be overlooked, because these amphibians are challenging targets for bowhunters and a source of some fine eating. A platter of frog legs is a real delicacy! Bullfrogs are widely distributed. Farm ponds are favorite spots. Lakes, bayous, swamps, canals, irrigation ditches, and stream and river banks are also good prospects. Usually there's no problem getting permission to hunt farm ponds, especially if you explain that you'll share the bounty.

It's possible to hunt frogs solo by using one of the variety of headlights that permit both hands to be free, but it's much more effective when done as a two-man team. That way the light can be more steadily directed, and if you're both bowhunters you can double the fun by taking turns shooting.

Some kinds of frog territory can be hunted effectively only by wading, but in other places a canoe or light aluminum flat-bottom boat is necessary. The main thing is to move as quietly as possible, because frogs are extremely shy. Any loud or unusual sound will cause them to submerge and disappear.

A light bow is sufficient to use for frogs, and arrows with three-pronged gig-type points are the best.

Some states have seasons and limits on bullfrogs, so it's wise to check out your local regulations before planning a hunt.

11

The King, and Other Birds

Not too many years ago the goal of most bowhunters was to bag some kind of big game, because it was commonly believed that only deer, elk, bears and other large animals could provide the kind of challenge worthy of testing their hunting and shooting skills.

This was before what could be called "the wild turkey revolution" began and caused some enormous changes to take place in the world of bowhunting. Once considered as somewhat incidental by archers, turkeys now rank right up at the top in the trophy category and on bowhunters' priority lists. To some, they have become the ultimate trophy.

There's good reason for this changed view of the challenge turkeys offer bowhunters, the proof being that many hunters with impressive records of big-game kills have yet to put an arrow into a gobbler—and this isn't because they haven't tried!

Significant, also, is that because turkey hunting has been such a fast-growing bowhunting sport, it has also had huge ramifications within the archery industry in regard to equipment design innovations.

The challenge of hunting turkeys has always been there, but the astounding rise of this bird to the position of being one of the most sought-after bowhunting prizes is a phenomenon that has much to do with availability.

The enormous increase in turkey populations was brought about by two concurrent practices. Highly successful restocking and restoration programs were introduced in the original turkey range, and at the same time new turkey populations were being developed in places where they had not existed before. In almost all instances, these "exotics" have flourished, and many states that previously had no tradition of turkey hunting can now offer hunters generous seasons and bag limits. The result of the combined efforts is that these magnificent game birds can now be legally hunted in more than three-fourths of the lower forty-eight states. Seasons vary from place to place. Some states have only spring seasons, some only fall dates, and still others allow hunting in both spring and fall.

TURKEY SPECIES

There are four races of wild turkeys in the United States, one with a range that includes

Three longbeard gobblers any bowhunter would like to carry home.

Judd Cooney looks over a nice gobbler bagged in his home state of Colorado.

well over half of the country, two with fairly large areas of distribution in the Southwest, and another that is found in only one state. Essentially, all are very much alike except for a few minor color variations on the wings and bodies, and some more noticeable differences in the tips of the tail feathers.

The best known and most numerous of these is the eastern variety. Originally, the territory it inhabited extended from Maine to Florida, west to Texas and northward through Nebraska to South Dakota. Since in recent years this species has been used to stock some of the states that were once barren of turkeys, its range has been further extended.

The eastern bird is special in hunters' hearts, because it is the subspecies that contributed the most to the great popularity turkey hunting now enjoys. Nearly all of the calls, calling techniques and hunting tactics were developed hunting them in places like Pennsylvania and the Deep South. Even at the turn of the century when turkey populations had vanished from many states, these places had huntable populations that allowed the sport to remain viable and consequently preserved the tradition. The eastern wild turkey was the one served at the Pilgrims' first Thanksgiving dinner, and it is the species most frequently featured in illustrations.

The Rio Grande turkey's home range was from central Texas into Mexico, sometimes overlapping slightly into the eastern bird's range to the north, and into the Merriam's to the west. Like the eastern bird's, the Rio Grande's boundaries have also been widened by transplanting.

The Merriam turkey occupied the most western range of all, which included Colorado, Arizona and parts of northern Mexico. They are now found in states farther north, among them South Dakota and Wyoming, and they have adapted well in these places.

The Osceola is native to the Florida peninsula, and it is the only species that has neither migrated nor been the subject of stocking at other locations. There is no reason to do so, mainly because of the abundance and availability of eastern birds for this purpose.

HUNTING TACTICS

All wild turkeys are alert, suspicious, elusive and deceptive. It has been said that wild turkeys exist in a state of constant nervousness, and anyone who has hunted them will agree to that.

One of the birds' most valuable assets is uncanny vision. The eye of a turkey may appear to be small and somewhat beady, but in reality the eyeball is quite large, with the capacity of much greater resolution than a human eye. In a sense, it could be compared with an extreme wide-angle camera lens, because it has enormous peripheral vision that comes close to allowing it to see to the rear.

Another thing: When looking around, a person's eye focuses on one object at a time. A turkey's eye, however, apparently focuses on *everything* at once. This "all-seeing" capability allows it to detect even the slightest movement. When veteran hunters declare that a wise old gobbler can spot the blink of an eye at forty yards, it's a statement that's hard to argue, especially if you've had personal experience with the birds.

Because of this keen eyesight, it's vital that a hunter be as nearly invisible as possible. This means not only total camouflage from head to toe, but also for the bow, arrows and other accessories. This is one particular area in which the bowhunter is disadvantaged over a gun hunter, because the latter can remain immobile up until the trigger is pulled. Being camouflaged often requires nothing more than breaking up the human outline. When a hunter wears camouflage, it isn't a person the turkey sees. What catches its eye is an *object* that doesn't belong in the scene. Just being camouflaged isn't sufficient for a bowhunter, because at some point the bow must be drawn. That means motion, and unless the hunter is thoroughly concealed, it's almost a sure thing that the bird will notice. That's why it's critical that particular attention be paid to the blind.

There are several options. Some light,

BOWHUNTING FOR TURKEYS

By Dennis Butler
Joelton, Tennessee

Hunting turkeys with a bow has been regarded by some as the ultimate challenge. It has also been called a fool's game. Nevertheless, many hunters have become accomplished in this difficult art.

The first step, and a very important one, is scouting. A successful hunt, whether it be for a trophy buck or a long-bearded gobbler, requires being in the right place at the right time. Scouting is the technique for finding that place. After you have decided on the area you want to hunt, start walking all the old roads and along open ridgetops. Visibility means security to turkeys, and they spend a great deal of time in open areas. As you walk along, look for tracks in the woods roads, and look for scratchings and dusting sites on the open ridges. Look for feathers and droppings, also, as both can distinguish between gobblers and hens.

Once you know the general area turkeys are using and after the hunting season has begun, go there at daylight, find a high vantage point, and listen for a gobble. You can often induce them to gobble by using an owl call at daylight or a crow or hawk call later in the morning. (But don't call to the turkeys during the scouting phase or you will be educating them.)

The way you set up to call is important. It's best if you're not able to see the turkey coming in until he is almost in position for your shot. If this is a crest of a hill, you can trick him by calling sixty or seventy yards below the crest. Then, when the excitement of his gobble tells you he is coming in, get up quickly and move to within twenty yards or so of the crest. When he comes over the top, he will be looking for the hen on down the ridge, and will be in range. Having a small cushion to kneel on is helpful as you lean beside a large tree for your setup. Another good setup, if properly done, is a blind and a folding stool. It's especially effective on the edge of a field.

I believe too much emphasis has been given to calling ability. A couple of basic calls such as the yelp and cluck are generally all that is required. Knowing when to call is much more important than the actual technique. You should never answer a gobbler as soon as he gobbles, because he will stop and expect the hen to come to him. Also, never call to a turkey while he's standing still and in the open. If you do, he will pinpoint your exact location and will spook when he doesn't see a hen. Instead, call when he walks behind a tree or when he is in a strut.

A bowhunter should limit his shot to the distance he can consistently hit a turkey's vital area—usually twenty-five yards or less. Practice in actual hunting situations, kneeling or sitting and using a broadhead-equipped arrow.

Dennis Butler has been bowhunting since 1977 and has hunted turkey for 10 years. He has taken 9 gobblers with a bow, all of them the eastern variety, and he's taken deer, elk and coyote. In January 1992, he took a mountain lion that was entered in the  *Pope and Young record book as sixth in the world. Dennis belongs to the Professional Bowhunters Society and the Montana Bowhunters Association.*

Turkeys are one of the most keenly observant and cautious of all creatures bowhunters seek. Total camouflage is very important, as demonstrated by this hunter using a box call.

portable, easily assembled blinds specially designed to meet bowhunters' needs are on the market. Camouflage netting can be used to construct very satisfactory blinds, and occasionally natural features like blowdowns, depressions in the ground, or small patches of cover can be made to work okay with just a few changes and adjustments.

The late Ben Rodgers Lee always maintained that successful turkey hunting consisted of 80% woodsmanship and 20% calling, and he said he wasn't entirely sure that a 90% to 10% ratio might not be a better estimate. Since Ben was a world-champion turkey caller and probably the best and most versatile turkey hunter of all time, his words are worth some thought.

The woodsmanship part is particularly important in this case, since without the skills described in the chapter on stalking, your chances of bringing home a bird are slim. It's essential that you have a good knowledge of turkeys and their habits: how they behave seasonally, their food preferences, and their general routes of travel. You should also be able to identify turkey signs in the woods and locate roosting sites. All this requires pre-season scouting and a lot of watching and listening. You don't just go into unfamiliar territory on opening day and start wandering around.

Calling is not only an important aspect of turkey hunting but also a skill that once perfected becomes a matter of personal pride. It's true that sometimes even the most basic and amateurish calling can be productive, but this is

This simple, easily assembled blind made from camouflage material and brush serves to mask the hunter's movements.

Turkey hunters in particular find compact, portable blinds like this ideal for setting up in places where there's little cover to offer concealment.

an exception that should be disregarded. The goal is to be consistently successful, and this takes practice and dedication.

In the spring, calling is the most important tool a hunter can possess for locating gobblers, getting their attention and luring them within range. The toms are trying to assemble harems, and hen yelps are the calls to which they are most likely to respond. However, if the gobbler already has a fairly large entourage of lady turkeys, convincing him he needs another can be very difficult. Yet this is what part of the challenge is all about, and what adds the electricity a hunter feels throughout the tense battle of wits and—figuratively speaking—words.

Calling works in the fall, also, but it is done differently and doesn't involve the gobbler-hen drama experienced in the spring. During this season, the old males generally travel together away from the hens and young jakes. The tactic that works best is to find a flock, run in and scatter them, then try to call them back in. They have the desire to be together and are eager to regroup.

The first hunters probably used their own voices to imitate turkey calls, and while some individuals still can do this, it's seldom practiced. Besides, it isn't necessary anymore. Virtually every kind of turkey call ever devised by man is available commercially, and these range all the way from ones that require little or no experience to those preferred by the experts. The difference is usually in the versatility and quality of sound that is made possible by the call.

TYPES OF CALLS

Basically, there are two kinds: friction calls and mouth calls. The former includes the traditional box calls, ones that use wood or plastic strikers scraped across slate or aluminum, hand-cranked devices that produces yelps, a spring-loaded call that can be operated with one hand, and many other variations.

This kind of box call can be operated with one hand and unobtrusively laid down when the time to draw nears.

The classic wing-bone call is an example of a mouth call. Sound is produced by sucking air in rather than expelling it. The tube type consists of a piece of thin surgical rubber stretched over a plastic cylinder, with sound created by holding the call against the lips, exhaling and causing the rubber to vibrate.

The small diaphragm call held inside the mouth is the favorite of bowhunters because it allows them to have both hands free at critical moments. It's a simple device: a piece of thin rubber in a U-shaped plastic or aluminum frame. The call is held against the palate with the tongue and sound is produced by a controlled breath release. The diaphragm call is more than practical, though: it's also the choice of experts. No other call can produce such a wide variety of turkey sounds, or ones that are as authentic.

The diaphragm call is held in the mouth, leaving both hands free. It's a type favored by many hunters, particularly when a bird is close and approaching.

There are many different kinds of turkey calls, but all are in two basic categories: those operated by mouth—the reed and diaphram kinds—and friction calls operated by hand.

When trying to get a response from a gobbler, especially in the spring, there are sounds other than "turkey talk" that are effective. A tom with mating on its mind is so excited and aggressive that it regards almost any kind of sound or noise as a challenge. Thunderclaps will sometimes do it, as will slammed car doors or train whistles.

These aren't things that can be depended upon, or made to happen at will. It's better to have one or more of the different kinds of game calls in your arsenal. These create sounds that are normally heard in the woods and aren't alarming, but which will still get a red-hot gobbler to reply. The best known and probably the most used of these is the owl-hooter, which duplicates the cry of the barred owl. Many hunters can produce this vocally, but there are also several commercial models that do it equally well. A crow call is a good choice, and hawk calls often get results when other kinds fail.

EQUIPMENT AND SHOOTING

While any bow of legal draw weight can be considered as adequate for turkeys, in the tense situations encountered by a turkey hunter where movement is such a critical factor, compound bows have one particular and very important advantage over stick bows: they permit a hunter to anticipate the right time to shoot and then to draw and hold until the moment arrives. This provides a grace period of several extra seconds that wouldn't be possible using other types of bows. Compound bows of lighter weight and a high degree of let-off make it easier to hold a draw for a longer period of time, but there are other things that deserve consideration. A heavier weight bow will deliver an arrow faster with a flatter trajectory, giving the bird less chance to react to either the motion or sound. Also, the greater stored energy will deliver more shocking power. A large broadhead with at least three blades, along with one of the devices that attach to the arrow behind the point to keep it from passing entirely through the bird, are advantages. The big broadhead will do a lot of internal damage, and it's more difficult for a gobbler to fly or run with an arrow in its body. Turkeys are as hard to kill as they are to hunt, so don't underestimate this.

Of all the species included in the big-game category, none offers a greater challenge to a bowhunter's shooting ability than the wild turkey. Size is the reason, of course. The entire body of a gobbler without feathers is no larger than that of the vital kill zone on the chest of a whitetail deer. Yet beyond that, the upper chest area on a gobbler into which a lethal arrow shot must be placed is only about the size of a grapefruit. The only other deadly possibilities are shots to the neck and head, which are even smaller targets.

This means a bowhunter must be capable of delivering arrows with pinpoint accuracy from a variety of shooting positions and under conditions that are usually far short of ideal. Developing this skill requires a lot of practice, and the best way to become proficient is to do it in places that match field conditions as closely as possible. Shoot from a blind, and from many different kneeling and standing positions. There are three-dimensional turkey targets that are ideal for this, since they can be arranged so as to provide head-on, profile or angled views.

If a turkey is shot and flies or runs, keep it in sight as long as you can and go after it right away. A lethally shot gobbler will sometimes fly 100 to 150 yards before dying, but if you aren't sure where it went, you can still lose it. Turkeys are extremely hard to spot in the woods because of their natural camouflage.

ACCESSORIES

Specially designed turkey hunting vests are available to accommodate all of the items bowhunters need, and the array of things that can be packed along are too numerous to mention. The important ones are the various calls, insect repellent, compact binoculars, a rangefinder, basic repair and replacement items, and a blaze orange vest or hat to wear when departing the woods, with or without game. Many states don't require these while hunting, but for safety's sake they should be worn at all other times.

OTHER GAME BIRDS

If all game birds flushed and flew like ringneck pheasants, more bowhunters would be likely to get involved in wingshooting.

This noble pheasant is big, showy and predictable, and bowhunters who pursue them have a commendably high rate of success. Ringnecks occupy open country, and hunters can usually depend upon having them burst into flight at close ranges, particularly if a dog is being used.

Ringnecks are exotic birds that were introduced into this country many years ago, and eventually adapted successfully from coast to coast in many of the northern U.S. states and the Canadian provinces. They're the favorite game bird of many hunters, and in several states of the Midwest and West big populations exist that not only provide great hunting for residents but also

Here's a happy hunter with a prize ringneck pheasant.

Blue and spruce grouse are easy targets for bow-hunters, since they show little fear of man. Both blunts and broadheads can be used to take grouse.

Prairie chickens are found only in certain locations, and they're nice trophies for bowhunters who hunt birds.

attract plenty of nonresidents from states that don't offer this kind of opportunity. Several places in the Western states provide some really challenging wingshooting for species like sharp-tailed grouse, sage grouse, greater and lesser prairie chickens, gray partridge, and blue grouse.

Not all of the birds available are tough targets. There are some easy pickings for spruce grouse all across Canada. This is a bird that can be taken without wingshooting, because they can be approached to within very close range as they perch on limbs. They have the nickname "fool hen," which is indeed appropriate. Oddly enough, the ruffed grouse, which in its U.S. range is considered one of the most wily of game birds, often exhibits the same kind of indifference in the Canadian woods and can be shot while it is sitting.

Wingshooting waterfowl doesn't have a large following among bowhunters, but some of the species like Canada geese are big enough targets to be tempting. Also, while duck populations are shrinking in most of the flyways, both Canada geese and snow geese are on the increase. Hunting them over decoys or pass shooting can be great sport for a bowhunter, and next to wild turkeys they're the toughest of all birds to bring down. Also, like gobblers, it takes a well-placed arrow to bring them down.

It must be remembered that these are migratory birds regulated by the U.S. Fish and Wildlife Service, and a federal stamp is required to hunt them. In many places, state waterfowl stamps are required in addition.

Often it's not necessary to make lengthy treks to get the chance to hunt ringneck pheasants and other kinds of large game birds such as wild turkeys and mallards, because all across the nation there are commercial hunting preserves that feature one or all of these species. The preserve system is a boon to hunters who want convenient access to assured action and either lengthy or year-round seasons. They have other benefits, too. They're excellent places to train young hunters, and they also offer elderly hunters an opportunity to enjoy time afield without too much exertion. Finally, they're ideal spots for professional people who have limited time to hunt.

Appendix B gives a listing of most U.S. and Canadian hunting preserves.

WINGSHOOTING

Wingshooting may at first appear to be extremely difficult, but it's a skill that most bowhunters can develop with a little practice. There's really nothing mysterious about it. Part of it is based on instincts and how to react to them.

A simple way to get the idea is to pick out a moving object and quickly point your finger at it. You'll find that you're almost always right on target. Now do the same thing with a bow in your hand and you'll most likely discover the

A bowhunter tries to pick out a target among a flock of flushing partridges.

Wingshooting practice with objects like paper plates or Frisbees thrown into the air can help develop the skills needed for this kind of hunting.

same thing. If the object was stationary, your eye would automatically mark the spot and your shot could follow through, but where motion is involved, your point of aim is where you anticipate the object will be seconds later.

Instinctive shooting, snap shooting and other aiming practices were talked about earlier, and individuals learning to wing shoot will have to discover which of these is the most suitable and comfortable. Once perfected, wing shooting becomes second nature in the same way it does for shotgunners. Practicing wing shooting can be done in the backyard with flu-flu arrows of the kind used for hunting. These heavily fletched arrows accelerate rapidly enough to be potent for game at short ranges, but they also lose velocity quickly. Because of this they're both safer and easier to find.

There are several options for targets on which to practice. One of the best is some form of the well-known Frisbee, since it can be effectively tossed either vertically or from angles. Some use targets made from corrugated pasteboard or Styrofoam plates, and while these work okay, unless several layers are glued together they're not as easy to throw. Black or red dots or bullseyes can be painted on these targets to establish a precise point of aim.

Some bowhunters who wish to go a few steps further in honing their wingshooting skills use the devices that throw clay pigeons. Some of these can be adjusted in order to better simulate the actual speed of a flushing or passing bird.

As in all shooting sports, there are true experts who accomplish feats almost beyond the imagination, and there are exhibition archers who are able to consistently hit objects as small as aspirin tablets tossed into the air.

Realistically, though, most bowhunters will be satisfied with being able to pick off a ringneck!

A medium-weight bow is fine for wing shooting. For hunting pheasants and grouse, some bowhunters use broadheads, but there are bird points made specially for this purpose that also work very well. Field points are all right for practice, but they aren't really satisfactory for downing game birds. In most cases, more than simple penetration is required to an adequate job, and if wild turkeys or geese are being shot on the wing, bigger, multi-blade points are necessary.

12

Varmints

The term "varmint" isn't as easy to define today as it once was. Many of the creatures formerly considered as predators or simply undesirable were legal to hunt year around without limits or restrictions. Now some of these are either fully or partially protected in many states.

There are some interesting examples of the changes that have occurred. For instance, not too many years ago black bears were classed as varmints rather than game animals in some locations. It also wasn't long ago that hawks, owls and even eagles were fair game for varmint hunters throughout most of their ranges. Shooting any kind of turtle or snake was okay, too, yet many reptiles and amphibians now occupy places on the protected lists in some areas.

Even with some species eliminated from the overall picture, bowhunters shouldn't be dismayed. There are still plenty of opportunities remaining. In fact, one species has increased in numbers so dramatically that no varmint hunter anywhere in the country can complain.

If you haven't guessed already, it's the coyote.

These animals were once mainly inhabitants of the Southwest, but in the last couple of decades they have migrated outward in all directions. This movement has been so extensive that they are present in every state in the nation, and most Canadian provinces as well. Studies show that some eastern states now have coyote densities that surpass those in the West where they have been present for centuries.

In many ways, the wily coyote could be classed as the king of the varmints. It is intelligent, crafty, fast, tough and best of all from a varmint hunter's standpoint, numerous. You may be under the impression that there are no coyotes in your vicinity, but a little investigation will prove you wrong. Not only are they prevalent in rural areas, but they have become well established in the suburbs, where they raid garbage cans, kill domestic dogs and cats, and on rare occasions, small children.

Hunting coyotes is mainly a calling-and-waiting game. Because of their keen senses, stalking these animals is all but impossible. They don't use regular routes of travel like deer, so sitting and waiting for them to appear doesn't work, either. However, they're suckers for the distress calls of rabbits and other small-game species on which

Coyote

they prey. If they get the idea there's a free meal to be had, they can't resist coming after it.

They also will respond to calls that imitate sounds of their own young being molested, especially if some red fox calls are included to make this animal the villain. There are many other options, because the coyote has an enormous curiosity and can be lured with a wide variety of bird and animal calls.

Since the advent of turkey decoys, it's been discovered that these are very effective coyote attractors. The animals investigate the calls, and the decoys convince them. Since hunters have learned this, the tactics have become a part of their bag of tricks for hunting coyotes at other times of the year.

Another strategy that works well with coyotes is to use fawn decoys at the times when deer are bearing their young. These infant animals are so desirable that upon spotting the decoys, coyotes often abandon all of their normal caution and rush headlong at what they think is an easy target.

Operating from a blind that offers good concealment is important, and for bowhunters a two-man team works best, with one person calling and the other doing the shooting. Coyotes are cautious and almost always circle the spot before coming in. There's no way to know from which direction they'll approach, so having two pairs of eyes scanning is a big advantage. In addition, this permits the caller to continue to coax the animal in while the shooter draws.

Night hunting for coyotes and other varmints was very popular at one time, but this form of the sport has been eliminated in those states that have spotlight laws designed to reduce deer poaching. The law is needed, but it's unfortunate that varmint hunters are restricted because of it.

Red and gray foxes can also be enticed by calls. Their habits and general behavior are very similar to those of the coyote, and long before the expansion of the coyote population in the East, these animals were favorites of varmint hunters. Mouse squeakers and bird and rabbit distress calls are the best for luring these artful predators. There are seasons on foxes in some states, but in a few places where traditional hunting with hounds is conducted, the red fox is protected.

The other large-size varmint that offers bowhunters widespread potential is the bobcat. Some states have now adopted seasons on them, though in almost all cases these are generous in length. So there's still plenty of opportunity

Red Fox

throughout this animal's broad range.

Bobcats respond to many of the calling tactics that are used for coyotes, and in areas where both are present it isn't unusual to have them show up almost as often. They're sometimes more aggressive than coyotes, which is evidenced by a few instances where bobcats actually pounced on hunters while they were calling.

Groundhogs occupy a large area of North America that encompasses most of the eastern United States, except for parts of the deep South, and they are in most Canadian provinces and eastern Alaska. These animals, often called woodchucks, are special favorites of varmint hunters because they're numerous and are regarded by most landowners as pests. They do economic damage to crops, and their holes are a hazard to livestock.

Rifle hunters pick off groundhogs at long ranges, but bowhunters must employ careful stalking tactics to get close enough to these burrowers to get off a shot. They're fond of open fields, which makes an approach all the more difficult, so hunting them is excellent practice in stealth and patience.

Bobcat

Groundhog

In the northern states, groundhogs hibernate during the winter, but in the southern states where the climate is more moderate, they merely estivate, emerging whenever there's a nice, sunny day. The prime time to go after groundhogs is in the spring when crops like soybeans are attaining six to eight inches in height. At this time they're out of their dens and foraging, and by watching a field where dens are known to be, it's fairly simple to spot them moving around. Such greenery is like manna to these rodents. Even if the crop isn't in the place where they have their burrows, they will sometimes travel fairly long distances to take advantage of the bounty.

Another animal that's a bonus for bowhunters has emerged on the scene, and that is the beaver. The widespread increase in the beaver populations and the damage they are causing to bottomland timber and small waterways have put them in the varmint category in many states. These are tough critters that can weigh more than 50 pounds, and it takes plenty of power and a good broadhead to kill them.

Beaver

Prairie Dogs

Wounded beavers seldom can be retrieved, since they dive and usually end up in a den that's all but impenetrable. For that reason, make sure when you're placing a shot that it will be lethal.

In the West, the varmint that offers the bowhunter the most opportunity is the prairie dog. It's a much smaller target than a ground-hog, and because these animals live in colonies, they're more difficult to stalk. Lots of eyes are watching all of the time. There are also several types of gophers in this region, many of which are legal to take.

While not necessarily high profile on the varmint list, there are places where skunks, porcupines, armadillos and badgers are plentiful and shouldn't be overlooked as possibilities for some extra shooting action.

Some bowhunters go after crows, because by calling them in to decoys there's the chance to get shots at them both perching and flying. Angry crows often can be brought to within a dozen or so yards and provide some exciting wingshooting. There is another enormous shooting opportunity available in the millions of starlings that blanket fields and lawns almost everywhere in the country. They're challenging targets for shooters who want to achieve pinpoint accuracy.

One of the biggest benefits offered by varmint hunting is that it provides the bowhunter with the chance to hunt and shoot at times of the year when the seasons are closed on other species. Regardless of what part of the nation you live in there are some kinds of varmints, large or small, that can be sought. It's just a matter of checking your state's hunting regulations to determine what's legal and when.

13

Fish

Bowfishing is another sport that broadens the archer's horizon of opportunity, and there are times when it can provide all of the action a bowhunter can handle.

A good example of this occurs in the spring when carp are spawning, or "shoaling" as it's also called. Large numbers of them move into shallow water and mill around. The result is a bonanza for bowhunters.

This might seem like shooting fish in a barrel, but it isn't that easy. A fish in a barrel can't go anywhere, but a big carp may head for parts unknown when it's hit with an arrow. Bowhunters often like to pick out the biggest fish to shoot, and since carp often attain weights of well over 20 pounds, they can get up a pretty powerful head of steam in a hurry!

That's why there's special equipment made for bowfishing that uses the harpoon gun principle. A reel attached to the bow is loaded with heavy fishing line, which is tied to the arrow. When a fish is hit and runs, the line plays out and the fish can either be retrieved by pulling or reeling it in or following it to where it stopped or died.

Another method that works well when shooting from a boat is to take along a rod and reel. Tie the line to the arrow, then remove fifteen to twenty yards of line from the reel and coil it away from your feet in the bottom of the boat. When the fish is shot, you'll have enough time to lay down the bow, pick up the rod, and be ready to play the fish.

Solid fiberglass arrows are favored for bowfishing, not only because of their toughness, but also since their weight makes it possible for them to be driven deeper into the water than wood, hollow glass or aluminum shafts. Rubber vanes that slip onto the arrow shaft are the most practical kind of fletching.

There are many point designs that work well for bowhunting fish, and either personal experience or professional advice can help to determine which you should use.

One nice thing about bowfishing is that the equipment isn't costly. Usually you can use your regular hunting bow; then it's simply a matter of getting a reel, a couple of arrows and some points.

Besides carp, there are many other types of

Bowfishing can be fun for archers looking for a new type of experience and a challenging sport.

fish bowhunters can seek. Streams and rivers in many parts of the country have spawning runs of suckers and buffalo that provide plenty of action. Some kinds are very good to eat. Throughout the southern United States the four species of gar—longnose, shortnose, spotted and alligator—hold great potential for the bowfisherman. These fish are throwbacks to prehistoric times, as their appearance suggests. Gar are slim and almost snakelike in appearance, with long, bony beaks and armor plates of tough scales. They vary considerably in size. The shortnose and spotted gar seldom exceed 3 feet in length, and the longnose sometimes reaches 5 feet. The alligator gar, however, can become a true giant by freshwater fish standards. Specimens of up to 10 feet in length and 300 pounds have been recorded, and ones in the 6- to 8-foot range aren't uncommon.

Because of their strength and powerful jaws, a hand gaff is recommended to land them, and wearing sturdy gloves is also a good idea. Big alligator gar can be dangerous, since they're very hard to kill and usually aren't mortally wounded by the harpoon arrow. Some individuals use a broadhead to administer the finishing touch, while others prefer a pistol shot to the head as a more positive solution before trying to land them. A 6-foot gar thrashing about in a boat can create havoc!

Talk about a real challenge! How about these huge carp that sometimes exceed 25 pounds.

Gar have a habit of floating just below the surface of the water on hot summer days, and this is an excellent time to go after them. You may see as many as a hundred in a school, so there won't be any shortage of action. The bonus gar provide is that they can be hunted throughout most of the year, and often they're present at the same places where carp, sucker and buffalo are found.

Night bowfishing for gar from a boat is also productive, especially for the larger fish. This is a two-man operation, of course, and it requires a powerful spotlight to locate the fish. It helps to have another form of illumination such as a gasoline lantern to provide enough light for shooting.

Wading is an effective method of going after spawning rough fish, whether it be in still or running water. The only problem is that it limits visibility. You can view a much larger area from a boat, and the extra height permits better shooting angles. Some bowfishermen increase this advantage by equipping their boats with high platforms on the bow much like those used by fishermen on saltwater bonefish flats.

One item that can be of special benefit to a bowfisherman is a pair of polarized glasses. These help overcome glare that makes it difficult or impossible to see objects underwater.

There's another matter concerning perceiving objects underwater that must be addressed.

Because of light refraction, fish aren't where the eye makes them seem to be. Shooting directly at them will result in the arrow passing well above the target. The solution is to aim low. How much you need to compensate depends on how far away the fish is and how deep it is. Trial and error will eventually enable you to be pretty accurate.

Freshwater bowfishermen have no shortage of places to go or species to seek. Almost every body of water of any size will have potential, and usually there are plenty of choices close to where you live. Consider all of the different kinds of rough fish that can be harvested, and you will recognize that there's a bonanza of opportunities.

There's another bonus that shouldn't be overlooked. Carp taken from clean waters are very suitable as table fare, and many people in this country and other parts of the world consider it a delicacy. Its reputation as being undesirable stems from the fact that it is commonly found

A bowfisherman stands ready to shoot as he and a companion cruise looking for shoaling carp.

in polluted waters not inhabited by gamefish. However, it's a different matter when it is occupying suitable habitat.

Gar, on the other hand, are not edible, and they can truly be classed as a nuisance. Shooting them provides bowhunters with a lot of fun, and ridding the waterways of them is a good deed.

The situation in saltwater used to be much the same, but this has changed very much in the last decade. Some species, such as sharks, skates, barracudas and various kinds of rays that

BOWFISHING—FUN AND FAST ACTION

By Deano Farkas
Easton, Pennsylvania

Bowfishing can make you a better bowhunter for both big and small game.

Equipment is simple and inexpensive. Any bow will do, though I prefer one in the 60-pound class to handle the heavy fish arrow.

Use solid fiberglass or fishgetter-type aluminum arrows weighing approximately 1500 grains. Heavy arrows will penetrate any rough fish in six to eight feet of water. I remove the rubber fletch from my bow for better accuracy, because bent rubber fletching may re-steer the arrow in the water.

As to reels, I prefer a spincast Zebco 808 when the fish are "hot and heavy." For large fish, 25 pounds or more, my choice is a simple hand-wind. Always remember safety. Press that button, and keep the line clear of your fingers and equipment.

My fish line is heavy, 90–120-pound braided. It is easy to handle and there is less chance of getting cut when you are fighting large fish. Also, a heavy line helps when you are trying to retrieve an arrow from the muck or tangled weeds. Always fasten the line to the rear of the fish arrow. If you fasten it to the front or tip, the shaft will fly sideways and you'll have poor penetration.

Use points with screw-on fronts. Arrows stuck in creek bottoms or logs can be removed easily by turning off the point. Carry extra front ends to replace any lost or dull points. Attach the points to shafts with 24-hour or 2-ton epoxy to give them better shock strength. I pin all my fish-points to the shaft by drilling a small hole through the point and shaft and inserting a fine aluminum or brass nail, cut to length.

Scout for pathways through lily pads and weedbeds. You can set up ambushes in these fish runs. Smoke trails (mud slicks) will also tell you fish are working in an area. Walk lightly so that carp resting or feeding near the bank will not dash to the middle of the river. And watch the sun position to avoid casting shadows on the water.

Most important: Know and obey the fish and game laws covering the rough fish species in your area.

Deano Farkas has been bowhunting seriously since 1961 and has hunted in 35 states and 6 Canadian provinces. He has taken over 250 big-game animals of many species, including 28 black bears, and numerous fish and small game. Several animals are in the Pope & Young record book. The largest fish was a 10-foot tiger shark that weighed 265 pounds. Deano has the ABC National Bow Record for a bow-taken turkey, has two Silver Broadhead awards from the NRA, and was named Bowhunter of the Year by Spector Bowhunters in 1981. He is a consultant to industry, a field editor for Bowhunting World, *and active in 35 outdoor and bowhunting organizations.*

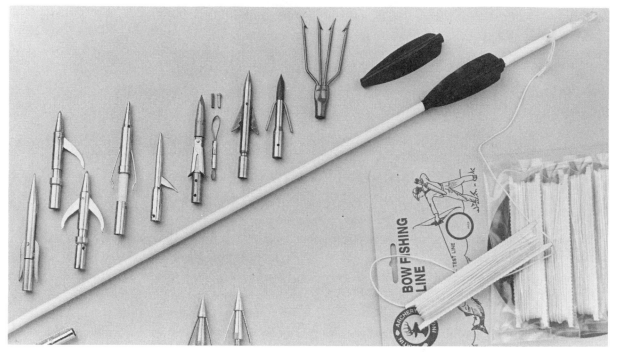

Special equipment for bowfishing includes stout lne that connects to a fiberglass arrow with rubber vanes. Various kinds of points can be used for both fish and frog hunting.

These bowfishermen are cruising the saltwater flats looking for stingrays.

were once popular with bowfishermen, are now either illegal to take or regarded as targets that shouldn't be taken. Part of the reason for this is that the populations of some of these fish have been heavily overharvested by commercial fishermen. Also, studies have shown that some, especially sharks, have very slow growth rates and can't replenish themselves fast enough to keep pace with the commercial demand. The stingray remains about the only target bowfishermen can seek legally or without twinges of conscience.

14

Field Games and Archery Competitions

Archery as a game has a long history. Its beginning was probably as simple as a couple of individuals with bows deciding to find which one could shoot the best. This possibly led to a rematch, or other challenges, and like any activity of this sort, these competitions ultimately became events that followed established rules.

Today archery activities run the gamut from simple backyard or field plinking to the stringent and formal structure of various world-class competitions. In between are the *target* and *field* events—the two major divisions in competitive archery. They are sponsored by various organizations, all of which have their own agendas and rules. There are many variations among these competitions, but in each case a game is called a "round," and an "end" is the number of arrows shot in succession before the score is recorded and arrows are pulled.

Target competition emphasizes the distance to the target, which normally is a round with scoring rings marked in centimeters that determine the score. A deviation of this is a paper target that simulates animal shapes. The round

is named for a potentially perfect score, thus a "600 Round" or a "900 Round" game. The end may be from three to six arrows, based on the target's size and distance.

A coveted trophy among target shooters is the Robin Hood, earned by driving the tip and shaft of the arrow deep into the end of another arrow already in the bullseye. Having a Robin Hood—arrows stuck end to end—above one's mantel is considered quite an achievement. It is the archer's "hole in one."

Field events are named for the type of target or the style of approach. Up to four archers, each using his or her distinguishable arrows, may shoot at the same target. Some common events are the Field Round, Hunters' Round and the Animal Round, and it is the latter category that has proved to be the most popular and best received by bowhunters.

The immense increase in interest in bowhunting has been a driving force in bringing many more archers into these activities, especially field archery, since—as was noted in the Introduction—so many archers today are

This foam deer silhouette placed at an undetermined distance gives the bowhunter and field archer the challenge of using the instinctive feel gained by experience in judging distances.

bowhunters whose main reason for being involved is to maintain a continuous, year-round practice regimen. Their participation has enhanced archery because it has added special features and events that weren't included traditionally. In the beginning field archery was a close copy of the rifle and handgun game that used animal silhouettes as targets. In the archery version, the targets depict various traditional animals such chickens, pigs, turkeys and rams that are made of plastic foam rather than metal. Dedicated archers appreciate the additional challenge of having to shoot at groups of three targets from various distances. The first target is a known distance appropriate for the species represented, but the next two force the shooter to estimate the distance. If the arrow topples a target, a hit is declared. A bow with a draw weight of at least forty pounds is standard for this event, and some competitors use much

heavier draw weights that will drop the ram target at seventy-five yards.

Sometimes these matches are timed events, which require the shooter to get off a large number of arrows very quickly. In such games sighting devices are virtually useless.

This type of competition is excellent for using the compound bow but also offers the opportunity for the barebow archer to practice instinct shooting.

Some other popular games are Clout, requiring arrows to be lobbed long distances at a single target, and Wand, a relic of an ancient game named for the thin vertical stick of wood that serves as the target.

One of the most significant of the more recent innovations, and the one that's by far the most exciting and authentic, is the three-dimensional, or 3-D, type of competition. These events use solid-bodied, life-size small-game,

Life-size, three-dimensional, or 3-D, targets with tough bodies into which hunting broadheads can be shot are extremely fine for bowhunting practice.

big-game, bird and varmint targets that must be shot at from unknown distances and a variety of positions, angles and elevations. Bowhunters find them exciting, and they are valuable in keeping both the hunter's shooting skills and the equipment constantly fine-tuned.

One version is called Yukon roving, in which the target is a life-size animal with the vital area marked but only visible at very close range. It is placed either thirty yards away in cover or forty yards in the open. Each participant has a turn selecting the target location, and sometimes shots must be from a kneeling or leaning position. One shot per round is allowed. A hit in the vital area earns a point while a hit elsewhere on the target deducts two points. No penalty is given for a miss.

Roving is a useful technique for bowhunters that provides field conditions and a variety of shots, depending on the terrain.

In addition to the established organizations, new ones have sprung up in recent years, and both old and new have begun to feature innovative kinds of competitive events that involve forms of shooting and equipment not previously known or sanctioned. New challenges appear continually: variations on timed games; night shoots that feature lighted targets; and shoots with targets that pop up randomly and must be shot at within a matter of seconds.

ONE BOWHUNTER'S STORY

The story of Rockie Jacobsen of Orofino, Idaho, illustrates how a bowhunter became interested and involved in field games, developed a high degree of skill in competition shooting, and saw that translated into hunting success and fulfillment:

"I began shooting a bow in 1968 at the age of sixteen. My first bow was a Bear recurve. Shooting instinctive was a great challenge and very

Practicing shooting 3-D targets in the backyard is a great way to keep in shape for hunting season.

Competition compound bows are sometimes radical in design, and these types have also become popular with bowhunters.

rewarding. I had some successful hunts, but it was the unsuccessful ones that taught me the most.

"As the years passed, archery became more and more advanced and more popular. In 1973 I switched to a compound bow. It seemed like the thing to do, since it was supposed to be a better way of shooting faster and being more accurate. I could pull more weight and hold less at full draw. This was all achieved by the round wheels put on the compound bow. But I soon found out there was more to archery than just shooting a bow.

"Archery attracted me mainly because of the hunting aspect. In the late seventies, archery tournaments became very popular, especially 3-D unknown yardages. These 3-D shoots are one of the best ways to help improve your archery skills for hunting. Here you learn to judge yardages, the right angle shots to be taken on animals, and how to shoot under pressure. But most of all, it is fun.

"I have been able to win a few local and state shoots and place high in national tournaments. It was in 1990 that I first put together a three-man team and entered the Western Triple

Crown archery tournament. My team, consisting of Don West, Tony Hyde and myself, took first place in the open class.

"This type of practice was invaluable. I have taken many different big-game animals such as deer, elk, bear, cougar; and I have hunted grouse, coyote and bobcat. Of all the animals I've taken the greatest thrill was bugling a bull elk to within bow range."

NAA AND FAA EVENTS

What has been, and continues to be, important to archery events and the organizations that sponsor them is the preservation of all the tradi-tional forms of equipment and shooting practices. The National Archery Association (NAA) and the Field Archery Association (FAA) have done this by closely defining what can and cannot be used in particular events.

The NAA, which is the sponsoring organization for Olympic shooting in the U.S., places great emphasis on excellence on the target line, whereas the FAA is oriented primarily toward hunting and simulation of actual field shooting situations.

The National Shooting Sports Foundation describes some of the NAA requirements this way:

"In NAA events, most any bow (other than

Here's a competition bow with an overdraw system that can be used for either tournaments or hunting.

compound) may be used providing it subscribes to the acceptable principle and meaning of the word bow as used in target archery; e.g., an instrument consisting of a handle riser, and two flexible limbs, each ending in a tip with a string nock. The bow is braced for use between the nocks only and in operation is held in one hand by its handle, while the fingers of the other hand draw, hold back and release the string.

"Arrow rests and an aiming aid such as a bowsight or bowmark are permitted as long as they are not electronic or do not use a lens or a prism for magnification. Stabilizers are also allowed."

These are obviously rules intended for users of traditional equipment such as longbows and recurve bows, so they are necessarily restrictive and prohibitive.

The Field Archery Association's rules are much broader and are attuned with current archers' preferences, and this has boosted participation by a great many more shooters in recent years. The rules state:

"In standard FAA events, equipment is divided into four categories: barebow, freestyle, competitive bowhunter and competitive freestyle bowhunter.

"*Barebow:* No sights or sight-marking devices of any kind or mechanical release devices.

"*Freestyle:* Practically any sighting or release device, stabilizer or arrow rest, is allowed.

"*Bowhunter:* Must conform to many of the same rules that apply to Barebow, except may add quiver to the bow and may shoot broadheads.

"*Bowhunter Freestyle:* Probably the most popular category, archers may use sighting devices and stabilizers, but no mechanical release."

OLYMPIC COMPETITION

Olympic archery competition uses the recurve bow. The limbs curve away from the archer to provide increased power. In a lever effect, it pro-pels arrows in excess of 150 miles an hour. These bows are usually of wood, fiberglass, and graphite or carbon composites, maximizing the properties of each material. The latest bows are of Syntactic Foam and ceramic, with stabilizers to reduce torque, or twisting, on release; fitted with sights and arrow rests. Most strings are of Fast Flight, a hydrocarbon product; others are of Kevlar, a material used in bulletproof vests. The latter often have "kisser buttons" attached that identify when the archer is at the correct anchor. Arrows are of either aluminum or graphite, with the point, the nock and the fletching attached to the shaft.

Strength is an obvious requirement for an Olympic-class archer. The ancient recurve bow, though made of improved materials and more aerodynamic, is lifted and drawn more than 312 times. With the average draw weight for a man of 50 pounds, that's a total of nearly 8 tons pulled over a four-day period. Women pull nearly five and a half tons with their 34-pound-average bows.

The accuracy required can be likened to standing on the goal line of a football field and hitting an apple under the opposite goal post!

WORLD TARGET ARCHERY

Internationally, the Fédération Internationale de Tir à l'Arc (FITA), or the International Federation for the Sport of Archery, sets target archery rules for member nations. There are three formats: the Single FITA Round, the Grand FITA Round, and the Olympic Qualification Round.

A Single FITA Round consists of 36 arrows shot from four distances—90, 70, 50 and 30 meters for men; and 70, 60, 50 and 30 meters for women—for a total of 144 arrows. These are fired at bullseye targets. The maximum possible score is 144 "10s" or 1440 points.

The Grand FITA round starts with a two-day Single FITA of 144 arrows. On the third day, the top 24 male and top 24 female archers play again, with a zero score beginning each new round. Six are eliminated in the morning, and 6 more in the afternoon. The semifinal round defines the top 8 competitors, and the final round determines the medal winners.

The new Olympic FITA Style Competition qualifiying round consists of 36 arrows fired from 90, 70, 50 and 30 meters for men and 70, 60, 50 and 30 meters for women. Each archer shoots 12 arrows on a 122-centimeter target at 70 meters. The top 32 women and the top 32 men compete in a single elimination match play competition until the winners emerge. Team qualification is determined when the first 16 men's and women's teams in the qualification round proceed to the elimination round. In the team competition, 27 arrows (3 by 9) are shot on the target.

APPENDIXES

Appendix A

National and International Archery and Bowhunting Organizations

There are quite a few international, national, regional, and local archery organizations that provide enthusiasts opportunity for additional involvement in the sport. The national and international organizations described here offer a good starting point for making new friends and promoting interests you feel are important.

AMERICAN ARCHERY COUNCIL
604 Forest Avenue
Park Rapids, Minnesota 56470
The AAC is a nonprofit organization that represents virtually all aspects of competitive archery and bowhunting. There are a number of affiliated organizations with a total membership of more than two million.

Mission Statement
The AAC is active in promoting competitive archery and bowhunting, supporting hunter education, and endorsing wildlife management.

AAC supports its position through youth education, contributions, legal action, legislative monitoring (state and federal), lobbying,

involvement with all outdoor user groups, and cooperative legal intervention on behalf of state bowhunting interests.

How to Join
Individuals may join and support one of the affiliated organizations. Direct contributions for specific projects or the AAC general fund may be sent to the American Archery Council Administrative Office (address above).

Contact the AAC Administrative Office for information on programs which raise funds for affiliates. Telephone: 218-732-7747.

ARCHERY RANGE AND RETAILERS ORGANIZATION
156 North Main Street, Suite D
Oregon, Wisconsin 53575
The Archery Range and Retailers Organization is a co-op comprising 95 leading archery pro shops in the USA. The member/stockholders perform as a cooperative buying group. It was incorporated in 1981 and was formerly known as the Archery Lane Operators Association.

Mission Statement
The ARRO is a strong group of elite archery retailers that builds consumer confidence by offering low-priced, top-quality archery merchandise.

How to Join
Member candidates must be a legitimate retailer and pass rigid screening tests. They must have the highest rated credit possible; be in a retail location; have been in business for at least three years and have grossed at least $50,000 in each of the past three years. Membership is limited to 500 member/dealers.

BOWHUNTERS OF AMERICA
1030 West Central Avenue
Bismarck, North Dakota 58501
Bowhunters of America (incorporating Bowhunters Who Care) is an organization actively working to protect the continuation of bowhunting in America and defend the sport against detractors. Started in 1989, the membership numbered 4,000 in 1992, and there are 27 affiliated state associations. BOA is a member of the

AAC, is a North American representative on the World Bowhunting Association Council, and is a major contributor to the Bowhunter Defense Coalition.

Members receive a quarterly magazine, voting rights, and sometimes a chance to win free hunts.

Mission Statement

The stated purposes and objectives are: A) to promote and foster fair chase hunting with the bow and arrow; B) to inform and educate bowhunters and the general public by promoting bowhunter education and providing information about the sport; C) to protect and defend bowhunting by assisting local, state and national groups in solving problems pertaining to bowhunting; D) to strengthen bowhunting by working with state and federal wildlife agencies in the wise use of our natural resources and the preservation of our wildlife and its natural habitat; E) to communicate all important bowhunting issues to the people; F) to promote and assist in the solution of environmental and conservation issues on a local, state and national level; G) to assist local and state bowhunting leaders and organizations in resolving legislative issues which adversely affect bowhunting; and H) to promote hunter safety and to promote and defend hunting as a legitimate sport and as a viable and necessary method of fostering the propagation, growth, conservation, and wise use of our renewable natural resources.

How to Join

Write BOA at the above address to request a membership application. There are eight levels of membership offered.

FRED BEAR SPORTS CLUB
4600 S.W. 41st Boulevard
Gainesville, Florida 32601
The late Fred Bear, founder of Bear Archery as well as the Fred Bear Sports Club, said: "When civiliza-

tion reaches the point where its people care nothing for their natural environment, it will cease to exist." Members may be eligible to win awards in the Bowhunting Division of the club, based on applications available at Bear Archery dealers and subject to the Award Approval Committee.

The club also offers a twice-yearly newsletter and free passes to the Fred Bear Archery Museum in Gainesville.

Mission Statement

The organization operates under a credo to protect outdoor ecology and support the proper wildlife management of the woods, fields and waters; to uphold the fish and game laws, preserve natural resources, and always compete honestly when engaged in outdoor sports. Members also adopt a nine-point "Rules of Fair Chase."

How to Join

It is not necessary to be a hunter or an archer to join, and there is no age limit. Contact you local Bear Archery dealer for a membership application, or write the organization directly at the above address.

INTERNATIONAL BOWHUNTING ORGANIZATION OF THE USA
P.O. Box 1349
Madisonville, Kentucky 42431
The IBO/USA was created in 1984. The organization is very active in three major areas: bowhunter defense, shooting skill standards, and club insurance.

In the area of bowhunter defense, activities are diverse and include media coverage, defense funds, lobbying, and support of WLFA and NBEF.

As to shooting skills, IBO promotes standardized shooting rules and classes, provides a national level of competition (the "Triple Crown" of bowhunting, with three national shoots in three different states), and

a world level of competition (the annual IBO/USA World Championship, with a series of sanctioned preliminary qualifying shoots in several states and coverage on ESPN). It also promotes scholarships.

The insurance program offers property damage, medical malpractice, and several types of liability coverage to club members.

IBO/USA has helped establish a Bowhunter Week in several states and has endorsed the National Bowhunter Educational Foundation (NBEF) program that perpetuates our bowhunting heritage.

IBO is part of the WLFA Bowhunting Defense Coalition created to protect the sport nationwide.

Mission Statement

IBO was formed to unify bowhunters and bowhunter organizations at an international level for purposes designed to promote, encourage and foster the art and sport of bowhunting, bowhunters' education, act as a liaison for the betterment of bowhunters, function as a clearing house for essential bowhunter information; and adhere to the basic ideal of the International Bowhunting Organization/USA which is the unification of bowhunting.

How to Join

Membership is open to individuals, families, and to any club, state organization, or association. Write the IBO/USA at the above address for an application form or to contribute to the Bowhunter Defense Fund. Membership includes a subscription to International Bowhunter.

INTERNATIONAL FIELD ARCHERY ASSOCIATION
31 Dengate Circle
London, Ontario
CANADA N5W 1V7
This is the world's governing body for field archery. Refer to the National Field Archery Association for membership information.

NATIONAL ARCHERY ASSOCIATION

1750 East Boulder Street
Colorado Springs, Colorado 80909

There are numerous archery organizations in the U.S., but the NAA is the National Governing Body for national and international competition.

NAA is a "Group A" member of the U.S. Olympic Committee (USOC), which sponsors all U.S. teams traveling to the Olympics and Pan Am Games. It is also a member of the Fédération Internationale de Tir à l'Arc (FITA), the international governing federation for archery. FITA dictates the eligibility requirements and competition rules for international and Olympic archery competition.

The NAA sponsors a number of programs for both beginning and elite archers, students, coaches and officials. The Resident Athlete Program allows archers to live and train full-time at the U.S. Olympic Training Center. The U.S. Archery Team consists of the top eight male and top eight female archers in the country. Team members conduct seminars and are scientifically tested to improve technique, nutrition and physical and mental training. The Junior Elite U.S. Archery Team also has eight top male and eight top female archers under 18. They are given a rigorous training and nutrition program. The Junior Olympic Archery Development (JOAD) program provides—through 175 clubs—archery instruction and tournament activities for thousands of young archers. The NAA conducts training camps for the three categories of archers mentioned. There is also a College Division that has over forty-five clubs and intercollegiate teams, and competitions decide the ten top men and ten top women each year.

Numerous state archery groups have organized and affiliated with the NAA to bring archery competition closer to the local level and provide year-long competition geared to the differing age and skill levels of their members.

Mission Statement

The NAA was formed to foster and promote the sport of archery. It sanctions and conducts tournaments, and chooses the U.S. representatives for international competitions such as those already mentioned, and world championships.

How to Join

Membership is open to everyone involved in archery, whether as a sport, hobby or craft. One and three year memberships are offered for adults, families, youths, full-time students and clubs. Membership includes a free NAA decal, six issues of *The U.S. Archer* magazine, the *NAA Newsletter,* and achievement pins which can be earned at NAA-sanctioned tournaments. To join, write the NAA at the address given above.

NATIONAL BOWHUNTER EDUCATION FOUNDATION

P.O. Box 2007
Fond du Lac, Wisconsin 54936

The National Bowhunter Education Foundation is a worldwide bowhunting foundation created to protect bowhunting privileges through sportsman education. It is a positive, proactive group. The NBEF presents the International Bowhunter Education Program (IBEP), taught by carefully selected volunteer instructors who generate 125,000 man-hours each year. The IBEP covers bowhunter responsibilities, proper equipment, safety, game laws, wildlife conservation, survival and first aid, bowhunting techniques and methods, and anti-hunting threats to bowhunting.

In 1992 the NBED planned to train more than 500 instructors and recruit the support and activity of thousands more. The educational training aids used are top-notch. NBEF-produced materials are also distributed by state fish and wildlife agencies for use in firearm safety and other courses. Some states have made the IBEP program mandatory for bowhunters, and others are interested in doing so.

The NBEF keeps a high profile through trade shows, national and international workshops, and joint efforts with other organizations. Much of this visibility is felt to be necessary because of the vital role NBEF plays in the fight to preserve the sport. Improving skills and ethics of the average hunter in the field is critical to lowering the statistics for unrecovered game and reducing the impact from animal-rights activists.

The NBEF is an affiliate of the AAF and is endorsed by more than a dozen top national and international sportsmen's organizations.

Mission Statement

The NBEF works to ensure the future existence of bowhunting through education and bowhunting information programs. Its goal it to perpetuate bowhunting by providing the fundamentals of good, safe bowhunting with an appreciation and respect for the environment, and to maintain the highest standards of the sport.

The educational program instills in bowhunters a responsible attitude, assists them in adopting exemplary behavior towards people, wildlife, and the environment.

Motto: "The Future of Bowhunting Depends on Bowhunter Education."

How to Join

The NBEF is a nonprofit foundation that offers four levels of individual sponsorship and five levels of group sponsorship. It is open to any person, business, association, publisher, guide/outfitter, organization or agency. Contributions are tax deductible.

Individual sponsors receive a quarterly newsletter, decals, and access to NBEF materials. Group sponsors may also use the NBEF logo in their literature along with an appropriate explanatory sentence.

Write the NBEF at the address above for information about becoming a sponsor.

NATIONAL FIELD ARCHERY ASSOCIATION
31407 Outer I-10
Redlands, California 92373

The National Field Archery Association is a nonprofit corporation dedicated to the practice of archery. Founded in 1939, it is the world's largest archery association with 50 chartered state associations and more than 1,000 affiliated clubs in the U.S. and other countries. It is a member of the International Field Archery Association (IFAA), the world's governing body for field archery.

The NFAA establishes shooting regulations, holds tournaments, maintains records and provides organized state associations and archery clubs with a well-rounded schedule of events. There are events and programs for Youth and Cub members, who have the opportunity to earn progressive merit patches as they advance in skill levels.

NFAA bowhunter programs offer recognition through awarding pins and certificates, and shooting skills can earn individuals a place on the 500 Club or the Perfect Club.

The events include national indoor/outdoor championship tournaments, a 3-D national tournament, shooting and equipment clinics, team events, a certified instructor school, sectional and state tournaments, indoor/outdoor leagues, and an indoor/outdoor Mail-in Match.

How to Join
The NFAA offers four levels of membership for individuals and three levels for families. All members receive a subscription to Archery Magazine, are eligible for NFAA-sponsored hunting award contests, and have access to various types of insurance. NFAA members are also members of the IFAA

and may compete in the IFAA World Championship. For a membership application, write to the address given above.

NATIONAL SHOOTING SPORTS FOUNDATION, INC.
555 Danbury Road
Wilton, CT 06897-2217

The National Shooting Sports Foundation is a nonprofit, educational, trade-supported association founded in 1960 whose interests cover all aspects of shooting. It was the NSSF that originated National Hunting & Fishing Day (officially proclaimed by Congress in 1972) as a means for recognizing the sportsman's contribution to wildlife conservation and to promote a better understanding of and more active participation in the shooting sports.

It was also the NSSF that originated the concept of a trade show dedicated to shooting, hunting and related outdoor industries. The inaugural SHOT Show was held in January 1979 in St. Louis, and the event now ranks as the 33rd largest trade exposition in the USA among the 8,000 shows held annually.

The SHOT Show provides manufacturers, dealers, and distributors with a marketplace and creates additional revenue for the NSSF programs promoting increased participation in shooting sports. Archery is one of the merchandise categories.

Mission Statement
NSSF was formed to create in the public mind a better understanding of and a more active participation in the shooting sports and in practical conservation.

How to Join
The NSSF welcomes participation by individuals and organizations in NHF Day. For information, write to "National Hunting Fishing Day" at the NSSF address listed above.

For complete rules and regulations governing competitive

archery, the NSSF recommends contacting the National Archery Association, the National Field Archery Association (both featured in this section), and Bowhunters Silhouettes International, P.O. Box 6470, Orange, CA 92667.

NORTH AMERICAN HUNTING CLUB
12301 Whitewater Drive, P.O. Box 3407
Minnetonka, Minnesota 55343

The North American Hunting Club began in 1978 when founder Paul Burke and his son Steve, avid outdoorsmen, decided hunters like themselves needed better information to make them more successful in the field. During its first year it numbered 1,500 hunters, and in 1992 it numbered 650,000.

The club's popularity skyrocketed with the first editions of its magazine *North American Hunter*. In April, 1992, it began a weekly TV show, "North American Outdoors," telecast to 58 million households on ESPN. The goal of the TV show is "to create a more knowledgeable audience with reinforced high ethical standards."

Club activities include: a computerized outfitter and guide rating service, outfitter-sponsored discounts on great hunting adventures, field testing and review of outdoor products, annual Big-Game Awards contest and President's Trophy, and chances to win free outfitted big-game hunts and outdoor products.

Though the club is not a bowhunters-only organization, it includes emphasis on bowhunting.

Mission Statement
The foremost goal of NAHC is to accurately portray hunters in the way that appeals most to ethical, dedicated sportsmen. It places special importance on getting members together to share their passion for hunting, and does all it can to recognize members' successes. To that end, it provides a forum for swap hunts.

How to Join

Write to the above address, or call 1-800-843-6232. (The umbrella organization, North American Outdoor Group, also sponsors the North American Fishing Club.)

POPE & YOUNG CLUB
P.O. Box 548
Chatfield, Minnesota 55923

The Pope and Young Club began in 1957 as a part of the National Field Archery Association's Hunting Activities Committee. It was named in honor of pioneer bowhunters Dr. Saxton Pope and Arthur Young, whose exploits early in the 20th Century drew national attention to the sport. In 1963 it became a separate incorporated scientific, non-profit organization, patterned after the prestigious Boone and Crockett Club. P&Y records the finest trophies of North American big game taken with the bow and arrow. The Club conducts ongoing recording periods, and every two years it presents appropriate awards for the finest trophies submitted, honoring the skulls, horns or antlers of various trophy-class big game species.

The Club is recognized worldwide as the official repository for bowhunting records. Its highest award is the ISHI Award, named for Ishi, the last surviving member of the Yana Indian tribe of northern California, a friend and bowhunting companion of Dr. Pope and Arthur Young. It is given only when a truly outstanding North American big-game trophy animal is deemed deserving of special recognition.

Pope and Young Club publications are available to individuals, wildlife agencies and conservation organizations.

Mission Statement

The Pope & Young Club has grown to epitomize sportsmanship and Fair Chase hunting. Today it fosters and nourishes bowhunting excellence and encourages responsible bowhunting by promoting quality hunting and sound conservation practices.

The Club remains dedicated to the perpetuation and sound management of wild animals and their habitat, as well as other beneficial wildlife practices. Members work actively behind the scenes, quietly supporting various educational, field research and game management programs with moral and financial backing. The Club's Conservation Committee investigates and selects worthy projects. In recent years financial grants totaling many thousands of dollars have been awarded in support of habitat preservation, big-game relocation, field research programs and educational projects.

How to Join

There are three classifications of membership: Associate, Regular and Senior. All new members must join as an Associate, and to qualify for membership the applicant must have taken, under the Rules of Fair Chase, one adult North American big-game animal with a bow and arrow. Regular and Senior Memberships have additional requirements.

For additional information, write the Club at the address given.

PROFESSIONAL BOWHUNTERS SOCIETY
P.O. Box 20066
Charlotte, NC 28225

The Professional Bowhunters Society is an organization of experienced bowhunters (numbering 600 regular and 2,000 associate members in 1992). It is a fraternity, or brotherhood, of some of the best bowhunters in the world. The term "professional" indicates a professional attitude and skill level. The group is dedicated to the belief that personal satisfaction in the sport must be measured in direct relation to the degree of challenge involved—in the hunting, more than the shooting.

PBS was founded in 1963 by seventeen accomplished bowhunters who wanted an organization that would serve the particular interests of serious bowhunters, most notably the need for bow weight requirements in target accuracy tests. The late Tom Shupienis, one of the founders, had this vision: "I see no reason why we cannot someday be the prime source of intelligent opinions and sophisticated respect in all matters relative to bowhunting's future, and PBS standards will be the goals of all bowhunters everywhere."

PBS has been active in important and controversial issues. Committees work in the areas of conservation, legislation, publicity, and education. It sponsors a National Affiliation Program serving state bowhunters' organizations and performing as an information clearinghouse.

Bowhunter Magazine is the official publication of the PBS.

Mission Statement

The PBS is dedicated to the advancement and preservation of bowhunting as a major outdoor sport. It encourages development of skill in bowhunting and the exchange of knowledge between bowhunters. Members work to improve the overall quality of all bowhunters, to understand their weapons, their capabilities, and to get the maximum effective performance from them.

How to Join

There are two levels of membership. Regular membership is limited to 500. Applicants must be 21 or older and must satisfy requirements dictating minimums for bow draw weight, arrow weight, and game taken. Furthermore, bowhunting, rather than target archery must be the applicant's primary interest. Associate membership is unlimited, and game kill requirements do not apply. Contact the address above for an application form.

SAFARI CLUB INTERNATIONAL
4800 West Gates Pass Road
Tucson, AZ 85745-9645

Safari Club International was founded in 1971 when C. J. McElroy, then living in Inglewood, California, organized four Safari Club chapters in the Los Angeles area. Since then, it has become a truly international organization representing more than a million hunters worldwide. SCI and its chapters have contributed millions of dollars to projects directly and indirectly benefiting wildlife.

SCI members are vitally interested in preserving the tradition of hunting. To introduce high-school age youth to wildlife management principles, the organization conducts the SCI American Wilderness Leadership School at Granite Ranch in Wyoming. The SCI Wildlife Museum is another educational tool at the World Headquarters in Tucson, Arizona, and the club has an active wildlife conservation education program that reaches thousands of school children and adults across the Southwest and in northern Mexico. Many SCI chapters participate in Sensory Safaris, where visually impaired children get their first "glimpse" of wildlife. SCI chapters and members are also deeply involved in governmental affairs at local, national and international levels.

Among the currently sponsored conservation projects are management and reintroduction of many species in North and South America, and in Africa.

Camaraderie is important in this organization, and the annual SCI Convention in Las Vegas is well publicized and draws attendees from all over the world.

Mission Statement

To promote conservation of the wildlife of the world as a valuable renewable resource in which hunting is one management tool among many; to stimulate conservation education programs and teacher training workshops emphasizing the wise use of renewable natural resources; to educate the public about the importance of wildlife conservation and the role of hunting in proper management of wildlife.

How to Join

Write Safari Club International for information about joining or about local chapters in your area.

THE WILDLIFE LEGISLATIVE FUND OF AMERICA

801 Kingsmill Parkway
Columbus, Ohio 43229-1137

The Wildlife Legislative Fund of America (founded in 1978) is an association of organizations dedicated to protecting the rights of sportsmen to hunt, trap and fish. It represents hundreds of sportsmen's clubs, in all benefiting over 750,000 American sportsmen with its legal, legislative and public relations expertise at the local, state and national levels.

The major effort is a program called "Protect What's Right," endorsed by mainline conservation organizations, the Department of the Interior and fish and wildlife agencies all over America.

The WLFA newsletter, *Update,* regularly incorporates "Bowhunter Defense Coalition NEWS." The WLFA Bowhunter Defense Coalition is a fast-growing arm that in 1992 included two-dozen national member organizations (major bowhunting clubs and national publications) and over forty-five state members. The WLFA is very active in providing training workshops in government and media relations to bowhunter leaders through the BDC.

The organization operates in 500 communities and 50 states, in Congress and the courts. It is active in state and federal wildlife regulatory processes and is waging a nationwide campaign to get the truth about our outdoor heritage to the uninformed public. To this end, it has been on the scene for outdoorsmen in ballot issue campaigns, legislative lobbying efforts and courtroom defenses. It operates a State Services Division, a National Affairs Office in Washington, D.C., a Legal Services Department, and a Public Relations Department.

WLFA provides training to member organizations in five areas. The Media Program offers a complete package of informational materials for use in all media. The Youth Program focuses on audio/visual materials that emphasize conservation with a pro-hunting slant. The Speakers Bureau Program covers everything from booking speeches to giving them and provides materials that assure a polished presentation. The Legislative Program is a full-scale program that deals with getting to know legislators and how to launch lobbying campaigns.

Mission Statement

The Wildlife Legislative Fund of America takes as its sole goal the preservation of our outdoors heritage. Today, our wildlife and our sports are under attack. A tide of government actions in the states and in Washington, D.C. threatens the very foundations of conservation. So that fathers and sons may continue to enjoy days afield, America's conservationists are protecting their legacy through the WLFA.

How to Join

Membership is open to both concerned individuals and clubs (who become associate organizations). By joining, members become part of a national network of sportsmen's clubs and take full advantage of an ongoing program that represents sportsmen's issues at the local, state, and national levels. All members receive the quarterly newsletter "Update" and legislative "Action Alerts," and have direct access to WLFA staff. Contact WLFA at the address above for additional membership information.

WOMEN HUNTERS OF AMERICA

P.O. Box 1052
Houma, Louisiana 70361

Women Hunters of America was formed in 1991 by a group of dedicated women hunters from Louisiana and Georgia to recruit and represent the estimated two million female hunters in the USA. The organization quickly signed up members from 35 states and Canada. It offers the opportunity for women hunters to get to know one another, to develop skills, and to become visible to hunting products manufacturers, retailers, outfitters and lawmakers.

WHOA sponsors "Outdoor Basics" courses and hunting workshops, offering education to adults and children.

The organization publishes a quarterly newsletter, "In Sight," that features general and organization news; gun and bowhunting tips; and wild game preparation, transportation, and cookery.

Mission Statement

WHOA is dedicated to the idea that women deserve to participate in a full range of outdoor hunting activity. It works to provide visibility to dedicated female hunters, to educate adults and children in all aspects of the outdoors, to work out solutions to gender-related problems (such as women being barred from hunting clubs, leases, and hunts without a male companion where these situations occur), and to foster more female participation in hunting competitions.

How to Join

Write to the address above, or call 1-504-868-0511.

Hunting and Shooting Preserves in the USA and Canada

This list is a directory of preserves that allow public access by membership or on a day basis. It is alphabetical by state and by name. Contact the individual locations for more information. (Source: National Shooting Sports Foundation)

ALABAMA
Season Oct. 1 – Mar. 31

Gunsmoke Plantation
Attn: Hern Holmes
Route 2, Box 15
Union Springs, AL 36089
Tel. 205-738-4642

Rockfence Hunting Reserve
Attn: Tim Larsen
P.O. Drawer 641
Lafayette, AL 36862
Tel. 205-864-0217

Selwood Farm & Hunting Club
Attn: O. V. Hill
Route 1, Box 230
Alpine, AL 35014
Tel. 205-362-7595

ARIZONA
Season: Oct. 1 – Mar. 31

Arizona Hunt Club Shooting Sports
Attn: Kent Henry
P.O. Box 1021
Mayer, AZ 86333
Tel. 602-632-7709

River's Edge Sporting Retreat
Attn: Norm Crawford
HCR Box 742
Benson, AZ 85602
Tel. 602-321-7096

ARKANSAS
Season: Oct. 1 – Mar. 31

Coley's Hunting & Fishing Resort
Attn: Lindsey or Laudis Coley
4700 S. Hwy. 367
McRae, AR 72102
Tel. 501-726-3239

Crowley Ridge Shooting Resort
Attn: Dale Horton
Route 1, Box 350
Forrest City, AR 72335
Tel. 501-633-3352

CALIFORNIA
Season: Sept. 1 – May 31

Circle H H Hunting Preserve
Attn: Fred & Jessie Hymes
HCR #1, Box 512
Nipton, CA 92364
Tel. 702-642-9405

Coon Creek Hunting Club
Attn: George Zents
2787 Pleasant Grove Road
Pleasant Grove, CA 95668
Tel. 916-656-2544

Creekside Pheasant Club
Attn: Larry Hamilton
Box 3640, Parkfield Route
San Miguel, CA 93451
Tel. 805-463-2349

Hayes Hunting Club
Attn: Sheila & Bob Hayes
P.O. Box 1373
Colusa, CA 95932
Tel. 916-473-2952

Lone Pine Pheasant Club
Attn: Bruce Ivey

P.O. Box 158
Lone Pine, CA 93545
Tel. 619-876-4595

McMain's Gamebird Club
Attn: Randy McMain
113 Blazeford Gulch Road
Oroville, CA 95966
Tel. 916-589-4257

Owens Valley Game Preserve
Attn: Charles Easton
P.O. Box 210
Olancha, CA 93549
Tel. 619-764-2831

Raahauge's Hunting Club
Attn: Mike Raahauge
5800 Bluff
Norco, CA 91760
Tel. 714-735-2361

Tulelake Lava Bed Gamebirds
Attn: Carl Arko or Steve Joseph
Route 2, Box 77
Tulelake, CA 96134
Tel. 916-664-3451

West Valley Upland Game Club
Attn: Robert Kloepfer
P.O. Box 257
Gustine, CA 95322
Tel. 209-854-6265

Willow Run Hunting Preserve
Attn: Chris Beane or Gary Alves
Route 1, Box 616
Glenn, CA 95943
Tel. 916-934-7533

COLORADO
Season: Year-round

Go-Fer Broke Hunt Club, Inc.
Attn: Jerry Shatley
19995 Myers Road
Colorado Springs, CO 80928
Tel. 719-683-3807

High Country Game Birds
Attn: Jim or Todd Pederson
33300 RD #25
Elizabeth, CO 80104
Tel. 303-688-3855

High Plains Hunting
Attn: Bruce or Sandi Vetter
57401 E. 88th Avenue
Strasburg, CO 80136
Tel. 303-622-4647

Jalmor Sportsmen's Club
Attn: Al Morse
47939 Elbert Co. Road 22
Ramah, CO 80832
Tel. 719-541-2854

Mt. Blanca Game Bird & Trout
Attn: Bill Binnian or Kathy Byers
P.O. Box 236
Blanca, CO 81123
Tel. 719-379-3825

Rocky Ridge Sporting Club
Attn: Mike Moreng & Dr. Robert Moreng
633 Gait Cr.
Ft. Collins, CO 80524
Tel. 303-221-4868

FLORIDA
Season: Oct. 1 – Apr. 20

J & R Outfitters
Attn: Joey or Liz O'Bannon
8400 S.W. Fox Brown Road
Indiantown, FL 34956
Tel. 407-597-4757

The Quail Den
Attn: Nick or Sydney Warhurst
3320 S.W. 85th Street
Ocala, FL 32676
Tel. 904-237-1504

GEORGIA
Season: Oct. 1 – Mar. 31

Big Sandy Plantation, Inc.
Attn: Robert "Bob" Davis, Jr.
Route 19, Box 400
Macon, GA 31201
Tel. 912-743-3727

**Callaway Gardens
Hunting Preserve**
Attn: E. L. Wilkins
P.O. Box 464
Pine Mountain, GA 31822
Tel. 404-663-5129

Dogwood Plantation Hunting
Attn: Bill Pullin
1409 Hwy. 42 South
McDonough, GA 30253
Tel. 404-957-7005

Foxfire Plantation
Attn: Jimmy Vaughn
P.O. Box 26
Thomasville, GA 31799
Tel. 912-226-2814

Quail Creek
Attn: Chuck May
P.O. Box 2846
Valdosta, GA 31604
Tel. 912-333-8611

Southeast Farms Preserve
Attn: James O. Jones
Route 1, Box 171
Preston, GA 31824
Tel. 912-828-5390

IDAHO
Season: Aug. 15 – Apr. 15

Flying B. Ranch
Attn: Michael Popp
Route 2, Box 12-C
Kamiah, ID 83536
Tel. 208-935-0755

Skyline Hunting Club
Attn: George Hyer
Route 2, Box 14A
Homedale, ID 83628
Tel. 208-337-4443

Wind Shadows Preserve
Attn: Diane Donndelinger
4608 Tio Lane
Nampa, ID 83686
Tel. 208-465-7643

ILLINOIS
Season: Varies

Briar Knoll Hunting & Fishing
Attn: Edward B. Johnson
Box 182
Amboy, IL 61068
Tel. 815-857-2320

Frisco Game Preserve
Attn: Norris Webb
RR 1
Ewing, IL 62836
Tel. 618-629-2527

Heggemeier Hunting Club
Attn: David & Robert Heggemeier
RR 2
Nashville, IL 62263
Tel. 618-327-3709

Hopewell Views Hunting Club
Attn: Rick Wombles
Route 2
Rockport, IL 62370
Tel. 217-734-9234

Huntley Game Farm
Attn: Rose B. Zerbel
10308 Crystal Lake Road
Huntley, IL 60142
Tel. 708-669-5600

Indian Ridge Hunting Preserve
Attn: Steve Clark
RR 3
Canton, IL 61520
Tel. 309-647-1464

Little Wabash Shooting Preserve
Attn: Gary L. Hartke
RR 2, Box 299-A
Neoga, IL 62447
Tel. 217-895-2677

Pinkston Hunting Preserve
Attn: Blaine Pinkston
P.O. Box 583
Pana, IL 62557
Tel. 217-562-5966

Riverwood Game Preserve
Attn: Sam Biswell
RR 1, Box 68
Tennessee, IL 62374
Tel. 309-776-4368

Salem Gamefields Hunt Club
Attn: Raymond Jones
RR 3, Box 445
Salem, IL 62881
Tel. 618-323-6623

Seneca Hunt Club
Attn: Dan or Sheila
P.O. Box 306
Maywood, IL 60153
Tel. 815-357-8080

Upland Bay Hunt Club
Attn: Bob Robinson
P.O. Box 337
Spring Grove, IL 60081
Tel. 815-678-4411

INDIANA
Season: Sept. 1 – Apr. 30

Flatrock Hunting Preserve
Attn: Merrill Carrigan
Route 1, Box 20
Milroy, IN 46156
Tel. 317-629-2354

Horrall Hunting Preserve
Attn: Mike Horrall
P.O. Box 131
Petersburg, IN 47567
Tel. 812-354-2657

J.E.M.P.
Attn: Ed Lewandowski
711 S. 21st Street
Chesterton, IN 46304
Tel. 219-926-1023

King Farms, Inc.
Attn: Eldred King
RR 1, Box 12
Parker City, IN 47368
Tel. 317-468-6706

Maier Hunting Farm
Attn: Marvin or Josephine
65450 Fir Road
Bremen, IN 46506
Tel. 219-633-4654

P.D.Q. Hunting Preserve
Attn: Jim Haines
64500 Elm Road
Bremen, IN 46506
Tel. 219-633-4044

Pleasant Valley Hunting Preserve
Attn: Rod Mace
RR 1, Box 140-A
Carbon, IN 47837
Tel. 317-548-2449

IOWA
Season: Sept. 1 – Mar. 31

Arrowhead Hunting Club
Attn: Gloria Mullin
RR1, Box 28
Goose Lake, IA 52750
Tel. 319-577-2267

Flood Creek Hunting Preserve
Attn: Dennis A. Straube
RR 2, Box 58
Nora Springs, IA 50458
Tel. 515-395-2725

Oakview Hunting Club
Attn: Ronald DeBruin
RR 2
Prairie City, IA 50228
Tel. 515-994-2094

Rock Ridge Game Preserve, Ltd.
Attn: Dale or Becky Davidson
Route 3, Box 159
Maquoketa, IA 52060
Tel. 319-652-5407

Safari Iowa Hunting Lodge
Attn: Larry L. Statler
RR 1, Box 151
Parnell, IA 52325
Tel. 319-668-1080

**Spring Run Shooting
Preserve, Inc.**
Attn: Martin & Barb Loos
Box 8364-A
Spirit Lake, IA 51360
Tel. 712-336-5595

Triple H. Hunting Preserve
Attn: Keith A. Hoelzen
Route 2, Hwy. 99
Burlington, IA 52601
Tel. 319-985-2253

Winchester Wild Game Club
Attn: Frank & Linda Schultz
RR 3, Box 42
Waverly, IA 50677
Tel. 319-352-4039

Winterset Hunt Club
Attn: Bob Sandahl
1012 Cedar Circle
West Des Moines, IA 50265
Tel. 515-224-0869

KANSAS
Season: Sept. 1 – Mar. 31

Blue Line Club
Attn: Bernie Janssen
Route 1, Box 139-A
Solomon, KS 67480
Tel. 913-488-3785

Cokeley Farms Hunting Preserve
Attn: Will Cokeley
Route 1, Box 149
Delia, KS 66418
Tel. 913-771-3817

High Noon Gunning Club
Attn: Mike Becker
RR 2, Box 40
Lindsborg, KS 67456
Tel. 913-227-2657

Lone Pine Shooting Preserve
Attn: Mike or Beth Hamman
Route 1, Box 79
Toronto, KS 66777
Tel. 316-637-2967

Mid America Adventure
Attn: Bob or Kathy Husband
11565 E. Plymell Road
Pierceville, KS 67868

Pawnee Wildlife, Inc.
Attn: Gregory O. Thomas
Route 5, Box 122-A
Fort Scott, KS 66701
Tel. 316-547-2450

Pheasant Creek
Attn: J. R. Dienst
P.O. Box 209
Lakin, KS 67860
Tel. 316-355-7118

Ravenwood Hunting Preserve
Attn: Ken Corbet
10147 Corbet
Topeka, KS 66610
Tel. 913-256-6444

Ringneck Ranch
Attn: Keith W. Houghton
HC 61, Box 7
Tipton, KS 67485
Tel. 913-373-4835

Shawnee Creek Preserve
Attn: Jon Holt
Route 2, Box 50-B
Columbus, KS 66725
Tel. 316-674-8563

Sullivan Wildlife
Attn: Shane & Mary Sullivan
Route 3, Box 119-B
Ulysses, KS 67880
Tel. 316-356-3924

Walnut Ridge Hunting Preserve
Route 1, Box 35-A
Walnut, KS 66780
Tel. 316-354-6713

KENTUCKY
Season: Sept. 1 – May 15

Knotty Pine Quail Farm
Attn: Paul Butterworth, Jr.
2511 Coldwater Road
Murray, KY 42071
Tel. 502-753-4029

LOUISIANA
Season: Varies

Big C Hunting Club
Attn: Paul Dickson or Owen Rigby
10045 Ellerbe Road
Shreveport, LA 71106
Tel. 318-861-0805

Wild Wings Hunting Preserve
Attn: Steve Bryan
Route 2, Hwy. 5531, Box 290
Downsville, LA 71234
Tel. 318-982-7777

MAINE
Season: July 1 – Nov. 30

Foggy Ridge Sports Center
Attn: Jim Olmsted
P.O. Box 211
Warren, ME 04864
Tel. 207-273-2357

MARYLAND
Season: Oct. 1 – Mar. 31

Chesapeake Gun Club
Attn: Chick Darrell
Route 1, Box 44
Henderson, MD 21640
Tel. 301-758-1824

Native Shore Hunting Preserve
Attn: Keith R. Leaverton
Route 6, Box 486
Easton, MD 21601

Sheaffer's Hunting Preserve, Inc.
Attn: John Wadley, Jr. or Pete
Sheaffer
P.O. Box 28
Centreville, MD 21617
Tel. 301-778-0185

MASSACHUSETTS
Season: Sept. 15 – Mar. 31

Hedgerow Kennel & Hunt Club
Attn: Patrick or Holly Perry
Route 32, RFD #2
Athol, MA 01331
Tel. 508-249-7115

Lissivigeen
Attn: Kevin & Carrie Coakley
221 Adams Road
Oakham, MA 01068
Tel. 508-882-3404

MICHIGAN
Season: Aug. 15 – Apr. 30

Big Creek Shooting Preserve
Attn: Steven A. Basi
P.O. Box 369
Mio, MI 48647
Tel. 517-826-3606

Circle M. Ranch
Attn: Lindy Hunt
13957 S. Straits Hwy.
Wolverine, MI 49799
Tel. 616-525-8216

P G W Hunt Club
Attn: Bud Gummer
9215 Jefferson Road
Lakeview, MI 48850
Tel. 517-352-6727

Rolling Hills Shooting Preserve
Attn: Curt Johnson
17025 McKenzie Street
Marcellus, MI 49067
Tel. 616-646-9164

Whisky River Hunt Club
Attn: Mike Damman
4555 Cambria Road
Hillsdale, MI 49242
Tel. 517-357-4424

Wild Wings Game Farm
Attn: James W. Avery
P.O. Box 1232
Gaylord, MI 49735
Tel. 616-584-3350

MINNESOTA
Season: Year-round

Charlie's Hunting Club
Attn: James Langan
Danvers, MN 56231
Tel. 612-567-2276

Clear Creek Outdoors, Inc.
Attn: Patrick LaBoone
Route 1, Box 53-A
Wrenshall, MN 55797
Tel. 218-384-3670

DeLange Hunting Preserve
Attn: John DeLange
Route 2
Marshall, MN 56258
Tel. 507-532-4784

Double Arrow Hunting Preserve
Attn: James Bramstedt
6524 145th Street North
Hugo, MN 55038
Tel. 612-429-6645

Gold Meadows Hunting Preserve
Attn: Joe Doubek
18506 260th Street
Richmond, MN 56368
Tel. 612-597-2747

LeBlanc Rice Creek Hunting
Attn: Gregg LeBlanc
Route 5, Box 213
Little Falls, MN 56345

Tel. 612-745-2451

Maple Landing Preserve
Attn: Mike & Deb Kolden
RR 3, Box 113
Erskine, MN 56535
Tel. 218-687-2175

Minnesota Horse & Hunt Club
Attn: Terry Correll, Manager
2920 220th Street
Prior Lake, MN 55372
Tel. 612-447-2272

Pearson Hunting Adventures, Inc.
Attn: Marvin R. Pearson
Box 1731
Minnetonka, MN 55345
Tel. 612-935-2514

Pheasant Dreams, Inc.
Attn: Greg Lefebure
15033 70th Street
Elk River, MN 55330
Tel. 612-441-7204

Pleasant Acres
Attn: Lester or Denice Zwach
RR 3, Box 144
New Ulm, MN 56073
Tel. 507-359-4166

Prairieland Hunting Club
Attn: Roger or Scott Doty
101 George Street
Alexandria, MN 56308
Tel. 612-763-3804

Spunk River Hunting Club
Attn: Tom or Donna Dickhausen
15718 390th Street
Avon, MN 56310
Tel. 612-746-2442

Stoney Flats Hunting Preserve
Attn: Jack Wenz or David Thoen
2550 South Shore Drive
Prior Lake, MN 55372
Tel. 612-447-1780

Wild Acres Hunting Club
Attn: Mary Ebnet
HC 83, Box 108
Pequot Lakes, MN 56472
Tel. 218-568-5024

Wild Marsh Hunting Preserve
Attn: Chris & Debbie Mortensen
13767 County Road #3
Clear Lake, MN 55319
Tel. 612-662-2292

MISSISSIPPI
Season: Oct. 1 – Apr. 30

Longleaf Plantation
Attn: George or Beth Alexander
P.O. Box 511
Lumberton, MS 39455
Tel. 601-794-6001

MISSOURI
Season: Sept. 1 – May 31

B & C Game Farms
Attn: Bill Sayre
Route 1, Box 47
St. Catherine, MO 64677
Tel. 816-258-2973

Baier's Den Kennels & Preserve
Attn: Bud Baier
Peculiar, MO 64078
Tel. 816-758-5234

Briggs Ranch Hunting Preserve
Attn: Russ Briggs
Route 3
Princeton, MO 64673
Tel. 816-748-3360

Hi Point Hunting Club
Attn: Alan Guffey
Route 1, Box 28
Breckenridge, MO 64625
Tel. 816-644-5708

Hunters Southern Prairie Preserve
Attn: Larry Thompson or Thomas
Thompson
Route 1, Box 207-E
Sedalia, MO 65301
Tel. 816-668-3937

Malinmor Sporting Estate
Attn: Rick Merritt
RR 4, Box 108
Eolia, MO 63344
Tel. 314-324-3366

Ozark Outfitters Farm Supply
Attn: Dusty Shaw or
Mark W. Risner
Thomasville Route, Box 60
Birch Tree, MO 65438
Tel. 417-764-3701

Pond Fort Kennels & Hunt Club
Attn: Marin & Helen Strubberg
8860 Highway North
O'Fallon, MO 63366
Tel. 314-327-5680

Snow White Enterprises
Attn: Carol L. Atherton
Route 1, Box 40
Carrollton, MO 64633
Tel. 816-542-3037

Squaw Creek Valley Gamebirds
Attn: Royce W. Clement
RR 1
Skidmore, MO 64487
Tel. 816-928-3248

Tall Oaks Club
Attn: Jeff Brand
295 Tall Oaks Road
Warrenton, MO 63383
Tel. 314-456-3564

Valley View Hunt Club
Attn: Tom Wolfe
P.O. Box 205
Climax Springs, MO 65324
Tel. 314-347-2280

Wing Tip Game Ranch & Kennel
Attn: John Rouse
Route 1
Cainsville, MO 64632
Tel. 816-893-5880

Yellow Rose Farm
Attn: Stephen & Susan Stiens
RR 1, Box 148
Skidmore, MO 64487
Tel. 816-928-3496

MONTANA
Season: Sept. 1 – Dec. 31

Fetch Inn Hunting Preserve
Attn: Tom & Jody Fo
P.O. Drawer 1429

Hamilton, MT 59840
Tel. 406-363-5111

**Western Montana
Wildlife Preserve**
Attn: Everitt Foust
10468 Moiese Valley Road
Moiese, MT 59824
Tel. 406-644-2285

NEBRASKA
Season: Sept. 1 – Mar. 31

Can Hunt
Attn: Todd Halle
Route 1, Box 128
Seward, NE 68434
Tel. 402-588-2448

Pheasant Haven
Attn: Earl or Scott Bruhn
P.O. Box 529
Elkhorn, NE 68022
Tel. 402-779-2608

Prairie Hills Hunt Club
Attn: John McElroy
1104 West Division
Grand Island, NE 68801
Tel. 308-226-2540

Swanson Hunting Acres, Inc.
Attn: Janet Swanson
Box 99
Niobrara, NE 68760
Tel. 402-857-3514

Tyson Farms Hunting Preserve
Attn: Tom and Sandy Tyson
Route 1, Box 110
Blair, NE 68008
Tel. 402-426-5963

NEVADA
Season: Sept. 1 – Apr. 30

Flying M Hunting Club
Attn: Jack Hedger
70 Pine Grove Road
Yerington, NV 89447
Tel. 702-463-5260

Topaz Sportsmen's Center
Attn: Evan L. Allred or George Asay
3851 Highway 208

Wellington, NV 89444
Tel. 702-266-3512

NEW JERSEY
Season: Sept. 1 – Apr. 15

Belleplain Farms Preserve
Attn: Nick Germanio
Box 222 Handsmill Road
Belleplain, NJ 08270
Tel. 609-861-2345

M & M Hunting Preserve
Attn: Anthony Matarese
Hook & Winslow Roads
Pennsville, NJ 08070
Tel. 609-935-1230

NEW MEXICO
Season: Sept. 1 – Mar. 31

C & L Hunting Reserve
Attn: Lloyd Lary
HCR 63, Box 565
Melrose, NM 88124
Tel. 505-372-6175

NEW YORK
Season: Sept. 1 – Mar. 31

Bill's Hunting
Attn: John M. or Linda K. Bills
RD 2, Box 288A
Mohawk, NY 13407
Tel. 315-823-1708

Catskill Pheasantry
Attn: Alex Papp
P.O. Box 42
Long Eddy, NY 12760
Tel. 914-887-4487

Coxsackie Shooting Preserve
Attn: Bill Schaefer
RD Box 27
Coxsackie, NY 12051
Tel. 518-731-2195

Forrestel Farm Hunting Preserve
Attn: Bill Keppler
4660 Water Works Road
Medina, NY 14103
Tel. 716-798-0222

Gray's Farms
Attn: David Gray
2839 Lockport Road
Oakfield, NY 14125
Tel. 716-948-9269

Highland Farm Pheasant Club
Attn: Joe Nastke
Box 193 Highland Road
Old Chatham, NY 12136
Tel. 518-784-2614

J. R. Shooting Preserve
Attn: Dick Nelson
P.O. Box 482
Palenville, NY 12463
Tel. 518-943-2069

Lido's Game Farm
Attn: Francine J. Laurents or Lido
RD 2, Box 277
Hillsdale, NY 12529
Tel. 518-329-1551

Pheasant Ridge, Inc.
Attn: Virginia A. Mallon
Route 40, P.O. Box 216
Greenwich, NY 12834
Tel. 518-692-9738

Spring Farm
Attn: Dave Schellinger
P.O. Box 301
Sag Harbor, NY 11963
Tel. 516-725-0038

T-M-T Hunting Preserve, Inc.
Attn: Thomas F. Mackin
RR #1, Box 297
School House Road
Staatsburg, NY 12580
Tel. 914-266-5108

The Austerlitz Club, Inc.
Attn: Terry Cozzolino
RD Box 182
Chatham, NY 12037
Tel. 518-392-3468

Valhalla Hunting Preserve
Attn: Ed Van Stine
Quigg Hollow Road, P.O. Box 703
Andover, NY 14806
Tel. 607-478-5222

NORTH CAROLINA
Season: Oct. 1 – Mar. 31

Adams Creek Gunning Lodge
Attn: Rusty or June Bryant
6240 Adams Creek Road
Havelock, NC 28532
Tel. 919-447-7688

Alligator River Shooting Preserve
Attn: Al Hollis
Route 2, Box 318-A
Columbia, NC 27925
Tel. 919-796-4868

Shady Knoll Preserve
Attn: John W. Maness
Route 1, Box 35
Asheboro, NC 27203
Tel. 919-879-3663

Six Runs Plantation
Attn: Rebecca Todd-Edwards
Route 1, Box 179
Rose Hill, NC 28458
Tel. 919-532-4810

NORTH DAKOTA
Season: Sept. 1 – Mar. 31

Bois De Sioux Hunting Preserve
Attn: Arlen Spear
18270 95 R. SE
Fairmount, ND 58030
Tel. 701-474-5879

Dakota Hunting Club & Kennel
Attn: George Newton
Box 1643
Grand Forks, ND 58206
Tel. 701-775-2074

Ringnecks Unlimited, Inc.
Attn: Steve or Deb Craine
Route 1, Box 12
Flasher, ND 58535
Tel. 701-597-3032

Spring Lake Hunting Preserve
Attn: Dianne Reuppel
HCR 1, Box 19-A
Baldwin, ND 58521
Tel. 701-673-3141

OHIO
Season: Sept. 1 – Apr. 30

Brier Oak Hunt Club
Attn: Kevin J. Schaeffer
8216 Star Route 113
Bellevue, OH 44811
Tel. 419-483-4953

Cherrybend Pheasant Farm
Attn: Holly & Mary Hollister
2326 Cherrybend Road
Wilmington, OH 45177
Tel. 513-584-4269

Elkhorn Lake Hunt Club
Attn: Samuel Ballou
4146 Klopfenstein Road
Bucyrus, OH 44820
Tel. 419-562-6131

Federal Valley Pheasant Hunting
Attn: Gene or Roseanna Hines
16171 E. Kasler Creek Road
Amesville, OH 45711
Tel. 614-448-6747

**Hidden Haven
Shooting Preserve, Inc.**
Attn. Ronald L. Blosser
9291 Buckeye Road
Sugar Grove, OH 43155
Tel. 614-746-8568

Pheasant Recreation, Inc.
Attn: Jack E. Carpenter
18376 London Road
Circleville, OH 43113
Tel. 614-477-1587

Pheasant View Farm
Attn: Mike Mulini
11625 Beloit Snodes Road
Beloit, OH 44609
Tel. 216-584-6828

Ringneck Ridge Sporting Club
Attn: Daniel C. Dishong
1818 C.R. 14
Gibsonburg, OH 43431
Tel. 419-637-2332

Stinson Farms Hunting Preserve
Attn: Manly Stinson

5920 Goodhope Road
Frankfort, OH 45628
Tel. 614-998-4977

Tallmadge Pheasant Farm
Attn: Jack & Nancy Tallmadge
#16 County Road 1950
Jeromesville, OH 44840
Tel. 419-368-3457

OKLAHOMA
Season: Oct. 1 – Mar. 31

Cimarron Hunting Preserve
Attn: Donald Miller
Route 1, Box 163
Hennessey, OK 73742
Tel. 405-853-2737

Five Cedars Ranch
Attn: Donna Duffy
P.O. Box 75
Chandler, OK 74834
Tel. 918-368-2331

Southern Ranch Hunting Club
Attn: Dean Caton
Route 2, Box 75
Chandler, OK 74834
Tel. 405-258-0000

OREGON
Season: Aug. 1 – Mar. 31

Noble Sporting Adventures
Attn: Don Noble
Route 2, Box 185-X
Milton-Freewater, OR 97862
Tel. 503-558-3675

Pheasant Ridge
Attn: Jeffrey Oakes
Route 1, Box 46-A
Tygh Valley, OR 97063
Tel. 503-544-2185

**Summer Ridge
Shooting Preserve**
Attn: Tim & Kathy McGuffin
3759 Reed Road
Vale, OR 97918
Tel. 503-473-3355

PENNSYLVANIA
Season: Sept. 1 – Mar. 31

**Angus Hunting &
Conservation Farm**
Attn: Jay Angus or John Angus
RD #1, Box 260
Latrobe, PA 15650
Tel. 412-423-4022

Cabin Creek Game Preserve
Attn: June or Stan Shaffer
RD 1, Box 602-C
Wrightsville, PA 17368
Tel. 717-252-1980

Gapview Hunting Preserve
Attn: Don or Harold Martz
RD 1, Box 85
Dalmatia, PA 17017
Tel. 717-758-3307

Gaybird Farms
Attn: Barney Berlinger
Box 1
Carversville, PA 18913
Tel. 215-297-5553

Hillendalae Hunt Club
Attn: Tom Crawford
RD 1, Box 390
Tyrone, PA 16686
Tel. 814-684-5015

Indian Run Country
Attn: David & Nancy Stutzman
Route 2, Box 207
Centerville, PA 16404
Tel. 814-967-2635

J D Z Game Farm
Attn: John Zaktansky
RD 2, Box 75
Watsontown, PA 17777
Tel. 717-649-5881

La-Da-Jo Pines
Attn: Larry Delp
RD 2, Box 67
New Ringgold, PA 17960
Tel. 717-943-2213

Medhia Shooting Preserve
Attn: Donald Singer

Route 1, P.O. Box 64
East Waterford, PA 17021
Tel. 717-734-3965

Pheasant Hill Farms
Attn: George S. Myers
RD 6, Box 331
Wellsboro, PA 16901
Tel. 717-724-3274

**Spruce Hollow
Hunting Farm, Ltd.**
RD 2, Box 353
Kunkletown, PA 18058
Tel. 215-826-5134

T.N.T. Shooting Grounds
Attn: Thomas Stewart
P.O. Box 236
Waltersburg, PA 15488
Tel. 412-677-2609

RHODE ISLAND
Season: Sept. 1 – Apr. 15

Addieville East Farm
Attn: Geoff Gabe
Box 248, 200 Pheasant Drive
Mapleville, RI 02839
Tel. 401-568-3185

SOUTH CAROLINA
Season: Oct. 1 – Mar. 31

Back Woods Quail Club
Attn: H. E. Hemingway
P.O. Box 187
Andrews, SC 29510
Tel. 803-264-3518

Brays Island Plantation
Attn: Tony Martin
P.O. Box 30
Sheldon, SC 29941
Tel. 803-846-3155

Broxton Bridge Plantation
Attn: Jerry Varn, Jr.
P.O. Box 97
Ehrhardt, SC 29081
Tel. 803-267-3882

The Oaks Gun Club
Attn: Tommy McClary

Route 2, Box 196-A
Georgetown, SC 29440
Tel. 803-527-1861

SOUTH DAKOTA
Season: Sept. 1 – Mar. 31

Dakota Dream Hunts, Inc.
Attn: Doug or Rich Converse
RR 2, Box 17
Arlington, SD 57212
Tel. 605-983-5033

Dakota Expeditions
Attn: Clint or Deanna Smith
HCR 4, Box 109
Miller, SD 57302
Tel. 605-874-2545

Dakota Ridge Hunting
Attn: James Dailey or Charles
Schomaker
RR 2, Box 67
Altamont, SD 57226
Tel. 605-874-2823

High Brass
Attn: Tom Koehn
RR 1, Box 4-X
Chamberlain, SD 57325
Tel. 605-734-6047

High Plains Game Ranch
Attn: Randy or Rhonda Vallery
HCR 76, Box 192
Nisland, SD 57762
Tel. 605-257-2365

Ingall's Prairie Wildfowl Hunts
Attn: Jim Ingalls
RR 1, Box 111
Bryant, SD 57221
Tel. 605-628-2327

James Valley Hunting Preserve
Attn: Harold or Jan Klimisch
Route 1, Box 39
Utica, SD 57067
Tel. 605-364-7468

**Pearson's Hunting
Adventures, Inc.**
Attn: Marvin R. Pearson
RR 1, Box 43
Forestburg, SD 57338
Tel. 612-935-2514

Stukel's Birds And Bucks
Attn: Frank Stukel
Route 1, Box 112
Gregory, SD 57533
Tel. 605-835-8941

The Hunt, Inc.
Attn: Eugene Warriner
P.O. Box 217
Blunt, SD 57522
Tel. 605-962-6472

TENNESSEE
Season: Year-round

Cookeville Dock's Preserve
Attn: Reece Nash
Route 2
Baxter, TN 38544
Tel. 615-858-2185

Hill and Dale Hunting Preserve
Attn: Bill Cannon
Route 8, Shady Lane
Murfreesboro, TN 37130
Tel. 615-890-5862

White Top Hunting Preserve
Attn: Joe Hicks
424 White Top Road
Bluff City, TN 37618
Tel. 615-538-8270

TEXAS
Season: Year-round

Cypress Valley Preserve
Attn: Mike Fields
P.O. Box 5783
Austin, TX 78763
Tel. 512-825-3396

Harper's Hunting Preserve
Attn: Gilbert & Clydeene Harper
Route 2, Box 484
Booker, TX 79005
Tel. 806-435-3495

Hawkeye Hunting Club
Attn: Jerry Waters
P.O. Box 27
Center, TX 75935
Tel. 409-598-2424

Landrum Creek Hunting Resort
Attn: John Martin

Route 7, Box 40
Montgomery, TX 77356
Tel. 409-597-4267

Lone Star Bird Hunts
Attn: Doug Davis
210 North Davis Avenue
Stephenville, TX 76401
Tel. 817-968-7972

Lone Star Hunting Club
Attn: Max Heatherington
Route 1, Box 1020
Ingleside, TX 78362
Tel. 512-776-7000

Possum Walk Ranch
Attn: Buddy Smith
Route 2, Box 174
Huntsville, TX 77340
Tel. 402-291-1891

Santa Anna Hunting Area
Attn: John R. Stearns
Roue 1, Box 102-A
Santa Anna, TX 76878
Tel. 915-348-9267

Upland Bird Country
Attn: Steve Stroube
P.O. Box 1110
Corsicana, TX 75151
Tel. 903-872-5663

UTAH
Season: Sept. 1 – Mar. 31

Hatt's Ranch
Attn: Rey Lloyd Hatt
Box 275
Green River, UT 84525
Tel. 801-564-3224

River Hollow Hunting Club
Attn: Randy A. Burbank
68 North 3rd East
Hyrum, UT 84319
Tel. 801-245-6150

VERMONT
Season: Sept. 1 – Mar. 31

Hermitage Inn Hunting Preserve
Attn: Jim McGovern
Box 457 Coldbrook Road

Wilmington, VT 05363
Tel. 802-464-3511

Tinmouth Hunting Preserve, Ltd.
Attn: Rick Faller
RD 1, Box 556
Wallingford, VT 05773
Tel. 802-446-2337

VIRGINIA
Season: Oct. 1 – Mar. 31

Forest Green Shooting Preserve
Attn: Danny Roberts
P.O. Box 361
Spotsylvania, VA 22553
Tel. 703-582-2566

Merrimac Farm Hunting Preserve
Attn: Dean N. McDowell
14710 Deepwood Lane
Nokesville, VA 22123
Tel. 703-594-2276

Oakland Shooting Preserve
Attn: David Pomfret
P.O. Box 1265
Orange, VA 22960
Tel. 703-854-4540

Orapax Plantation
Attn: Tom Dykers
3831 River Road West
Goochland, VA 23063
Tel. 804-556-6585

WASHINGTON
Season: Year-round

Banks Lake Rod & Gun Club
Attn: Jim L. Pitts
HCR 2, Box 357-A
Coulee City, WA 99115
Tel. 509-632-5502

Landt Farm Shooting Preserve
Attn: Ellwood Landt
W. 16308 Four Mound Road
Nine Mile Falls, WA 99026
Tel. 509-466-4036

Pac's Pheasant Hunts
Attn: Tim Wolf

Box 4391
Spokane, WA 99202
Tel. 509-838-6070

R & M Game Birds Preserve
Attn: Mac or Rodger Ford
495 Fisher Hill Road
Lyle, WA 98635
Tel. 509-365-3245

WEST VIRGINIA
Season: Year-round

Foxy Pheasant Hunting Preserve
Attn: Gene Abelow
Route 1, Box 437
Kearneysville, WV 25430
Tel. 304-725-4963

**Kincheloe Pheasant
Hunting Preserve**
Attn: Paul Hughes
Route 2, Box 88-A
Jane Lew, WV 26378
Tel. 304-884-7431

WISCONSIN
Season: Year-round

Bearskin Wildlife Reserve
Attn: Gail R. Winnie
8915 Church Road
Harshaw, WI 54529
Tel. 715-282-5362

Big Rock Hunting Preserve
Attn: Chuck Birkenholz
W 15664 Chuck Road
Gilman, WI 54433
Tel. 715-668-5557

Blonhaven
Attn: Jim Clark
P.O. Box 12
Milton, WI 53563
Tel. 608-868-3176

Blue Wing Hunt Club
Attn: Bill Maass
P.O. Box 117
Elkhart Lake, WI 53020
Tel. 414-894-3318

Fence Line Hunt Club
Attn: Richard Prihoda
10759 W. 8 Mile Road
Franksville, WI 53126
Tel. 414-425-8112

Geneva National Hunt Club
Attn: John Treslley
555 Hunt Club Court
Lake Geneva, WI 53147
Tel. 414-245-2100

Hawe Hunting Preserve
Attn: Tom Hawe
2594 Blueberry Lane
Waldo, WI 53093
Tel. 414-528-8388

Isaacson's Pheasant Pharm
Attn: Sylvia Isaacson
Route 1, Box 365
Sarona, WI 54870
Tel. 715-635-9586

Kidder Game Farm
Attn: Warren/Nancy/Clark Kidder
1582 W. County N.
Milton, WI 53563
Tel. 608-868-2376

Martin Fish & Game Farm
Attn: James H. Martin
W 10681 Hwy. 127
Portage, WI 53901
Tel. 608-742-7205

Oak Hill Hunting Preserve
Attn: Paul & Janet Snider
W. 8718 Forest Avenue
Eldorado, WI 54932
Tel. 414-921-2776

Oakwood Kennel & Game Farm
Attn: Ronald or Dianne Norman
7149 Badger Lane
Allenton, WI 53002
Tel. 414-488-5852

Pheasant City Hunt Club
Attn: Bill or Debbie Scallon
Route 1, Box 272
Markesan, WI 53946
Tel. 414-324-5813

River Wildlife
Attn: Max Grube
444 Highland Drive
Kohler, WI 53044
Tel. 414-457-0134

Schmeiser's Hunting Preserve
Attn: Jeff or Pat Schmeiser
N 5744 Sackett's Drive
Medford, WI 54451
Tel. 715-785-7349

Sioux Creek Hunt Club
Attn: Fred Bannister
Box 27
Chetek, WI 54728
Tel. 715-924-4811

Smokey Lake Reserve
Attn: P. C. Christiansen
P.O. Box 100
Phelps, WI 54554
Tel. 715-545-2333

Spring Valley Hunting Preserve
Attn: Lyle Yaun
15201 Lang Road
Orfordville, WI 53576
Tel. 608-879-2628

**Strebig's Game Farm &
Shooting Preserve**
Attn: Tim Strebig
N 3215 CTHE
Medford, WI 54451
Tel. 715-748-2883

Tamarack Game Farm
Attn: Stan Lorenz
Route 2, Box 138-C
Colfa, WI 54730
Tel. 715-632-2346

Thunderbird Game Farm
Attn: Len Leberg
W Box 23119 Thunderbird Road
Chilton, WI 53014

Top Gun Farms
Attn: David Fiedler
N 3249 River View Road
Juneau, WI 53039
Tel. 414-349-8128

Tumm's Pine View Game Farm
Attn: James Tumm
Route 2, Box 240
Fall Creek, WI 54742
Tel. 715-877-2434

Wern Valley Sportsmens Club
Attn: Steve & Patti Williams
S-36W-29903 Wern Way
Waukesha, WI 53188
Tel. 414-968-2400

Wild Wings Hunting Preserve
Attn: Ron or Joy Nolan
N 865 Hwy. W
Campbellsport, WI 53010
Tel. 414-533-8738

**Woods and Meadows
Hunting Resort**
Attn: Scott Goetzka
Route 1, Box 40
Warrens, WI 54666
Tel. 608-378-4223

WYOMING
Season: Aug. 1 – Mar. 31

Big Horn Canyon Ranch
Attn: Jim Roach
P.O. Box 282
Big Horn, WY 82833
Tel. 307-674-9097

Clear Creek Hunting Preserve
Attn: Matthew S. McAdams
3004 US Hwy. 14-16 East
Clearmont, WY 82835
Tel. 307-737-2237

Muddy Ridge Gamebirds
Attn: Ken or Kathi Metzler
387 Mo. Valley Road
Shoshoni, WY 82649
Tel. 307-856-4965

Wyoming Wings
Attn: Rod Johnson & Tom Ofero
68 E. Johnson Road
Wheatland, WY 82201
Tel. 307-322-3604

CANADA
Season: Sept. 1 – Apr. 30

Springfield Game Farm
Attn: Gunter Mesa
Box 6, Group 4, RR 1
Anola, Manitoba
CANADA R0E 0H0
Tel. 204-866-2624

Wild Wings Sporting Clays
Attn: Rick Tams
RR 4
Innisfail, Alberta
CANADA T0M 1A0
Tel. 403-227-1232

Winnipeg River Gamebird Coop
Attn: Luc Vincent or Guy Bruneau
Box 118
St. George, Manitoba
CANADA R0C 1V0
Tel. 204-367-8611

Appendix C

Shooting Ranges and
Archery Clubs in the USA

This list is alphabetical by state and by club name. The codes for types of archery are given after the name as: (O) outdoor archery; (F) field archery; and (I) indoor archery. Contact the ranges or clubs directly for additional information. (Source: The National Shooting Sports Foundation, 555 Danbury Road, Wilton, CT 06897.)

ALABAMA

**Sand Mountain
Shooter's Club (O)**
Attn: Daniel Cooper
Bloodworth Road
Boaz, AL 35957
Tel. 205-593-8027

Styx River Shooting Center (O, F)
Attn: Joe Coleman
P.O. Box 543
Robertsdale, AL 36567
Tel. 205-964-6066

ALASKA

**Chugiak Chapter Izaak Walton
League of America (O)**
Attn: Lynn Hosack
P.O. Box 670650
Chugiak, AK 99567
Tel. 907-688-3967

**Fort Wainwright Skeet &
Trap Club (O)**
Attn: Jim Bowers
P.O. Box 35046
Ft. Wainwright, AK 99703
Tel. 907-353-7869

ARIZONA

Douglas Rifle & Pistol Club (O)
Attn: John Behrens
P.O. Box 3582
Douglas, AZ 85608
Tel. 602-364-8213

**Fort Huachuca Skeet &
Trap Center (O)**
Attn: Charlie Cornett
P.O. Box 334
Sierra Vista, AZ 85613
Tel. (day) 602-538-7712;
(eve) 602-458-6188

Scottsdale Sportsman Club (F)
Attn: Thomas Hayes
Eldorado Park
Scottsdale, AZ 85251
Tel. 602-967-8226

Wickenburg Sportsmans Club (O)
Attn: Gene Gutowski
Box 1581
Wickenburg, AZ 85358
Tel. 602-427-3658

ARKANSAS

Arkansas Bowhunters Assn. (O)
Attn: H. Keith Noble
P.O. Box 9902
Little Rock, AR 72219
Tel. 501-224-6141

**North Little Rock Public
Shooting Range (O)**
Attn: George Neal
1221 W. Maryland Avenue
North Little Rock, AR 72116
Tel. 501-835-7644

CALIFORNIA

**Arrowhead Fish & Game
Conservation Club, Inc. (O)**
Attn: Barbara Morrison
Highway 173, Box 567
Lake Arrowhead, CA 92352
Tel. (day) 714-337-0747

Beale Rod & Gun Club (O, F)
Attn: Manager
9CSG/SSYG
Beale AFB, CA 95903
Tel. 916-788-2473

Carmel Gun Club (O)
Attn: Manager
P.O. Box 1575
Monterey, CA 93940

Mother Lode Gun Club (O)
Attn: Manager
c/o Gun Sport
Jamestown Road
Sonora, CA 95370
Tel. 209-984-4160

**Nevada County
Sportsmen, Inc. (O, F)**
Attn: Kent Boothby
11296 Banner Mountain Trail
Nevada City, CA 95959
Tel. (day) 916-265-5131;
(eve) 916-273-5488

COLORADO

Durango Gun Club (O, F, I)
Attn: John Leonard
576 Florida Road
Durango, CO 81302
Tel. 303-247-4607

**Northern Colorado Rod &
Gun Club, Inc. (O)**
Attn: Manager
Owl Canyon Road, P.O. Box 1298
Ft. Collins, CO 80522
Tel. 304-493-1148

**Western Sportsman
Gun Club (O)**
Attn: Bob Tesch
9500 Coalton Road
Louisville, CO 80020
Tel. 303-665-0480

CONNECTICUT

**Guilford Sportsmen's
Association (O, F)**
Attn: Harry DeBenedet
Hart Road, P.O. Box 286
Guilford, CT 06437

Mystic Rod and Gun Club (O, F)
Attn: Paul Altman
Box 181
Mystic, CT 06355
Tel. 203-536-8309

**Pachaug Outdoor
Club (O, F, I)**
Attn: Michael Rinne

692 Norwich Road
Plainfield, CT 06394
Tel. (evening) 203-564-8417

**Suffield Sportsmens
Assn., Inc. (O, F)**
Attn: Art Sladyk
c/o 187 Copper Hill Road
West Suffield, CT 06093
Tel. (evening) 203-644-3070

Wooster Mountain Gun Club (O)
Attn: Joe Chapman
P.O. Box 1254
Danbury, CT 06810
Tel. 203-794-9716

DELAWARE

Ommelanden Range (O, F)
Attn: George Long
Route 9
New Castle, DE 19720
Tel. (day) 302-328-2256
(eve) 302-322-2962

FLORIDA

**Central Florida Rifle & Pistol
Club, Inc. (O)**
Attn: Manager
P.O. Box 15165
Orlando, FL 32858

Gateway Rifle & Pistol Club (O)
Attn: Warren Schryer
9301 Zambito Road
Jacksonville, FL 32210
Tel. 904-771-2937

Wyoming Antelope Club (O, F)
Attn: John Gluck
3699 126th Avenue, P.O. Box 724
Pinellas Park, FL 34290
Tel. (day) 813-327-5023
(eve) 813-347-8469

GEORGIA

Country Sportsman (O, I)
Attn: Helmut Cawthon
2626 Callier Springs Road
Rome, GA 30161
Tel. (day) 404-235-4366;
(eve) 404-291-4601

De Kalb Firing Range (O)
Attn: T. C. Stevens
3905 North Goddard Road
Lithonia, GA 30058
Tel. 404-428-8965

**Northeast Georgia Firearms
Range & Gunsmith Shop (O)**
Attn: Gene Bristow
Route 1, Box 2000, Gumlog Road
Lavonia, GA 30553
Tel. 404-356-8722

IDAHO

Cassia Rod & Gun Club (O, F)
Attn: J. L. Keen
Box 184
Burley, ID 83318

Parma Rod & Gun Club (O, F)
Attn: Gary Beaver
Parma, ID 83660
Tel. (day) 208-722-6701;
(eve) 208-722-5585

**Rupert Rifle &
Pistol Club & Jr. Div. (I)**
Attn: Walt Charles
Route #1, Box 99
Rupert, ID 83350
Tel. 208-436-3344

**Sandpoint Rifle &
Pistol Club (O, I)**
Attn: Willard Piehl
1114 Lake Street
Sandpoint, ID 83864
Tel. 208-263-3572

**Sportsman's Rod &
Gun Club (O)**
Attn: Harley Lekvold
366th CSG/SSRT, Bldg. 2222
Mt. Home AFB, ID 83648
Tel. (day) 208-828-6093;
(eve) 208-587-3683

Whitebird Gun Club, Inc. (O)
Attn: Penny Wiesnor
Whitebird Creek Road
P.O. Box 128
Whitebird, ID 83554
Tel. 208-839-2284

ILLINOIS

Aurora Sportsmen's Club (O, F, I)
Attn: Benjamin Eaton
P.O. Box 414
Aurora, IL 60507

Bristol Shooting Ranges (O)
Attn: Steven Zywczak
Highway AH
Bristol, IL 60087
Tel. 312-362-1986

Chillicothe Sportsmen's Club (O)
Attn: Lowell Bennett
Yankee Lane
Chillicothe, IL 61523
Tel. (evening) 309-274-5586

Foosland Sportsmen's Club (O)
Attn: Ronald Carpenter
Route 47
Foosland, IL 61845
Tel. 218-846-3155

Lincoln Sportsmen Club (O)
Attn: Paul Berger
Old Route 66
Lincoln, IL 62656

**Plug & Pellet
Sportsman Club (O)**
Attn: Dave Picchioni
Centerville Road
Rockford, IL 61107
Tel. 815-399-3984

Richmond Hunt Club (F)
Attn: Mike Daniels
Route 173
Richmond, IL 60071

INDIANA

**Deer Creek Conservation
Club (O, F)**
Attn: Manager
P.O. Box 127
Gas City, IN 46933

**Elkhart Conservation
Club (O, F)**
Attn: Mike Bowman
U.S. 20 W

Elkhart, IN 46513
Tel. (evening) 219-862-4776

**Evansville Chapter, Izaak Walton
League of America (O, F)**
Attn: Martin Vincent
P.O. Box 2468
Evansville, IN 47714
Tel. 812-897-2746

**Fall Creek Valley Conservation
Club (O, F)**
Attn: Donn Bonner
State Road 109
Anderson, IN 46016
Tel. (evening) 317-649-2623

IOWA

Anamosa Bow Hunters (O, F, I)
Attn: Randall Townsend
206 N. Garnavillo
Anamosa, IA 52205
Tel. 319-462-4083

Central Range (I)
Attn: Craig Stockel
2100 White Street
Dubuque, IA 52001
Tel. 319-582-8514

**Council Bluffs Rifle & Pistol
Club, Inc. (O)**
Attn: David Head
P.O. Box 1042
Council Bluffs, IA 51502
Tel. (day) 712-322-0565;
(eve) 712-322-6477

**Dickinson County Chapter, Izaak
Walton League of America (O)**
Attn: Larry Webber
Pioneer Beach Road
Spirit Lake, IA 51360
Tel. 712-336-2202

Fairbank Gun Club (O)
Attn: G. W. Galleger
Fairbank, IA 50629

**Ireton Sportsman's
Club (O, F)**
Attn: Mark Wells
Ireton, IA 51027

Tel. 712-278-2598

**Laurens Sportsmens Club &
Jr. Div. (O, F)**
Attn: Fred Eaton
Main Street
Laurens, IA 50554
Tel. 712-845-4330

**Marshall County
Chapter, Izaak Walton
League (O, F)**
Attn: Ed Moore
12th Avenue, Route 2
Marshalltown, IA 50158
Tel. 515-752-1021

**Oskaloosa Chapter, Izaak Walton
League of America (O)**
Attn: R. R. Scharff
Oskaloosa, IA 52579
Tel. 515-673-8994

Rock Rapids Gun Club (O)
Attn: John Appel
North Boone Street
Rock Rapids, IA 51246
Tel. 712-472-3468

Shootin' Range, Inc. (I)
Attn: Daryl Schoppe
Highway 30W
State Center, IA 50247
Tel. 515-483-2656

**Tryhedron Bowhunters
Assn. (O, I)**
Attn: Ritch Stolpe
413 Pearl Street
Sioux City, IA 51101
Tel. 712-255-5132

**Volga Valley Conservation
Club (O)**
Attn: Dan Burkhart
Box 15
Fayette, IA 52142
Tel. 319-425-3331

Winnebago Archery Club (O)
Attn: John Carlson
P.O. Box 7
Lake Mills, IA 50450
Tel. 515-592-6122

KANSAS

**Geary County Fish &
Game Assn. (O, F)**
Attn: E. L. Augustine
P.O. Box 631
Junction City, KS 66441
Tel. 913-238-8727

**Liberal Recreational Shooting
Range (O)**
Attn: Gary Lucas
1601 E. Eighth Street
Liberal, KS 67901
Tel. 316-626-0133

The Bullet Hole (I)
Attn: Richard Stovall
6201 Robinson
Overland Park, KS 66202
Tel. 913-432-0050

KENTUCKY

**Boyle County Fish &
Game Club (O)**
Attn: Dewey Small
Route 300
Junction City, KY 40440
Tel. 606-854-6511

Buck Creek Sportsman's Club (F)
Attn: C. B. Lowe
Young Road
Glasgow, KY 42142
Tel. (day) 502-651-9121;

Daviess County Fish & Game (O)
Attn: Nell or Chris Tharp
1370 South Chestnut Grove Road
Lewisport, KY 42301
Tel. 502-264-1865

Fishtrap Sportsman's Club (O)
Attn: Harold Rowe
Route 194
Phyllis, KY 41554
Tel. 606-835-4303

French Range (O, F)
Attn: Ed Peterson
U.S. Hwy 31W
Ft. Knox, KY 40121
Tel. 502-624-2712

Knob Creek Range (O, F)
Attn: Kenny & Holly Sumner
Route 1, Box 85C
West Point, KY 40177
Tel. 502-922-4457

LOUISIANA

**American Hunter Trap &
Skeet Range (O, F)**
Attn: Tom Mincher
Covington, LA 70433
Tel. (day) 504-892-2521;
(eve) 504-845-3433

Caddo Rifle & Pistol Club (F)
Attn: Dick Gunther
Jones Mabry Road
Shreveport, LA 71105
Tel. (day) 318-221-2688;
(eve) 318-797-1511

**Florida Parishes Skeet &
Gun Assn (O)**
Attn: L. B. Ponder
Box 217, Amite, LA 70422
Tel. (day) 504-748-8025;
(eve) 504-748-6700

MAINE

**Boothbay Region Fish &
Game Assn. (O)**
Attn: Membership Director
Dover Road, Box 107
East Boothbay, ME 04544

**Buxton & Hollis Rod &
Gun Club (O, F)**
Attn: Royal Hoskins
Deer Pond Road, P.O. Box 497
Bar Mills, ME 04004
Tel. (evening) 207-727-5271

Durham Rod & Gun Club (O)
Attn: Jan Litchfield
Route 136
Freeport, ME 04210
Tel. 207-353-8487

**Freehold Lodge Club/Omega
Dev. Group (F)**
Attn: George Fennell
South Meadow Road
Perry, ME 04667
Tel. 207-726-5093

Knox County Fish & Game (F)
Attn: Manager
Alford Lake
Hope, ME 04847
Tel. (evening) 207-785-4758

Lincoln County Rifle Club (O)
Attn: Richard Varick
Business Route 1
Damariscotta, ME 04543
Tel. (evening) 207-563-3061

**Sanford-Springvale Fish & Game
Protective Assn. (O, F)**
Attn: Carl Townsend
Old Berwick Road, P.O. Box 788
Sanford, ME 04073
Tel. (day) 207-438-2608;
(eve) 207-324-9377

**Scarborough Fish &
Game Assn (O, F)**
Attn: Joe Newcomp
Holmes Road, P.O. Box 952
Scarborough, ME 04074
Tel. 207-883-2797

MARYLAND

**Bethesda-Chevy Chase Chap.
IWLA (O, F)**
Attn: Robert Chapman
Izaak Walton Way, P.O. Box 542
Poolesville, MD 20837
Tel. (evening) 301-972-7334

MASSACHUSETTS

**Fall River Rod &
Gun Club (O, F, I)**
Attn: Mike Brillo
Sanford Road
Westport, MA 02723
Tel. 617-673-4535

**Fin, Fur & Feather Club
of Mattapoisett (O, F)**
Attn: Marc Folco
P.O. Box 102
Fairhaven, MA 02719
Tel. (day) 617-993-6430
(eve) 617-995-6772

**Framingham Sportsmens
Assn. (O, F, I)**
Attn: Diane Rodger
Lumber Street
Hopkinton, MA 01748
Tel. (day) 617-435-9985;
(eve) 617-879-4466

Gardner Fish & Gun Club (O)
Attn: Allen Gross
Clark Street, Box 396
Gardner, MA 01440
Tel. (evening) 617-632-6463

**Haverhill Hound Rod &
Gun Club, Inc. (O)**
Attn: Joe Pachucki
Chadwick Road, P.O. Box 770
Haverhill, MA 01830
Tel. (day) 617-372-2552;
(eve) 617-372-0853

**Leominster Sportsman
Assn. (O, F, I)**
Attn: Victor DeFelice
1455 Elm Street, Box 484
Leominster, MA 01453

Maynard Rod & Gun Club (O, F)
Attn: Larry Hartnett
P.O. Box 339
Maynard, MA 01754
Tel. 617-897-9873

Nipmuc Rod & Gun Club (O, F)
Attn: Manager
West Main Street, Fiske Mill Road
Upton, MA 01568
Tel. 617-473-9778

**Plymouth Rod &
Gun Club (O, F)**
Attn: Dick Ragazzini
South Meadow Road, P.O. Box 3121
Plymouth, MA 02361
Tel. 617-747-1312

**Rutland Sportsmen's
Club (O, F, I)**
Attn: Manager
Pleasantdale Road
Rutland, MA 01543
Tel. 617-886-4721

Sippican Rod & Gun Club (O)
Attn: Steven Hall
Dexter Lane, P.O. Box 282
Rochester, MA 02770
Tel. 617-759-2044

**Springfield Sportsmen's
Club (O, F)**
Attn: Club Manager
Wood Hill Road
Monson, MA 01057
Tel. 413-267-9652

**Tyngsboro Sportsmen
Club (O, F, I)**
Attn: Manager
P.O. Box 65
Tyngsboro, MA 01879

Wayland Rod & Gun Club (O)
Attn: Paul Ramsey
4 Meadowview Road
Wayland, MA 01778
Tel. 617-877-4587

MICHIGAN

Cass City Gun Club (O, F)
Attn: Richard Mika
Cass City, MI 48726
Tel. (evening) 517-872-3976

Century Gun Club (O)
Attn: Walter Mills
Newberg Road
Oak Park, MI 48237
Tel. 313-541-8486

**Chick-Owa Sportsman's
Club (O, I)**
Attn: Don Bosch
Ottagon Road, P.O. Box 61
Zeeland, MI 49464
Tel. 616-772-1154

**Fenton Lakes Sportsman's
Club (I)**
Attn: John Cadiex
1140 Butcher Road, P.O. Box 188
Fenton, MI 48430
Tel. 313-629-7964

**Fin & Feather Club of Mason
County (F)**
Attn: Dick Van Atta
Darr Road, Box 402
Ludington, MI 49431
Tel. 616-843-4632

**Grand Blanc Huntsman's
Club (O)**
Attn: Bill Jones
9046 South Irish Road
Grand Blanc, MI 48439
Tel. (day) 313-236-4781;
(eve) 313-233-5392

**Isabella County Sportsmen's
Club (O, F)**
Attn: Kent Wheeler
Winn & Millbrook Roads
Winn, MI 48896
Tel. 517-866-2643

**Jackson County Outdoors
Club (O, I)**
Attn: G. William McCleery
5480 Benton Road
Jackson, MI 49201
Tel. 517-764-4931

**Lake Superior Sportsman's
Club, Inc. (I)**
Attn: Joe Kukavick
Highway M64 West
Ontonagon, MI 49953
Tel. (evening) 906-884-2768

Maple Grove Gun Club (O, I)
Attn: Doug Prevost
2-4545 21 Mile Road
Mt. Clemens, MI 48045
Tel. (day) 313-949-0020;
(eve) 313-949-1430

Munith Rod & Gun Club (O)
Attn: William Rupright
Fitchburg Road
Munith, MI 49259

Tel. (day) 517-569-2099;
(eve) 527-788-8478

**New Buffalo Rod &
Gun Club (O, F)**
Attn: Ed Kliss
Kruger Road
Union Pier, MI 49129
Tel. 616-469-1624

**Portage Lake
Sportsmen's Club (F)**
Attn: William Hockings
Chassell-Painesdale Road, P.O. Box
56
Chassell, MI 49916
Tel. 906-482-5311

Qua-Ke-Zik Club (O, F)
Attn: John Black
Foreman Road
Lowell, MI 49331
Tel. 616-897-5128

**Saginaw Field &
Stream Club (O, F)**
Attn: Charles Duncan
Gleaner Road, P.O. Box 2092
Saginaw, MI 48605
Tel. 517-793-0772

Southern Michigan Gun Club (O)
Attn: Robert Himebauch
809 E. Crosstown Parkway
Kalamazoo, MI 49001
Tel. 616-344-5964

**Tony's Gun Shop &
Range, Inc. (O)**
Attn: George Hewitt
23031 Pennsylvania Avenue
Wyandotte, MI 48192
Tel. 313-283-0030

**Tulip City Rod &
Gun Club (O, F)**
Attn: Steve Vanderhill
Riley Street
Holland, MI 49424
Tel. 616-392-3568

**Wetern Wayne County
Conservation Assn. (O, F)**
Attn: Robert Laich

6700 Napier Road
Plymouth, MI 48170
Tel. (day) 313-425-1685;
(eve) 313-453-9843

MINNESOTA

Buffalo Gun Club (O)
Attn: Wally Shelstad
Highway 55 E
Buffalo, MN 55313
Tel. 612-682-4585

**East Grand Forks Rod &
Gun Club (O, F)**
Attn: Greg Strausbaugh
P.O. Box 87
E. Grand Forks, MN 56721
Tel. (day) 701-777-2577
(eve) 701-772-8123

**Gopher Rifle &
Revolver Club, Inc. (O)**
Attn: E. M. Berntson
P.O. Box 18023
Minneapolis, MN 55418
Tel. 612-571-1618

**Hancock
Sportsmen's Club (O, F)**
Attn: Larry Krupke
433 Pacific Avenue
Hancock, MN 56244
Tel. (day) 612-392-5178;
(eve) 612-392-5320

**Mid-Range Marksmanship
Center (O, I)**
Attn: Stuart Anderson
Marksmanship Center Road
Hibbing, MN 55746
Tel. (day) 218-262-1093;
(eve) 218-263-5126

**Minnetonka
Sportsmen's Club (O)**
Attn: Ed Sakry
County Road 15, P.O. Box 351
Mound, MN 55364
Tel. (evening) 612-474-6338

**Montgomery
Sportsmens Club (O)**
Attn: Steve Pagel

Highway 21 & 5th Street South
Montgomery, MN 56069
Tel. (day) 612-364-5431;
(eve) 612-364-8959

Oakdale Gun Club (O)
Attn: Dick Bauer
10386 10th Street North
Lake Elmo, MN 55042
Tel. 612-459-5073

**United Northern Sportsmens
Club of Minnesota (O)**
Attn: Ralph Levine
8755 Rice Lake Road
Duluth, MN 55803
Tel. 218-525-7181

MISSISSIPPI

**Leake County
Sportsmen's Club (O)**
Attn: James Freeny
Route 3
Carthage, MS 39051
Tel. 601-267-9202

Lynn Creek Hunting Club (O, F)
Attn: Wayne Boler
Section Line Road
Union, MS 39365
Tel. (evening) 601-656-7543

Natchez Trace Gun Club (O)
Attn: Paul Floyd
County Road
Houston, MS 38851
Tel. (day) 601-456-2381;
(eve) 601-456-4612

Starkville Gun Club (O)
Attn: Gary Bunner
Starkville, MS 39759
Tel. (day) 601-323-3542;
(eve) 601-324-2125

MISSOURI

**Buzzard Glory
Hunting Lodge (O, F)**
Attn: Russell Turner
Weatherby, MO 64497
Tel. (day) 816-749-5416;
(eve) 816-749-5443

**Green Valley Rifle &
Pistol Club (O)**
Attn: Don Martin
P.O. Box 162
Columbia, MO 65205

Gun Exchange Club (F)
Attn: Manager
Highway 67N
Poplar Bluff, MO 63901
Tel. 314-686-3200

Hi Point Hunting Club (O)
Attn: Alan Guffey
Breckenridge, MO 64625
Tel. 816-644-5708

**Mid America
Game Bird Assn. (O)**
Attn: Jon Nee
636 East 97 Street
Kansas City, MO 64131
Tel. 816-941-2472

**Missouri Gun &
Quail Club, Inc. (O)**
Attn: Mel Treu
County Road F, P.O. Box 91
Wright City, MO 63390
Tel. 312-486-5111

The Bull's Eye (I)
Attn: Ron Sperber
3676 Market Street
St. Louis, MO 63110
Tel. 314-535-3555

MONTANA

**Billings Rod &
Gun Club (O, F)**
Attn: Manager
Box 33
Billings, MT 59102

**Colstrip Rod &
Gun Club (O, F, I)**
Attn: Glen Westervelt
Highway 39
Colstrip, MT 59323
Tel. (day) 406-748-2533;
(eve) 406-748-2509

NEBRASKA

Big Mac Sports Club (O, F)
Attn: Manager
315 East A
Ogallala, NE 69153

Central City Sportsmans Club (O, F)
Attn: Bob Cline
Central City, NE 68826
Tel. (evening) 308-946-2861

Karp & Krow Club (O)
Attn: Gerald John
Old River Road
Ord, NE 68862

**Lincoln Chapter, Izaak Walton
League of America (O)**
Attn: Delmer Miller
RR 1, Box 101C
Bennet, NE 68317
Tel. 402-488-1640

NEVADA

**White Pine
Shooting Complex (O, I)**
Attn: Ed Deschamps
South Industrial Road,
P.O. Box 1002
Ely, NV 89301
Tel. 702-289-3231

NEW HAMPSHIRE

Associated Sportsman Club (O)
Attn: Carl Baldwin
Royalston Road
Fitz William, NH 03447

Chester Rod & Gun Club (F, I)
Attn: Edward Fallon
Route 102
Raymond, NH 03038
Tel. 603-434-0577

**Major Waldron
Sportsmens Assn. (O, I)**
Attn: Lester Waterhouse
Route 9, P.O. Box 314
Barrington, NH 03825
Tel. (day) 603-652-7061;
(eve) 603-664-5544

**Nashua Fish &
Game Club Inc. (F)**
Attn: Wilfred Oikle
Manchester Street
Nashua, NH 03060
Tel. (evening) 603-889-5895

Piscatague Fish & Game (O, F)
Attn: Manager
Tuttle Lane
Greenland, NH 03801

**Plaistow Fish &
Game Club (O, F)**
Attn: Robert Weber
May Ray Avenue
Plaistow, NH 03865
Tel. (day) 603-382-9773;
(eve) 603-382-8698

NEW JERSEY

Antler Gun Club (O)
Attn: Peter Rapetti
Weymouth Road
Ventnor City, NJ 08406
Tel. (day) 201-823-9830;
(eve) 201-823-3152

Fin Fur & Feather Club (O)
Attn: John Sichik
Yardville, NJ 08610
Tel. (day) 201-298-6300;
(eve) 201-581-0041

Mullica Hill Rifle & Pistol Club (O)
Attn: Paul Dare
111 Ward Avenue
Audubon, NJ 08106

**Quinton
Sportsmens Club, Inc. (O, F)**
Attn: Johnathan Sparks
Jericho Road
Quinton, NJ 08072
Tel. (day) 609-339-3876
(eve) 609-935-7014

**United Sportsmens
Assn. of N.A. (O, F, I)**
Attn: Skip Myers
Elmer Greenville Road
Elmer, NJ 08080
Tel. 201-589-7218

NEW MEXICO

Angel Fire Sportsmans Club (O)
Attn: Manager
Box 181
Angel Fire, NM 87710
Tel. (day) 505-377-2416;
(eve) 505-377-2590

**Carlsbad
Sportsmans Club (O, F, I)**
Attn: Tom Vining
P.O. Box 1603
Carlsbad, NM 88220
Tel. 505-887-1570

Inn of the Mountain Gods (O)
Attn: Johnathan Adams
P.O. Box 259
Mescalero, NM 88340
Tel. (day) 505-257-5141;
(eve) 505-257-9770

Picacho Gun Club (O)
Attn: J. Eggenberger
P.O. Box 594
Las Cruces, NM 88001
Tel. 505-522-6445

NEW YORK

**Allied Sportsmen
of Western NY (O, F, I)**
Attn: Frankl Merrill
12846 Clinton Street
Alden, NY 14004
Tel. 716-937-3469

Calverton Shooting Range (O)
Attn: Manager
395 Nugent Drive
Calverton, NY 11933
Tel. 516-727-9881

Camden Rod & Gun Club (O)
Attn: David VanDyke
Moran Post Road, Box 38A1
Canastoth, NY 13316
Tel. 315-697-9009

**Classic and Modern Arms
Unlimited (O, F, I)**
Attn: Rufus Newman
P.O. Box 28185

Queens Village, NY 11428
Tel. 718-843-1182

**Coxsackie
Sportsmens Club (O, F, I)**
Attn: Jack Larson
Schoolhouse Road
Coxsackie, NY 12051
Tel. 518-945-1284

Creekside Gun Shop (O, I)
Attn: Manager
Mail Street
Holcomb, NY 14469
Tel. 716-657-6131

Galway Fish & GameClub (F, I)
Attn: Tom Nowicki
Route 29
Galway, NY 12074
Tel. (evening) 518-882-9075

Hartland Conservationist Club (O)
Attn: Ken Berner
Orangeport Road
Gasport, NY 14067
Tel. 716-772-7372

**Hendrick Hudson Fish & Game
Club (O, F)**
Attn: Arthur Milanese
Route 66
Poestenkill, NY 12140
Tel. 518-477-9257

Huntington Rifle & Pistol (O)
Attn: Jack Fass
Spagnoli Road
Melville, NY 11749
Tel. 516-531-8474

Kodiak Hunting Assn. (O)
Attn: Nicholas Loter
6718 Ft. Hamilton Parkway
Brooklyn, NY 11204
Tel. (evening) 718-232-6238

**Marbletown
Sportsman's Club (O, F)**
Attn: Paul Brasky
Peak & Scarawan Road
Stone Ridge, NY 12401
Tel. (day) 914-687-7621
(eve) 914-331-9415

**Massena Rifle &
Gun Club (O, F, I)**
Attn: John Hurd
Route 37
Massena, NY 13662
Tel. 315-769-9207

**Nassau Sportsmans
Club (O, F, I)**
Attn: Thomas Gill
Boyce Road
Nassau, NY 12123
Tel. (day) 516-766-2680;
(eve) 518-766-2558

**Oakfield Rod &
Gun Club, Inc. (O)**
Attn: Lou Lagoe
Maltby Road
Oakfield, NY 14125
Tel. 716-948-5686

Oneida Rifle Club (O)
Attn: Joseph Sochan
Randal Road
Oneida, NY 13421
Tel. (evening) 315-363-2092

R C Club (F, I)
Attn: Vic Pape
New Baltimore Road
Ravena, NY 12158
Tel. (evening) 518-767-2029

**Richmond Boro
Gun Club (O, F)**
Attn: Anthony Racioppo
Claypit Road
Staten Island, NY 10314
Tel. 212-943-2900

**Salem Fish &
Game Club (O, I)**
Attn: Rupert Jennings
Salem, NY 12865
Tel. (evening) 518-677-2691

**Stuyvesant Rod &
Gun Club (I)**
Attn: Sebastian Pepi
64-69 Dryharbor Road
Middle Village, NY 11379
Tel. (evening) 718-326-7350

**Tonawandas
Sportsmens Club, Inc. (O, I)**
Attn: Paul Gilbert
Killian Road
Tonawanda, NY 14120
Tel. (day) 716-705-1909;
(eve) 716-692-2161

Trenton Fish & Game Club (O, F)
Attn: Herbert Chapple
Utica Road, P.O. Box 113
Holland Patent, NY 13304
Tel. 315-865-4136

**Tri-States Rod &
Gun Club, Inc. (O, F)**
Attn: Manager
North Orange Street
Pt. Jervis, NY 12771

Turnpike Rod & Gun Club (O)
Attn: Al Dwyer
County Route 410
Westerlo, NY 12054
Tel. (evening) 518-439-3997

Victory Rifle & Pistol Club (I)
Attn: Edward Sofo
Palisade Street & Lily Pond Avenue
Staten Island, NY 10314
Tel. (evening) 718-761-7591

**Watertown
Sportsmen, Inc. (O, F)**
Attn: Andre' Charlebois
Dry Hill Road
Watertown, NY 13601
Tel. 315-788-3924

**West Albany Rod &
Gun Club, Inc. (O, F, I)**
Attn: Arnis Zilgme
100 Willoughby Drive
Albany, NY 12205
Tel. (day) 518-783-2704;
(eve) 518-869-7934

**Willsboro Fish &
Game Club, Inc. (O, F)**
Attn: Wayne Ashline
Fish & Game Road
Willsboro, NY 12996
Tel. (day) 518-963-4273;
(eve) 518-873-2198

NORTH CAROLINA

Lenoir County Wildlife Club (O)
Attn: Freddie Dawson
17 Summerhill Terrace
Kinston, NC 28501
Tel. 919-522-3387

Old Hickory Gun Club (O)
Attn: Louis Levy
Dalewood Road
Rocky Mount, NC 27804
Tel. (day) 919-443-8043;
(eve) 919-443-5911

**Seymour-Johnson
AFB Gun Club (O, F)**
Attn: Ben Ansedt
Bldg. 2010, Seymour-Johnson AFB
Goldsboro, NC 27520
Tel. 919-736-5405

NORTH DAKOTA

**Grand Forks AFB
Rod & Gun (O)**
Attn: Gary Braun
Grand Forks AFB
Grand Forks, ND 58205
Tel. (evening) 701-746-7851

OHIO

**A&A Shooting and
Hunting Club (O)**
Attn: Al Spolarich
12006 Fenstermaker Road
Nelson Township, OH 44231
Tel. 216-548-8753

Ashland Lake Gun Club (O)
Attn: Terry Snyder
Route 42
West Salem, OH 44287
Tel. 216-749-0769

**Ball and Arrow Primitive
Weapons (F)**
Attn: Manager
Route 39
Roswell, OH 44654

Captina Sportsman Club (O)
Attn: Clarence Harrigan

Route 7
Powhatan Point, OH 43942

**Conneaut Fish &
Game Club (O, F)**
Attn: Virginia Gagat
Keefus Road
Conneaut, OH 44030
Tel. 216-593-3028

**Defiance County
Fish & Game Club (O, F)**
Attn: Warren Spencer
State Route 15
Defiance, OH 43512

**East Palestine
Sportsmen Club (O)**
Attn: Chuck McGuire
State Line Road
E. Palestine, OH 44413
Tel. 216-426-2393

**Eastern Ohio
Conservation Club (F)**
Attn: J. Hellwig
RD 4, West Calla Road
Salem, OH 44460
Tel. 216-533-4371

**Erie County
Conservation League (O)**
Attn: John McClure
US Route 250, P.O. Box 476
Sandusky, OH 44870
Tel. 419-626-6526

Fairfield Sportsmen's Assn. (O, F)
Attn: Jeffrey Schaefer
6501 River Road
Harrison, OH 45030
Tel. 513-793-3639

**Fulton County
Sportsmens Club (I)**
Attn: Lonnie Blosser
County Road 14
Wauseon, OH 43567
Tel. (day) 419-337-3422;
(eve) 419-337-7146

**Leipsic Fishing &
Hunting Assn (O, F)**
Attn: Richard Okuley

RD H, Box 88
Ottawa, OH 45875
Tel. (day) 419-538-6021;
(eve) 419-539-6592

Madison County
Fish & Game Assn. (O, F)
Attn: David Coverdale
Madison Lake
London, OH 43140

Meeker Sportsman Club (O)
Attn: Douglas Hickman
State Route 309
Marion, OH 43392
Tel. (day) 614-499-3757
(eve) 614-382-4335

Middletown
Sportsmen's Club (O)
Attn: Bert Walls
6945 Michael Road
Middletown, OH 45042
Tel. 513-422-5112

Milford Gun Club (O)
Attn: Fred Schuerman
Milford, OH 45150
Tel. 513-831-4667

Oak Harbor
Conservation Club (O)
Attn: Milton Mann
South Gordon Road, P.O. Box 144
Oak Harbor, OH 43449
Tel. (day) 419-837-9168;
(eve) 419-898-0518

Pickaway County
Sportsmen, Inc. (O, F)
Attn: Dick Redman
8100 State Route 22
Circleville, OH 43154
Tel. 614-474-4882

Portage-Summit
Field & Stream (O)
Attn: Kenneth Zeigler
8504 State Route 224, P.O. Box 3036
Cuyahoga Falls, OH 44223
Tel. 216-773-5701

Stryker Sportsman Club (O)
Attn: Ronald Walker
309 West Hamilton Street
Bryan, OH 43506
Tel. 419-636-2727

Tri-County Sportsmen's League
Attn: Roland Chaney
Box 124
New Comerstown, OH 43832
Tel. 614-545-9245

Vienna Fish &
Game Club (O, F, I)
Attn: Manager
Route 193
Youngstown, OH 44512

Williams County Conservation
League (O, F, I)
Attn: Hobart McKarns
Bryan, OH 43506
Tel. (evening) 419-636-1386

Wolf Creek
Sportmens Assn. (O, F)
Attn: Thomas Rymers
349 Teachout Road
Curtice, OH 43412
Tel. 419-693-3985

OKLAHOMA

Kiamichi Rifle & Pistol Club (O)
Attn: Manager
P.O. Box 1931
Idabel, OK 74745
Tel. (day) 405-286-6667;
(eve) 405-286-2774

McCurtain County
Archery Assn. (O, F)
Attn: Mike Love
Kulli Road
Idabel, OK 74745
Tel. (day) 405-286-2176;
(eve) 405-286-3072

Oil Capital Rod &
Gun Club (O, F)
Attn: Richard Erickson
P.O. Box 52131
Tulsa, OK 74152
Tel. 918-438-2326

Tulsa Red Castle Gun Club (O)
Attn: Robert Hinds
P.O. Box 4302
Tulsa, OK 74159
Tel. (day) 918-581-7300;
(eve) 918-743-5276

OREGON

Josephine County Sportsman's
Assn. (O, F, I)
Attn: Range Master
P.O. Box 663, Sportsmans Park
Grants Pass, OR 97526
Tel. 503-476-2040

Tri-County Gun Club (O)
Attn: Donald Williams
P.O. Box 372
Sherwood, OR 97140
Tel. 503-642-5873

PENNSYLVANIA

Allegheny Country
Rifle Club (O, F)
Attn: Jack Schell
112 Ramage Road
Pittsburgh, PA 15214
Tel. (day) 412-821-9942;
(eve) 412-931-3888

Arrick Sportsmen's
Club (O, F)
Attn: Mike Tumas
Ridge Road, Box 350
Library, PA 15219
Tel. (day) 412-431-5326;
(eve) 412-835-5184

Bob's Gun Shop &
Indoor Range (O)
Attn: Bob McDowell
U S Route 99
McKean, PA 16426
Tel. 814-476-7523

Bobtown Rod &
Gun Club (O, F, I)
Attn: Manager
Franklin Street, Box 36
Bobtown, PA 15315
Tel. (evening) 412-839-7460

**Boyertown Rod &
Gun Assn. (O, F)**
Attn: Bob Lewis
P.O. Box 296
Pottstown, PA 19464
Tel. 215-326-1370

**Buchanan Valley Rod & Gun
Club (F)**
Attn: Harold Cook
Club Road
Arendsville, PA 17307
Tel. (day) 717-761-2730;
(eve) 717-677-9357

**Bucks County Fish &
Game Assn. (O, F, I)**
Attn: William Johnson
Turk & Wells Road
Doylestown, PA 19040
Tel. 215-672-2374

**Buffalo Valley
Sportsmen's Assn. (F)**
Attn: Allen Zimmerman
Sportsmens Club Road
Mifflinburg, PA 17844
Tel. (evening) 717-966-0173

Bull Creek Rod & Gun Club (O)
Attn: Wilbur Shotton
Bull Creek Road
Tarentum, PA 15084
Tel. 412-224-4442

**Butler City Rifle & Pistol Club
(O, F, I)**
Attn: Darrell Filges
East Butler Road
East Butler, PA 16029
Tel. (evening) 412-285-8181

**Cochranton Area
Sportsman Club (O, F)**
Attn: Russell Barngrover
Route 173
Cochranton, PA 16314
Tel. (day) 814-724-1400;
(eve) 814-425-7967

**Crowfoot Rod &
Gun Club (O, F, I)**
Attn: Robert Learzaf
Crowfoot Road, P.O. Box 319

Murrysville, PA 15668
Tel. (day) 215-793-3095
(eve) 215-322-9315

Dunbar Sportsmens Club (O)
Attn: John Maddas
1st Avenue, Bryson Hill
Dunbar, PA 15431
Tel. (evening) 412-277-4258

**Evans City
Sportsmen's Club (F, I)**
Attn: Gary Rader
Box 172
Evans City, PA 16033

**Falls Township Rifle & Pistol
Assn. (O, F)**
Attn: President
354 Newbold Road, P.O. Box 11
Fairless Hills, PA 19030
Tel. 215-295-6565

**Friedensville Rod &
Gun Club (O)**
Attn: Mike Mish
RD 3, Box 179
Center Valley, PA 18034
Tel. (evening) 215-791-4666

**Gem City Gun
Club, Inc. (O, F, I)**
Attn: W. David Atkinson
P.O. Box 7079
Wesleyville, PA 16510
Tel. 814-899-6823

**Greater Pittsburgh
Trap & Skeet (O, F)**
Attn: Tex Freund
Bulger, PA 15019
Tel. 412-796-1251

**Green Hills Sportsmens
Club (O)**
Attn: Edward Freese
Route 10
Morgantown, PA 19540
Tel. 215-856-7424

**Greencastle
Sportsman's Assn. (O, F, I)**
Attn: T. D. Zullinger
P.O. Box 193

Greencastle, PA 17225
Tel. 717-597-2815

Guthsville Rod & Gun Club (O)
Attn: Secretary
Valley G, Hausdohl Road
Orefield, PA 18069
Tel. 215-395-9121

**Harrisburg Hunters &
Anglers (O, F, I)**
Attn: Lee Leidich
6611 Hunters Run Road
Harrisburg, PA 17111
Tel. 717-545-1361

**Hollidaysburg Consolidated
Sportsmens Assn. (O, F)**
Attn: Jimmie Miller
Route 22
Hollidaysburg, PA 16648
Tel. 814-742-8784

**Jenner Community
Sportsmen Assn. (O, F)**
Attn: David Livingston
Laurel Hill Mountain
Jennerstown, PA 15531
Tel. 814-629-9127

Keystone Sportsmen's Club (O)
Attn: Randy McCoy
RD 1
Creekside, PA 15732
Tel. 412-783-6638

**Lake Edinboro Sportsmen's
League (O, F)**
Attn: John Amy
Edinboro, PA 16412
Tel. 814-734-7784

**Lappawinzo Fish &
Game Assn. (O, F)**
Attn: Andrew Hensel
Main Street
Northampton, PA 18067
Tel. (evening) 215-262-8732

**Little Fishing Cr.
Rod & Gun Club (O, F)**
Attn: Manager
P.O. Box 424
Millville, PA 17846

**Logan's Ferry
Sportsmen's Club (O)**
Attn: H. L. Haerr
Sardis Road, P.O. Box 14047
Plum Boro, PA 15239

Manheim Sportsmen's Assn. (F, I)
Attn: Edward Pfoutz
Oak Tree Road
Manheim, PA 17545
Tel. 717-665-2587

**McDonald Sportsmen
Assn. (O, F, I)**
Attn: F. J. Blanchard
Nobletown Road, P.O. Box 130
McDonald, PA 15057
Tel. (day) 412-796-2271;
(eve) 412-926-2158

**Mill Creek Sportsmens
Assn., Inc. (O, F, I)**
Attn: Judy VanDusen
1877 Windy Hill Road
Lancaster, PA 17602
Tel. (evening) 717-397-0496

**Mt. Joy Sportsmen's
Assn., Inc. (O)**
Attn: Jim Hoffmaster
P.O. Box 83
Mt. Joy, PA 17552
Tel. (evening) 717-273-8574

Murrysville Gun Club (F)
Attn: William Funk
Gun Club Road
Murrysville, PA 15668
Tel. 412-327-0551

**Northern York City
Game & Fish Assn. (F)**
Attn: Gary Wiley
Bremer Road
York, PA 17403
Tel. 717-843-9592

**Paletown Rod &
Gun Club, Inc. (O)**
Attn: Henry Krikory
P.O. Box 237
Quakertown, PA 18951
Tel. 215-536-6696

**Parks Township
Sportsmen's Club (O)**
Attn: Don Sproull
RD 1, Box 3398
Leechburg, PA 15656
Tel. 412-842-2393

Pine Creek Sportsmen's Club (O)
Attn: David Reed
Box 192
Templeton, PA 16259
Tel. 412-868-2392

Pine Run Sportsmen's Club (O, I)
Attn: James DeLarre
Blackwoods Road
Freedom, PA 15074

**Pitcairn-Monroeville
Sportsmen's Club (O, F)**
Attn: Manager
Johnston Road, P.O. Box 145
Pitcairn, PA 15140
Tel. (evening) 717-793-4967

**Quemahoning
Rod and Gun Club (I)**
Attn: John Adams
RD 1
Hooversville, PA 15936
Tel. (evening) 814-798-8661

Renton Rod & Gun Club (O)
Attn: Louis Rosen
Plum Street Ext.
Renton, PA 15239
Tel. 412-793-0770

Richland Sportsmen's Assn. (O, I)
Attn: Leonard Leschinsky
P.O. Box 16
Wildwood, PA 15091

**Ridge & Valley
Rod & Gun Club (O)**
Attn: Bob Tucker
South Blue Church Road, P.O. Box 2
Coopersburg, PA 18036
Tel. (evening) 215-282-4810

**Saegertown Area Sportsmen's
Club (O, F)**
Attn: Dale Beers
Venango Road

Saegertown, PA 16433
Tel. (evening) 814-763-4577

**Salisbury-Elk Lick
Hunting Club (O, I)**
Attn: John Zimmerman
Salisbury, PA 15558
Tel. (evening) 814-662-2082

**Shannock Valley Sportsmen's
Club (O, F, I)**
Attn: Manager
Yatesboro, PA 16263

**Shenecoy
Sportsmen Club (O, F)**
Attn: Gary Shoemaker
Route 26
McConnellstown, PA 16647
Tel. (evening) 814-658-2155

**Slippery Rock
Sportsmen's Club (O, F)**
Attn: William Matthews
Kiester Road
Slippery Rock, PA 16057
Tel. (evening) 412-794-6069

**Souderton-Harleysville
Game Fish & Forestry Assn. (F)**
Attn: Richard Schneider
Whites Mill Road
Lansdale, PA 19446
Tel. 215-855-9339

**Springtown
Rod & Gun Club (O)**
Attn: Paul Miller
Springtown, PA 18081
Tel. 215-346-8473

**Stockertown
Rod & Gun Club (O, I)**
Attn: Manager
Lafever Road
Stockertown, PA 18083
Tel. 215-759-9255

**Templeton
Rod & Gun Club (O, F)**
Attn: Kent Greenwalt
Templeton, PA 16259
Tel. 412-868-2183

Trafford Gun Club (O, F)
Attn: Hank Pascoe
First Street Ext., P.O. Box 3
Trafford, PA 15085
Tel. (day) 412-681-9159
(eve) 412-372-6230

Trent Rod & Gun Club (O)
Attn: Dale Pritts
Seven Springs Road
Somerset, PA 15501
Tel. (evening) 814-443-4457

Tri-County Sports Club (F)
Attn: Dale Bennett
Silvania, PA 18623
Tel. 717-869-1363

York & Adams County Game & Fish Assn. (O, F, I)
Attn: Rudy Ecker
Country Club Road
Abbotstown, PA 17331
Tel. (evening) 717-632-5249

York Chapter, IWLA (O, F)
Attn: William Shaffer
Ironstone Hill Road
Loganville, PA 17342
Tel. (evening) 717-428-2883

RHODE ISLAND

Wallum Lake Rod & Gun Club (F)
Attn: David Mills
Brook Road, P.O. Box 489
Harrisville, RI 02839
Tel. 401-568-3843

SOUTH DAKOTA

Black Hills Rod & Gun Club (O, F)
Attn: Will Cooper
Main Street, Box 436
Lead, SD 57754
Tel. (day) 605-584-3527
(eve) 605-584-3379

Brookings Rifle & Pistol Club (I)
Attn: Tom Raines
221 Main Avenue
Brooking, SD 57001

Tel. (day) 605-692-6294
(eve) 605-693-4086

Hecla Sportsman Club (O, F)
Attn: Jay Osterloh
Highway 37
Hecla, SD 57446
Tel. (day) 605-994-2050
(eve) 605-994-2512

Mellette County Sportsman's Club (I)
Attn: Jeannine Woodward
Highway 44
White River, SD 57579
Tel. (day) 605-259-3135
(eve) 605-259-3255

Milbank Trap Club (I)
Attn: David McCulloch
Highway 15
Milbank, SD 57252
Tel. (day) 605-432-6793
(eve) 605-432-5091

TENNESSEE

Bend of the River Public Shooting Center (O, F)
Attn: Charlie Pardue
Highway 136
Cookeville, TN 38501
Tel. 615-528-2010

Cleveland Hunting, Rifle, and Pistol Club (O, F)
Attn: Secretary
Leadmine Road, P.O. Box 3661
Cleveland, TN 37311
Tel. (day) 615-476-3750
(eve) 615-476-8810

Down Range, Inc. (O)
Attn: Ron Venn
602 Gallaher View Drive
Kingston, TN 37763
Tel. 615-376-1138

Henry Horton Skeet & Trap Range (O, F)
Attn: Charles Rogers
Highway 31
Chapel Hill, TN 37091
Tel. (day) 615-359-4531
(eve) 615-359-1236

Memphis Sport Shooting Assn., Inc. (O, F)
Attn: James Norris
9428 Old Brownsville Road
Memphis, TN 38134
Tel. 901-829-3905

TEXAS

A Place to Shoot (O)
Attn: Ralph Voss
Moursund Boulevard
San Antonio, TX 78221
Tel. 512-628-1888

Arlington Sportsman's Club (O, F)
Attn: Joe Schaefer
P.O. Box 117
Arlington, TX 76010
Tel. (day) 817-460-1102
(eve) 817-274-3752

Camp Cullen (YMCA)
Attn: Neil Rosenbaum
FM 356
Trinity, TX 75862
Tel. 409-594-2274

Clear Creek Gun Range (O)
Attn: Ernest Randall
306 Crystal
League City, TX 77573
Tel. (day) 713-337-1722
(eve) 713-554-6391

Corpus Christi Pistol & Rifle Club (O)
Attn: Richard Appleman
FM 763
Corpus Christi, TX 78415
Tel. 512-852-1212

Elm Fork Shooting Park, Inc. (F)
Attn: Dennis Reed
10751 Luna Road
Dallas, TX 75220
Tel. (day) 214-556-0103
(eve) 214-401-0303

Fort Bliss Rod & Gun Club (O)
Attn: Roy Kline
P.O. Box 6118, Bldg. 11617
Ft. Bliss, TX 79916
Tel. 915-562-8956

**Galveston Rifle &
Pistol Club, Inc. (O)**
Attn: Glenn Hood
P.O. Box 3001
Galveston, TX 77552
Tel. 409-744-2887

Lake Houston Gun Club (O)
Attn: Jim Nauter
15220 Garrett Road
Houston, TX 77044
Tel. (day) 713-456-9009
(eve) 713-451-6549

**Laredo Rifle &
Pistol Club (O, F)**
Attn: Jim McManus
P.O. Box 1771
Laredo, TX 78044
Tel. 512-727-6267

Midland Shooters Assn. (O, F)
Attn: Gene Love
FM 1213
Midland, TX 79711
Tel. 915-563-4479

Orange Gun Club (O)
Attn: James Stimac
Route 8, Box 1298
Orange, TX 97630
Tel. 409-883-5771

Palacios Gun Club (O)
Attn: Gene House
Palacios, TX 77465
Tel. 512-972-3985

**Targetmaster Indoor
Shooting Center (I)**
Attn: Manager
1717 South Jupiter
Garland, TX 75042
Tel. 214-343-4545

UTAH

Hill Rod & Gun Club (O, F)
Attn: R. D. Walker
P.O. Box 187
Clearfield, UT 84015
Tel. (day) 801-777-6767
(eve) 801-545-1405

**Lee Kay Center
for Hunter Education (O, F)**
Attn: Brad Bird
6000 W. 2100 S.
Salt Lake City, UT 84120
Tel. 801-972-1326

VERMONT

Sportsmen, Inc. (O, F)
Attn: David Putnam
Guilford Street, P.O. Box 313
Brattleboro, VT 05301

VIRGINIA

**Arlington/Fairfax Chapter, Izaak
Walton League of America (O, F)**
Attn: Gerry Stephenson
Mt. Olive Road, P.O. Box 366
Centreville, VA 22020
Tel. (day) 202-694-3995
(eve) 703-978-8332

**Arrowhead
Gun Club (O)**
Attn: Milton Mills
Route 49
Chase City, VA 23924
Tel. 804-372-4581

National Sportsman Assn. (O)
Attn: Charles Rogers
P.O. Box 190
Woodbridge, VA 22194
Tel. (day) 703-494-2593
(eve) 703-690-1543

**Nottaway Wildlife
Assn. Range (O)**
Attn: Michael Clifford
P.O. Box 81
Nottaway, VA 23955
Tel. 804-645-9315

**Portsmouth-Norfolk
County Chapter of Izaak Walton
League Assn. (O)**
Attn: Treasurer
Skeet Road, P.O. Box 6276
Portsmouth, VA 23703
Tel. 804-484-0287

Stonewall Rifle & Pistol Club (O)
Attn: Manager
P.O. Box 441
Staunton, VA 24401

WASHINGTON

Cedar River Bowmen
Attn: Dan West
SE Duthie Hill Road
Issaquah, WA 98027
Tel. (day) 206-281-6383
(eve) 206-883-6773

Granite Falls Sportsmen Club (O)
Attn: Manager
Box 293
Granite Falls, WA 98252

**Jefferson County
Sportsmen's Club (O, F)**
Attn: Michael Edwards
Gun Club Road, P.O. Box 737
Port Townsend, WA 98368
Tel. 206-385-1301

Kenmore Gun Ranges (O, F, I)
Attn: Range Master
1031-228th SW
Bothell, WA 98021
Tel. 206-481-8686

Marksman Range (I)
Attn: Manager
11003 Canyon Road
E. Puyallup, WA 98373
Tel. 206-535-4363

Nanook Skeet/Trap Range (O, F)
Attn: Jack Ross
P.O. Box 546
Ft. Greely, WA 98733

Tacoma Sportsmen's Club (O, F)
Attn: Office Secretary
16409 E. Canyon Road
Puyallup, WA 98373
Tel. 206-537-6151

WEST VIRGINIA

**Kincheloe Pheasant Farm &
Shooting Preserve (O)**
Attn: Paul Hughes

Jane Lew, WV 26378
Tel. (evening) 304-884-7431

WISCONSIN

**Dalton Rod &
Gun Club (O, F)**
Attn: Rellis Morgan
Box 67
Dalton, WI 53926

**Door County
Rod & Gun Club (I)**
Attn: Conrad Eggers
Mathey Road
Sturgeon Bay, WI 54235
Tel. (evening) 414-494-1009

**Indianhead Rifle and
Pistol Club (F)**
Attn: Richard Coquillette
806 River Street
Spooner, WI 54801
Tel. (day) 715-635-2483
(eve) 715-635-8208

**Jones
Shooting Center (I)**
Attn: Kevin Jones
856 North Main Street
Seymour, WI 54165
Tel. 414-833-7078

**La Farge
Trapshooters (I)**
Attn: La Verne Campbell
Bickle Road
La Farge, WI 54539
Tel. (day) 608-625-2180
(eve) 608-625-4301

**Lakeview
Trap Club (O)**
Attn: JoAnn Karklus
South 80 W, 14401 Schultz Lane
Muskego, WI 53150
Tel. (day) 414-679-3766
(eve) 414-422-9025

**Luxemburg
Sportsmen's Club (O, F, I)**
Attn: R. F. Stodola
Highway 54
Luxemburg, WI 54217

**Manitowoc
Gun Club (O, F)**
Attn: Mike Wicklacz
Clover Road, P.O. Box 201
Manitowoc, WI 54220
Tel. (day) 414-683-2498
(eve) 414-682-6555

**McMiller
Sports Center (O, F)**
Attn: Manager
Kettle Moraine State Forest
Eagle, WI 53119
Tel. 414-594-2182

Reedsburg Outdoor Club (O, F, I)
Attn: William Friede
Luedtke Road
Reedsburg, WI 53959
Tel. (day) 608-524-4341
(eve) 608-524-3427

Smoky Lake Reserve (O)
Attn: P. C. Christiansen
Highway 17
Phelps, WI 54554
Tel. 715-545-2333

**Springbrook
Sportsman's Club (O)**
Attn: Manager
Springbro
ok Road, P.O. Box 589
Oshkosh, WI 54901

**St. Croix Valley
Rod & Gun Club (O, F, I)**
Attn: Manager
1042 Sommers Street North
Hudson, WI 54016
Tel. 715-386-9955

**Stoughton Conservation
Club (O, F, I)**
Attn: David Everett
984 Collins Road
Stoughton, WI 53589
Tel. (evening) 608-873-8537

Superior Shooting Sports (O)
Attn: Timothy Magnuson
1313 Grand Avenue
Superior, WI 54880
Tel. 715-394-7893

**Triangle Sportsmen's
Club, Inc. (O)**
Attn: H. Kurtz
Town Line Road
E. Troy, WI 53120
Tel. (evening) 414-642-5416

**Van Dyne Sportsmen's
Club (O, F)**
Attn: Manager
Winnebago-Fond du Lac Road,
P.O. Box 8
Van Dyne, WI 54979
Tel. 414-688-5595

Appendix D

Government Regulating Agencies

The following listings give addresses of state agencies in the USA and agencies in the Canadian provinces. (Source: National Wildlife Federation.)

STATE AGENCIES

Alabama Dept. of Conservation
Division of Game and Fish
64 North Union Street
Montgomery, AL 36130

Alaska Dept. of Fish & Game
P.O. Box 3-2000
Juneau, AK 99802

Arizona Game & Fish
2222 West Greenway Road
Phoenix, AZ 85023

**Arkansas Game &
Fish Commission**
#2 Natural Resources Drive
Little Rock, AR 72205

California Dept. of Fish & Game
1416 9th Street
Sacramento, CA 95814

Colorado Division of Wildlife
6060 Broadway
Denver, CO 80216

**Connecticut Dept. of
Environmental Protection**
State Office Bldg.,
165 Capitol Avenue
Hartford, CT 06115

**Delaware Division of
Fish and Wildlife**
P.O. Box 1401
Dover, DE 19903

**Florida Game and
Freshwater Fish Commission**
Farris Bryant Building
620 South Meridian
Tallahassee, FL 32399

**Georgia State Game and
Fish Division**
Floyd Towers East, Suite 1366
205 Butler Street, S.E.
Atlanta, GA 30334

Division of Forestry & Wildlife
1151 Punch Bowl Street
Honolulu, HI 96813

Idaho Fish & Game Department
600 S. Walnut, P.O. Box 25
Boise, ID 83707

Illinois Dept. of Conservation
Lincoln Tower Plaza
524 S. Second Street
Springfield, IL 62701-1787

Indiana Div. of Fish and Wildlife
607 State Office Building
Indianapolis, IN 46204

**Iowa Department of
Natural Resources**
Wallace State Office Building
East 9th and Grand Avenue
Des Moines, IA 50319

**Kansas Department of
Wildlife and Parks**
Box 54-A, Rural Route 2
Pratt, KS 67124

**Kentucky Dept. of Fish &
Wildlife Resources**
#1 Game Farm Road
Frankfort, KY 40601

**Louisiana Dept.
Wildlife and Fisheries**
2000 Quail Drive, P.O. Box 98000
Baton Rouge, LA 70898

**Maine Dept. of Inland
Fisheries & Wildlife**
284 State Street, Station #41
Augusta, ME 04333

**Maryland Department of
Natural Resources**
Tawes State Office Building
Annapolis, MD 21401

**Massachusetts Div. of
Fisheries & Wildlife**
Department of Fisheries,
Wildlife and Environmental
Law Enforcement
100 Cambridge Street
Boston, MA 02202

**Michigan Dept. of
Natural Resources**
Stevens T. Mason Bldg.,
Box 30028
Lansing, MI 48909

**Minnesota Dept. of
Natural Resources**
500 Lafayette Road
St. Paul, MN 55155-4020

**Mississippi Dept. of
Wildlife, Fisheries and Parks**
P.O. Box 451
Jackson, MS 39205

Missouri Dept. of Conservation
2901 N. Ten Mile Drive,
P.O. Box 180
Jefferson City, MO 65102

**Montana Dept. of
Fish, Wildlife, and Parks**
1420 E. Sixth Avenue
Helena, MT 59620

**Nebraska Game &
Parks Commission**
2200 North 33rd Street,
P.O. Box 30370
Lincoln, NE 68503

Nevada Department of Wildlife
P.O. Box 10678
Reno, NV 89520

**New Hampshire Fish and
Game Department**
2 Hazen Drive
Concord, NH 03301

**New Jersey Div. of Fish, Game
and Wildlife**
CN 400
Trenton, NJ 08625

**New Mexico Game and Fish
Department**
Villagra Building
Santa Fe, NM 87503

**New York Division of
Fish and Wildlife**
50 Wolf Road
Albany, NY 12233

**North Carolina Wildlife
Resources Commission**
512 N. Salisbury Street
Raleigh, NC 27611

**North Dakota Game &
Fish Department**
100 North Bismark Expressway
Bismark, ND 58501

Ohio Division of Wildlife
Fountain Square
Columbus, OH 43224

**Oklahoma Dept. of
Wildlife Conservation**
1801 North Lincoln,
P.O. Box 53465
Oklahoma City, OK 73152

Oregon Dept. of Fish & Wildlife
P.O. Box 59
Portland, OR 97207

Pennsylvania Game Commission
2001 Elmerton Avenue
Harrisburg, PA 17110-9797

**Puerto Rico Department of
Natural Resources**
P.O. Box 5887
Puerta De Tierra
San Juan, PR 00906

**Rhode Island Dept. of
Environmental Management**
Division of Fish and Wildlife
Washington County Government
Center
Wakefield, RI 02879

**South Carolina Wildlife &
Marine Resources Dept.**
Rembert C. Dennis Bldg.,
P.O. Box 167
Columbia, SC 29202

**South Dakota Dept. of
Game, Fish and Parks**
Sigurd Anderson Building,
445 E. Capitol
Pierre, SD 57501-3185

**Tennessee Wildlife
Resources Agency**
Ellington Agricultural Center, P.O.
Box 40747
Nashville, TN 37204

**Texas Parks & Wildlife
Department**
4200 Smith School Road
Austin, TX 78744

**Utah Division of
Wildlife Resources**
1596 W. North Temple
Salt Lake City, UT 84116

**Vermont Fish & Game
Department**
103 S. Main Street, 10 South
Waterbury, VT 05676

**Virginia Dept. of Game and
Inland Fisheries**
4010 W. Broad Street,
P.O. Box 11104
Richmond, VA 23230

Washington
Department of Wildlife
600 North Capitol Way
Olympia, WA 98504

West Virginia Div. of
Wildlife Resources
1900 Kanawha Blvd., East
Charleston, WV 25305

Wisconsin Dept. of
Natural Resources
Box 7921
Madison, WI 53707

Wyoming Game &
Fish Department
5400 Bishop Blvd.
Cheyenne, WY 82002

AGENCIES IN CANADIAN PROVINCES

ALBERTA

Director of Wildlife
Fish and Wildlife Division
Department of Energy and Natural
Resources
Petroleum Plaza, South Tower
9945-108 Street
Edmonton, Alberta
CANADA T5K 2C9

BRITISH COLUMBIA

Director, Wildlife Branch
Ministry of the Environment
Parliament Buildings
Victoria, British Columbia
CANADA V8V 1X5

MANITOBA

Director, Wildlife Branch
Natural Resources Division
Department of Natural Resources
Room 302, Legislative Building
Winnipeg, Manitoba
CANADA R3C 0V8

NEW BRUNSWICK

Director
Fish and Wildlife Branch
Department of Natural Resources
Centennial Bldg., P.O. Box 6000
Fredericton, New Brunswick
CANADA E3B 5H1

NEWFOUNDLAND

Wildlife Division
Department of Culture,
Recreation and Youth
P.O. Box 4750
St. Johns, Newfoundland
CANADA A1C 5T7

NORTHWEST TERRITORY

Chief,
Wildlife Management Division
Department of Renewable
Resources
Legislative Building
Yellowknife, Northwest Territory
CANADA X1A 2L9

NOVA SCOTIA

Wildlife Division
Department of Lands and Forests
Toronto Dominion Bank Building
1791 Barrington Street
P.O. Box 698
Halifax, Nova Scotia
CANADA B3J 2T9

ONTARIO

Wildlife Director
Outdoor Recreation Group
Ontario Ministry of Natural
Resources
Whitney Block, Queen's Park
Toronto, Ontario
CANADA M7A 1W3

PRINCE EDWARD ISLAND

Minister
Community and Cultural Affairs
11 Kent Street, P.O. Box 2000
Charlottetown, Prince Edward
Island
CANADA C1A 7N8

QUEBEC

Director,
Fish and Game Branch
Quebec Ministere Du Loisir, De La
Chasse Ed De La Peche
150 est boul, St.-Cyrille
Quebec City, Quebec
CANADA G1R 4Y1

SASKATCHEWAN

Director,
Wildlife Branch
Saskatchewan Park and Renewable
Resources
Legislative Building
Regina, Saskatchewan
CANADA S4S 5W6

YUKON TERRITORY

Chief of Wildlife Management
Wildlife Branch
Department of Renewable
Resources
P.O. Box 2703
Whitehorse, Yukon Territory
CANADA Y1A 2C6

Photo Credits

All photos by Aubrey Watson unless otherwise credited.

Americase: page 39 (top)
API Outdoors, Inc.: page 50 (right)
Barnett International: page 22
E.W. Bateman & Co.: pages 37 (lower left), 38
Bear Archery Co.: pages 20, 23, 121 (bottom)
Bear/Jennings Archery: page 76
Ben Pearson Archery, Inc.: page 20
Bracklynn Archery: page 50 (top left)
Bry, Ed, North Dakota Game & Fish Dept.: pages 132 (top), 133 (bottom)
Cadieux, Charles L., Bureau of Sports Fisheries &
      Wildlife: page 132 (bottom)
Cooney, Judd: pages 117, 125, 126, 127
Farkas, Deano: pages 137, 140 (bottom)
Game Tracker: page 78 (lower left)
Golden Key-Futura, Inc.: page 77
Greany, J. Malcolm, Bureau of Sports Fisheries & Wildlife: page 63
Haddon, E. P., U.S. Fish & Wildlife Service: pages 62, 64, 66, 70
Hawk Associates: page 78 (upper right)
Hunting Classics, Ltd.: page 39 (center)
Kalambach, E. R.: U.S. Fish & Wildlife Service, pages 131, 134
Lawrence, H. Lea: pages 17, 34, 61, 65, 79 (lower right), 121 (top)
Martin Archery, Inc.: page 140 (top)
New Archery Products Corp.: page 77
Nickels, Jon, U.S. Fish & Wildlife Service: page 67
Oneida Labs, Inc.: page 19
Ranging: page 79 (top left and right)
R.L.H. Archery Products: page 78 (upper left)
San Angelo Sports Products: page 39 (bottom)
Sapp, Richard: page 115
Saxon International, Inc.: page 21
Silver Creek Industries: page 81 (lower right)
Sonic Technology Products, Inc.: page 81 (lower left)
U.S. Fish & Wildlife Service: page 69
Vista Rea-Salisbury Enterprises: page 133 (top)
Vivion, Mike, U.S. Fish & Wildlife Service: page 68